DATE DUE

		DISCARD	

BLENDED LEARNING IN PRACTICE

BLENDED LEARNING IN PRACTICE

A Guide for Practitioners and Researchers

EDITED BY AMANDA G. MADDEN, LAUREN MARGULIEUX,
ROBERT S. KADEL, AND ASHOK K. GOEL

FOREWORD BY RICHARD A. DEMILLO

The MIT Press
Cambridge, Massachusetts
London, England

This book was set in ScalaSans and Scala by Toppan Best-set Premedia Limited. Printed and bound in the United States of America.

Library of Congress Cataloging-in-Publication Data

Names: Madden, Amanda G., editor. | Margulieux, Lauren editor. | Kadel, Robert S., editor. | Goel, Ashok K., 1953- editor.
Title: Blended learning in practice : a guide for practitioners and researchers / edited by Amanda G. Madden, Lauren Margulieux, Robert S. Kadel, and Ashok K. Goel ; foreword by Richard A. DeMillo.
Description: Cambridge, MA : The MIT Press, [2019] | Includes bibliographical references and index.
Identifiers: LCCN 2018024093 | ISBN 9780262039475 (hardcover : alk. paper)
Subjects: LCSH: Blended learning--United States. | Computer-assisted instruction--United States. | Flipped classrooms--United States. | Curriculum planning--Education--United States. | Blended learning--United States--Case studies. | Computer-assisted instruction--United States--Case studies. | Flipped classrooms--United States--Case studies. | Curriculum planning--Education--United States--Case studies.
Classification: LCC LB1028.5 .B5695 2019 | DDC 371.3--dc23
LC record available at https://lccn.loc.gov/2018024093

10   9   8   7   6   5   4   3   2   1

Amanda Madden: To my husband, Chris, whose skill in writing and teaching never fails to inspire, and for his support and encouragement

Lauren Margulieux: For my husband, Justin, who supports me in everything I do

Robert Kadel: For my wife, Stephanie, and sons, Samuel and Liam, who supported our relocation to Atlanta so that I could join a new and wonderful academic family at Georgia Tech

Ashok Goel: For my sons, Gautam and Kunal

CONTENTS

CONTENTS

This book was conceived in the fall of 2015 after a discussion between several of the editors and a call for sharing resources on blended learning on the Center for 21st Century Universities' listserv. Several of the editors and authors discovered that they had each independently tried experiments with blended learning but hadn't found much of use in the literature or clear guidelines on how to do it. Shortly thereafter, a call was put out to Georgia Tech faculty to share their experiences with blended learning and we conceived of an edited volume that would be of use to those looking for similar guidance.

As its title suggests, this volume bridges the gap between rigorous research on blended learning and blended learning in actual practice. It is intended for the deliberative educator who seeks not only to develop new courses and programs in blended learning, but also to assess the effectiveness of learning, to reflect on the educational experience, and to use data and evidence to continuously improve blended learning. Thus, our audience for this book includes instructors who seek to experiment with blended learning, instructional support personnel including instructional designers, research scientists, and teaching assistants, as well as education administrators, policymakers, and strategic consultants seeking insights into how blended learning can be executed, supported, and evaluated at a programmatic or institutional level.

Blended learning itself is a kind of bridge between traditional in-person learning and the modern movement of online education. It seeks to combine the benefits of the two: the face-to-face interactions as well as the personal advising and mentoring of the former, with the scale, asynchrony, and flexibility of the latter. Georgia Tech has long been a center of innovation in online education and blended learning. This volume not only highlights several recent efforts on blended learning at Georgia Tech but also abstracts some common emerging themes. Perhaps more importantly, it illustrates how one institute's support can lead to educational innovations on the one hand, and how individual faculty initiatives can influence an institute's culture on the other.

The book consists of thirteen chapters plus a conclusion, ranging from case studies to discussions of research methods to novel approaches at the frontiers of blended learning. The authors are primarily the course instructors, some of whom have been supported in their research by scientists in Georgia Tech's Center for 21st Century Universities. Other instructors have tried the method on their own with departmental or institutional support. The disciplines of the included chapters vary from computing to engineering to English composition to international affairs. The level of education varies from freshman composition and introductory computing to graduate education in artificial intelligence and health informatics. The scale varies from small residential sections to large online classes, from a single interdisciplinary residential class to multiple, geographically distributed sections.

We hope that the experiences and lessons described in this volume will encourage deliberative educators around the world to experiment with blended learning in their classes. Each chapter in this book points to the need for additional future research. Blended learning is one of the newest innovations to come to higher education, and research on it, while increasingly popular, is still in its adolescence. We encourage interested educators and researchers to join us and others in the field in being deliberative and deliberate not only in classes that promote better learning outcomes but in doing research—

designing studies that will gather data, test hypotheses, draw conclusions, and contribute to the growing body of knowledge on blended learning. For our part, we plan on future volumes that incorporate the newest research on blended learning, highlighting its challenges as well as its benefits, and providing guidance for future work that will contribute to the efficacy of blended learning.

Atlanta, Georgia
March 2018

ACKNOWLEDGMENTS

We would like to thank the Center for 21st Century Universities at Georgia Tech (C21U) for providing partial support and resources for conceiving and editing this volume. We would also like to thank our colleagues in various departments—especially the contributors to this volume for writing and revising their various chapters through multiple iterations. We also thank MIT Press—particularly our acquisitions editor, Susan Buckley, and her assistant, Noah Springer—for patiently guiding us in preparing this volume. Finally, we would like to thank the two anonymous reviewers whose thoughtful critiques helped us shape the book.

Amanda Madden would like to thank Rebecca Burnett for introducing her to the scholarship of teaching and learning and always supporting pedagogical experiments outside the box.

Lauren Margulieux would like to thank Mike McCracken for his feedback on the early stages of her blended learning work and the Center for 21st Century Universities for providing a focal point for blended learning work at Georgia Tech.

Robert Kadel would like to thank the hard-working, innovative staff and graduate students in Georgia Tech's Center for 21st Century Universities,

Georgia Tech Professional Education, and Donald Webster in Georgia Tech's College of Engineering for early collaboration on blended learning research.

Finally, Ashok Goel would like to thank the Georgia Tech Online Master of Science in Computer Science program, Georgia Tech's Commission on Next in Education, and the students and teaching assistants in the Georgia Tech course on Knowledge-Based Artificial Intelligence from fall 2014 through fall 2017.

FOREWORD

Georgia Tech's Center for 21st Century Universities (C21U) was conceived in 2011 as a living laboratory for fundamental change in higher education. It was important to us that C21U not be viewed primarily as a research center for studying fundamental change, but rather as a kind of garage where teachers, technologists, and tinkerers would put together and try out new approaches to learning that might effect fundamental change. One of the center's first projects was the exploration of new pedagogies that might be enabled by the ready availability of online, remixable, and scalable courseware that was being generated in impressive quantities as we designed and distributed massive open online courses (MOOCs). That project took concrete form when a steady stream of Georgia Tech faculty began blending online and in-person materials into new learning experiences that we thought better served the needs of students who were attempting to master a flood of challenging material via older lecture/recitation methods.

Beginning with simple pilots that flipped the roles of lectures and homework, we began tackling some of the difficult problems in organizing and achieving repeatable, predictable outcomes for large, multisection gateway courses in engineering and computer science. It seemed at the outset like a simple initiative, but we realized quickly that without a solid research basis, we would have no way of knowing whether flipped classrooms—or any of the other methods for blended learning experiences—had any effect at all on learning outcomes, cost of operations, access and availability, or any of the dozen other factors of interest to us. Fortunately, we had insisted that MOOC developers be accompanied by instructional designers and educational researchers. In fact, every minute of video courseware and every online assessment was already part of a package deal. We were not going to throw courseware in scattergun fashion at students in the hope that some of it would be worthwhile. We could not guarantee success for every online offering, but we would have a disciplined way of gauging the relative success of each course. One consequence of this decision was to raise the height of the barrier to entry for an instructor. Instructional staff and administrators clearly felt the weight of this responsibility. It did not appreciably deter instructors from redesigning courses in this new format, but the amount of effort needed to mount a successful course using online materials became well known among Georgia Tech's professors and instructional staff. It was not something to be undertaken lightly.

The effect of these decisions startled me. Not surprisingly, the idea of flipped classrooms was initially attractive to many instructors, who saw it as a way to reduce their own effort by prerecording lectures that students would have to navigate on their own. I noticed an uptick of interest in blended learning from instructors who had shown little prior interest in pedagogical matters. This usually took the form of a purchase request for handheld HD video recorders to be placed at the back of a lecture hall. Quashing these projects resulted in an entertaining series of skirmishes that usually ended when it became clear how much work was involved in implementing blended learning.

More significantly, serious educators began to ask for help and supporting materials that we thought were readily available to them. C21U is a small operation and we did not have a large staff of full-time support specialists to answer questions. C21U's associate director, Michael McCracken, and his student, Lauren Margulieux (who contributed greatly to this volume), began to turn out FAQ entries that would serve as an online guidebook for instructors. The task was much larger than we anticipated. Basic facts about research methodologies, experimental design, and statistical analysis of results were not part of the repertoire of tools for even highly technical STEM instructors. A guidebook was needed. Margulieux and McCracken began to capture and chronicle the research and design techniques. The growing number of tenure-track faculty involved in the project were a rich source of lessons learned, and as the university began to rely more and more on blended learning, the idea occurred to the editors of this volume that making this material available in book form might be a valuable service for institutions, teachers, and administrators of all kinds who are contemplating walking the same path that we had started down in 2011.

This volume—which we expect to grow and be augmented over time—is aimed at instructors considering blended learning in their own classroom. We have incorporated our own experience to anticipate the questions we know are uppermost in the minds of teachers daunted by the prospect of ripping apart the careful scaffolding that has been the hallmark of lecture-format courses and replacing it with effective blended classroom materials. This book also addresses others who are often left out of more technical discussions. We know, for example, that administrators are important partners in developing and deploying new pedagogical tools. This book will help administrators make an informed case to instructors about the nature and benefits of blended learning. Finally, the editors and contributors are all educational researchers in their own right and this volume provides a rich source of case studies and examples for other researchers to use as they structure similar projects.

The book will help tame what to many educators feels like the Wild West when it comes to anticipating wholesale change in educational delivery. Much research has been undertaken on this topic, but blended learning is implemented in a wide spectrum of ways and with varying degrees of involvement or commitment in the undetaking. And make no mistake—to create a well-blended classroom is an undertaking.

Richard A. DeMillo
Executive Director, Center for 21st Century Universities (C21U)
Charlotte B. and Roger C. Warren Professor of Computing and Professor of Management
Georgia Institute of Technology

INTRODUCTION

Amanda G. Madden, Lauren Margulieux, Robert S. Kadel, and Ashok Goel

Higher education is unquestionably facing a number of profound changes. Student demographics are shifting dramatically from a generation ago—the student population is now more diverse, students start college later, and adults are returning to school or acquiring more skills in record numbers. The needs of the 21st-century workforce and a changing professional landscape are shaping curricula, degrees, and skill acquisition. Technology is changing the classroom experience for both student and teacher. And while some facets of the university will remain the same, many aspects of higher education will be unrecognizable in twenty years.

Blended learning, which combines face-to-face and online learning, is at the forefront of this ongoing, rapid transformation of higher education. Blended classrooms infuse learning with technology-supported instruction and often include a combination of synchronous and asynchronous learning. In a popular configuration known as "flipped" classrooms, lectures are often given outside of class time via media like online videos (Osguthorpe and Graham, 2003; Day and Foley, 2006; Margulieux, McCracken, and Catrambone, 2016). This can include the use of adaptive textbooks or videos in lieu of lectures (Valiathan, 2002). Other variations include redistributing class time to focus on problem solving, group activities, laboratory experiments, and other types of hands-on engagement and active learning. The important takeaway is that blended learning shifts the role of the instructor from a transmitter of content to a facilitator of learning; the role of the student changes from a receiver of content to a creator of knowledge. This shift can have a large impact on the experience of both teachers and students that positively affects outcomes.

While configurations of blended classrooms are as varied as goals and contexts, the motivations behind rethinking the traditional lecture in the brick-and-mortar classroom are more straightforward and focus on improving learning outcomes (Garrison and Kanuka, 2004). Studies show that blended learning fosters deeper conceptual understanding, increased mastery of content, and enhanced metacognitive skills essential for further learning and success in the workforce (López-Pérez et al., 2011; Owston, York, and Murtha, 2013). Secondary gains include increased student engagement and the formation of learning communities (Strayer, 2012). Indeed, research shows that students in blended learning classes have higher test scores, enhanced content mastery, self-perception of expertise, and greater satisfaction (Bishop and Verleger, 2013; Biddix, Chung, and Park, 2015). The blended classroom also provides adaptability, flexibility, and space for the instructor to tailor the learning experience and to make rapid interventions with the class as a whole (Beatty, 2014; Bergmann and Sams, 2014; Picciano, 2014).

At the same time, there are very real barriers to experimenting with blended learning in practice despite the growing body of evidence that makes the case for it. Instructors may find it daunting to try out blended learning, especially on their own. As several contributors to this volume point out and as is noted elsewhere, redesigning and blending a course can prove frustrating and time consuming (Bergmann and Sams, 2014; Kenney and Newcombe, 2011; Picciano, 2014). Sometimes institutional barriers to adoption present themselves. These can include lack of support for new initiatives or outright skepticism (Porter et al., 2016). Technological barriers should not be ignored as access to technology and other resources can greatly impact whether an instructor can pilot the method (Taplin, Kerr, and Brown, 2013). Finally, the physical space can often be a challenge for blending classes in traditional lecture halls (Bergmann and Sams, 2012).

In the addition to these barriers, the issue of scale is one of the larger obstacles to the implementation of blended learning, as many authors in this volume attest. For classes with hundreds of students—large-scale introductory courses, for example—blending the classroom can be difficult as it requires a great deal of initial attention and effort on the part of the instructor (Ferri et al., 2014). In-class pacing and direction can pivot rapidly in blended classrooms as it is particularly important to focus more on actively facilitating and guiding students. This can require changes in attention and a different toolbox.

Assessment can also offer barriers to widespread adoption. While research indicates that blended learning leads to greater learning gains, sometimes these gains can be difficult to quantify. Much of the current research relies heavily on qualitative measurements like student feedback surveys. More work needs to be done in pinpointing difficult-to-measure students' cognitive gains and experience and teachers' experience and workload (Henrie et al., 2015). Not only does more research need to be done in this area but new methods should be developed.

The horizon of possibilities for blended learning are widening each day. With the advent of massive open online courses (MOOCs) and open courses at scale, for example, or new developments in learning management systems (LMSs) that enable timely feedback and automated assessments on a larger scale, inventive instructors are increasingly adopting the pedagogy. For instance, some are using videos developed for MOOCs to enable blended learning (Rayyan, 2015; Fisher et al., 2015). LMSs, such as Canvas, D2L, and Blackboard, can also facilitate blended learning by providing more data on student behavior and cognitive gains (Dias et al., 2015; Zacharis, 2015). Additionally, with the advent of learning analytics and the influx of big data in education, researchers are increasingly able to quantify gains in learning outcomes and achievement, including in blended classrooms (Carbonaro et al., 2017; Saqr, Fors, and Tedre, 2017).

This volume offers a cross-section of studies across an institution that provides a number of insights and perspectives on how some of the challenges in executing blended learning can be met. The chapters address issues of course design, assessment, technology, and learning outcomes. The contributors to this volume represent wide backgrounds from science to engineering, from technical communication to international affairs. This diversity in discipline and approach provides a range of perspectives on implementation, support, theoretical underpinnings, and best practices.

Before unpacking details, it's first necessary to clarify the use of the term *blended learning* in this volume. Margulieux, McCracken, and Catrambone's (2016) definition of blended learning was adopted. The terminology often used to describe blended learning can conflate the terms *flipped, mixed,* and *hybrid* (Picciano, 2014). Beginning with analyzing existing definitions of blended, hybrid, flipped, and inverted learning to find common features, Margulieux et al. developed the MIX taxonomy to give consistent definitions to courses that mix face-to-face and online instruction. The MIX taxonomy (see figure 1.1) is based on two important dimensions: instruction type and instruction medium. Instruction type describes whether students are receiving content (for example, lectures) or receiving help while applying content (for example, help while solving problems or feedback on a project). Instruction medium describes whether students receive instruction directly from their instructor, whether the instructor is using technology to support instruction, and whether students are receiving instruction through technology, even if they are in the same room as the instructor or the content is simply a recording by the instructor. The taxonomy focuses solely on instruction provided to students. It does not include other aspects of the course, such as whether students form study groups outside of class.

Margulieux et al. (2016) used these dimensions to categorize several class types (see figure 1.1) but the two that are most relevant to this volume are blended and flipped. A blended course includes instruction that both delivers content and aids application of content; instruction comes from both the instructor and technology. Flipped courses are a subtype of blended courses that delivers content through technology and provides support during application of content. For example, students watch videos and learn via a smart

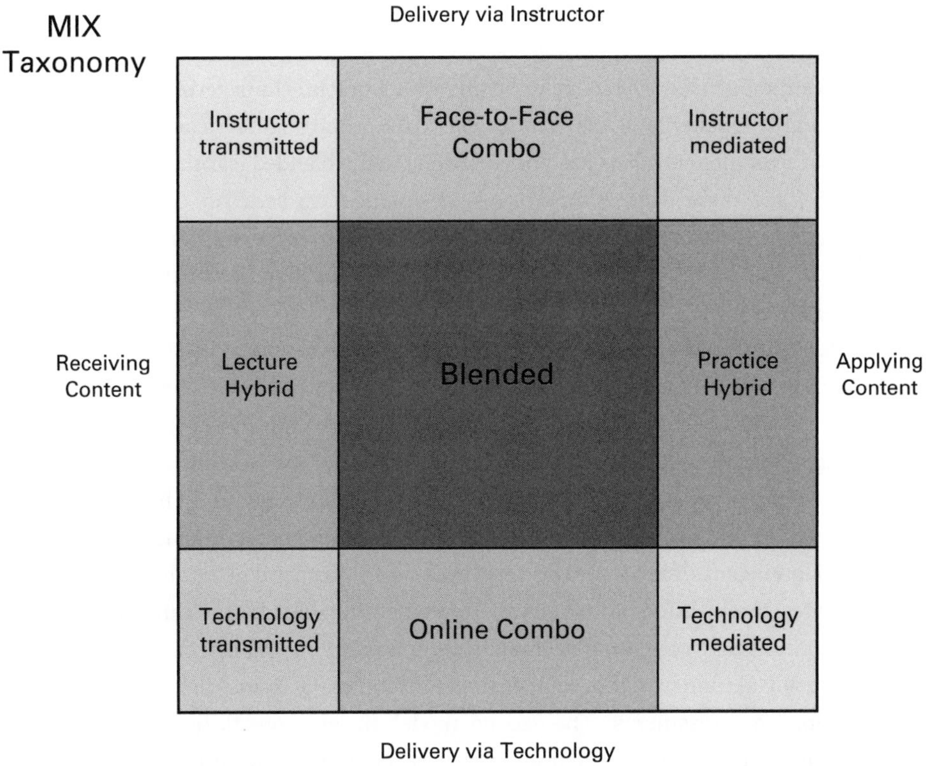

MIX
Taxonomy

Delivery via Instructor

Instructor transmitted	Face-to-Face Combo	Instructor mediated
Lecture Hybrid	Blended	Practice Hybrid
Technology transmitted	Online Combo	Technology mediated

Receiving Content

Applying Content

Delivery via Technology

Figure 1.1
The Mixed Instructional eXperience (MIX) taxonomy provides terminology to consistently categorize mixed instruction courses. Reprinted from *Educational Research Review*, vol. 19, Lauren Margulieux, Michael McCracken, and Richard Catrambone, "A Taxonomy to Define Courses That Mix Face-to-Face and Online Learning," 104–118, copyright (2016), with permission from Elsevier.

textbook outside of class and then come to class to do labs with instructor or TA supervision.

To aid the reader, each chapter begins with a precise characterization of the learning components of the blended class based on the MIX taxonomy. This type of structured analysis has not been done in the blended learning literature before, and these direct comparisons are intended to be a key contribution of this book. Each of the three parts of this volume includes information on how course content, instruction, tools, and class makeup define the student experience.

Part I, "New Issues and Approaches," consists of empirical studies that examine novel issues and approaches at the frontier of blended learning. In chapter 2, "Three Models for Blending Classes in a Multisection Course," Bonnie Ferri, Joyelle Harris, and Aldo Ferri examine how teaching a multiple-section course in a blended format provides an opportunity to maintain consistency in addition to promoting better student-instructor interactions. To provide guidance for those who seek to design a similar course, this chapter provides three different models of implementing blended learning across multiple-section courses. The first is a centralized model of course design where all sections of the course share resources, learning materials, and summative assessments. The second model allows more flexibility for the instructors. Instructors synchronize their schedule but choose the depth and presentation of some course topics and major summative assessments. The final model considered is distributed, where faculty have access to the same course resources but conduct their classes without coordination. Finally, the chapter introduces evaluation criteria and guidelines for determining which model might work best for a given department or faculty. Each of the models solves consistency problems across multisection courses and allows for blending on a larger, programmatic level.

In chapter 3, "Preliminary Evidence for the Benefits of Online Education and Blended Learning in a Large Artificial Intelligence Class," Ashok Goel describes a multiyear study with traditional, online, and blended approaches in a large computing class on artificial intelligence for both undergraduate and graduate students. He first describes an online course on the same topic (Goel and Joyner, 2016). In the first year of the study, he found that the students in the online section did slightly better on several learning assessments than residential students in a parallel section. In the second and third years, students in the residential class were asked to watch the video lessons prior to coming to the class. Instead of utilizing lectures, class time was used mostly for discussions of the concepts and methods described in the videos and for working on exercises in small groups. Goel found that the residential students using blended learning performed as well as the online students on the same assessments. He concludes by reflecting on the pedagogical experiment and presents guidelines for designing similar classes.

David Joyner's chapter, "Building Purposeful Online Learning: Outcomes from Blending CS1301" (chapter 4), describes using blended learning to pilot one section of a computer science course. The chapter begins with course design and discusses the production of the MOOC and the use of online components providing content delivery and feedback. Students who took a linked face-to-face class and students who took the blended class during the same semester were assessed and surveyed. Student performance was measured through a standardized computer science assessment. Student demographic information, as well as expectations for the course and perceptions after taking the course, were measured through surveys. Joyner concludes that students in the online section showed no signs of being disadvantaged by the course design but reported higher levels of satisfaction with the course material.

In chapter 5, "An Innovative, Blended, Project-Based Health Informatics Course," Mark L. Braunstein and several coauthors outline the use of blended learning in Georgia Tech's Introduction to Health Informatics graduate seminar. The Health Informatics course is taught both as a traditional on-campus graduate seminar and as an online course in Georgia Tech's Online Master of Science in Computer Science program (OMSCS). In both versions of the course, students view online materials developed by the course instructor outside of class. Likewise, students in both sections form teams of four to six members to develop real-world apps in consultation with healthcare professionals. Connecting students with diverse backgrounds and experiences in an inherently multidisciplinary field proved extremely beneficial.

Part II, "Conducting Research in Blended Courses," examines doing educational research on blended learning and provides some guidelines for both instructors and researchers. Many instructors report not knowing how to conduct research on blended learning in the classroom. To orient those not familiar with Scholarship of Teaching and Learning (SOTL), its own field with research designs, methodology, and modes of analysis, Robert S. Kadel and Lauren Margulieux begin this section with "Research Methods in Blended Learning" (chapter 6). The chapter walks instructors who are not familiar with social science research methods, or perhaps just need a refresher, through the decision points of conducting research in a classroom. As noted, the choice of research design depends on what question you are trying to answer. Accordingly, Kadel and Margulieux familiarize readers with a discussion of both qualitative and quantitative research methods. Next, they consider the spectrum of research design, including the pros and cons of choosing different methods, focusing on the research methods and analyses that will help an instructor scientifically evaluate his or her classroom and produce publishable educational research. At the end of the chapter are resources readers can use to further explore the topic.

Illustrating a qualitative study, Rebecca E. Burnett, Olga Menagarishvili, and Andy Frazee's contribution in chapter 7, "Student Attitudes about Teamwork in Face-to-Face and Blended Technical Communication Classes," presents a qualitative study examining blended learning in a writing-intensive environment. Students were enrolled in an upper-level capstone course linking computer science and technical communication, a requirement for computer science majors at Georgia Tech. Beginning with the premise that students are less positive and engaged in both online and large writing classes, their study contradicts these commonplace assumptions by examining a blended course in technical communication with larger-than-average enrollments.

In chapter 8, "Analyzing Quantitative and Qualitative Data for Blended Learning," Lauren Margulieux and Robert S. Kadel follow up on their previous research method chapter. In particular, they focus on how to collect data, discuss different considerations in ensuring that the data provides accurate measures of what is being studied, and explain why it is important to be specific about whom you are collecting data from. Starting with some of the fundamental concepts of understanding quantitative data and analyses, they describe the statistical analyses appropriate for various types of data and research questions. The chapter concludes with a description of how to analyze qualitative data.

In the last chapter in part II, "Blended Dynamics—Does Size Matter?" (chapter 9), Donald R. Webster, Robert S. Kadel, and Amanda G. Madden examine the learning outcomes of employing active problem solving in a blended dynamics course, comparing a face-to-face class and blended courses of various sizes. The outcomes in the blended course were nearly identical to those of the face-to-face class despite a substantial difference in the classroom environment and the student-to-instructor ratio. The authors conclude that the experiment in scaling the blended classroom pedagogy to a larger class successfully created an effective learning environment.

Part III, "Course Design Case Studies: Solving Common Teaching Issues," focuses on how to design a blended learning classroom. Each of the instructors in this section noted problems in traditional classrooms that they wanted to address, including enhancing student engagement, incorporating more active learning strategies, approximating real-world problem solving, and reaching nonmajors. In chapter 10, "Blending a First-Year Composition Course Using *Assassin's Creed II*," Amanda G. Madden tackles the common problem of the lack of student engagement in a required course for nonmajors. Focused on improving learning outcomes, she prototyped a blended learning design for her course. Using the popular videogame *Assassin's Creed II* as one of the course textbooks and as a stand-in for some of the lectures, she designed similarly immersive student in-class activities designed to foster active learning. After completing these activities and playing the game, students were then asked to demonstrate their mastery of historical content and writing skills. This blended design promoted student engagement, critical thinking, and content mastery.

Similarly interested in promoting student engagement, Lauren Margulieux blended an undergraduate research method course for psychology and computer science students. In chapter 11, "Blended Learning in a Midlevel, Required Course with Students from Two Majors," she describes her strategies. As students needed to learn how to transfer their knowledge outside the classroom to their environment, she made applied activities an important component of learning in the course. To measure student understanding, students completed an activity for each textbook reading that allowed the instructor to adapt short, targeted lectures on student misconceptions. By describing a major success and a major failure from the course, class design, and classroom space, Margulieux points the way to blending upper-level research classes.

Joseph M. Le Doux's chapter, "The Problem-Solving Studio: An Approach for Structuring Face-to-Face Learning Activities in the Flipped Classroom" (chapter 12), offers guidance on how to create and implement effective in-class learning activities in a blended learning classroom. The chapter provides a detailed description of three learning activities that introduce students to two important cognitive tools engineers use to solve problems: diagramming and estimation. Each exercise described in the chapter leverages the features of the learning environment in the problem-solving studio by requiring students to actively engage in reading, diagramming, estimating, and problem solving, reflecting on their own and with their peers, while being apprenticed by the instructor. These step-by-step instructions are intended to serve as helpful guides for instructors to experiment with and fine-tune to suit their learning objectives, teaching style, and the classroom's culture.

In "Global Issues and Leadership: Georgia Tech as a Laboratory for the Future of Education" (chapter 13), Joe Bankoff and Kenneth J. Knoespel examine blended learning in an international affairs seminar. After designing the course for students from various disciplinary backgrounds and different institutions, they offered a fourteen-week seminar that students in Atlanta took in tandem with students at Sciences Po, Paris. Because the seminar took place in a real-time international setting, this blended format enabled students to practice leadership in a real global environment where diverse participants provided differences in perspective.

In chapter 14, the concluding chapter, we tie together the major themes and implications of the book.

* * *

The aim of *Blended Learning in Practice* is to give readers a vision of the deliberative educator. A deliberative educator not only has a passion for their content domain but also a desire to share that passion with others using tools and strategies that improve student learning. It is not enough to be an expert on one's subject matter in order to teach well. Among other things, one also needs to define learning goals, adopt teaching strategies, evaluate course materials, and design assessments to be an effective instructor.

While no single pedagogical framework can claim to be appropriate for all topics, classes, or student types, blended learning's flexibility provides tools applicable for many different combinations of tasks and environments. The chapters in this volume, and the research that undergirds them, provide a broad swath of information relevant to blended learning in different disciplines. We hope that readers will be deliberate in choosing what to try and deliberative in studying their own implementation of a blended classroom.

References

Beatty, B. (2014). Hybrid courses with flexible participation: The HyFlex course design. In L. Kyei-Blankson & E. Ntuli (Eds.), *Practical applications and experiences in K-20 blended learning environments*. Hershey, PA: Information Science Reference.

Bergmann, J., & Sams, A. (2012). *Flip your classroom: Reach every student in every class every day*. Eugene, OR: International Society for Technology in Education.

Bergmann, J., & Sams, A. (2014). *Flipped learning: Gateway to student engagement*. Eugene, OR: International Society for Technology in Education.

Biddix, J. P., Chung, C. J., & Park, H. W. (2015). The hybrid shift: Evidencing a student-driven restructuring of the college classroom. *Computers & Education, 80*, 162–175.

Bishop, J. L., & Verleger, M. A. (2013, June). *The flipped classroom: A survey of the research*. Paper presented at the 120th ASEE Annual Conference & Exposition, Atlanta.

Bonk, C. J., & Graham, C. R. (2012). *The handbook of blended learning: Global perspectives, local designs.* Hoboken, NJ: Wiley.

Carbonaro, M., Montgomery, A., Mousavi, A., Dunn, B., & Hayward, D. (2017, June). Learning analytics in a blended learning context. In J. Johnston (Ed.), *Proceedings of EdMedia 2017* (pp. 62–66). Washington, DC: Association for the Advancement of Computing in Education (AACE).

Day, J., & Foley, J. (2006). Evaluating a web lecture intervention in a human-computer interaction course. *IEEE Transactions on Education, 49*(3), 420–431.

Dias, S. B., Hadjileontiadou, S. J., Hadjileontiadis, L. J., & Diniz, J. A. (2015). Fuzzy cognitive mapping of LMS users' quality of interaction within higher education blended-learning environment. *Expert Systems with Applications, 42*(21), 7399–7423.

Ferri, B. H., Majerich, D. M., Parrish, N. V., & Ferri, A. A. (2014). *Use of a MOOC platform to blend a linear circuits course for non-majors.* Paper presented at the 121st ASEE Annual Conference & Exposition, Indianapolis.

Fisher, D. H., Burge, J., Maher, M. L., & Roth, J. (2015). Blended CS courses using massive, open, online courses (and other online resources). *Proceedings of the 46th ACM Technical Symposium on Computer Science Education* (pp. 703–703). New York: ACM.

Garrison, D. R., & Kanuka, H. (2004). Blended learning: Uncovering its transformative potential in higher education. *Internet and Higher Education, 7*(2), 95–105.

Goel, A., & Joyner, D. (2016). An experiment in teaching cognitive systems online. *International Journal for the Scholarship of Technology Enhanced Learning, 1*(1), 3–23.

Henrie, C. R., Bodily, R., Manwaring, K. C., & Graham, C. R. (2015). Exploring intensive longitudinal measures of student engagement in blended learning. *International Review of Research in Open and Distributed Learning, 16*(3), 131–155.

Lim, D. H., Morris, M. L., & Kupritz, V. W. (2007). Online vs. blended learning: Differences in instructional outcomes and learner satisfaction. *Journal of Asynchronous Learning Networks, 11*(2), 27–42.

López-Pérez, M. V., Pérez-López, M. C., & Rodríguez-Ariza, L. (2011). Blended learning in higher education: Students' perceptions and their relation to outcomes. *Computers & Education, 56*(3), 818–826.

Margulieux, L. E., McCracken, W. M., & Catrambone, R. (2016). Mixing face-to-face and online learning: Instructional methods that affect learning. *Educational Research Review.* doi:10.1016/j.edurev.2016.07.001.

Osguthorpe, R. T., & Graham, C. R. (2003). Blended learning environments: Definitions and directions. *Quarterly Review of Distance Education, 4*(3), 227–233.

Owston, R., York, D., & Murtha, S. (2013). Student perceptions and achievement in a university blended learning strategic initiative. *Internet and Higher Education, 18*, 38–46.

Picciano, A. G. (2014). Big data and learning analytics in blended learning environments: Benefits and concerns. *Interactive Journal of Artificial Intelligence and Interactive Multimedia, 2*(7), 35–43.

Picciano, A. G. (2014). *A critical reflection of the current research in online and blended learning.* Lifelong Learning in Europe (LLinE), 4

Porter, W. W., Graham, C. R., Bodily, R. G., & Sandberg, D. S. (2016). A qualitative analysis of institutional drivers and barriers to blended learning adoption in higher education. *Internet and Higher Education, 28*, 17–27.

Rayyan, S. (2015). Upper level physics MOOCs for online and blended learning. *Bulletin of the American Physical Society, 60*(5).

Saqr, M., Fors, U., & Tedre, M. (2017). How learning analytics can early predict underachieving students in a blended medical education course. *Medical Teacher, 39*(7), 1–11.

Strayer, J. F. (2012). How learning in an inverted classroom influences cooperation, innovation and task orientation. *Learning Environments Research, 15*(2), 171–193.

Taplin, R. H., Kerr, R., & Brown, A. M. (2013). Who pays for blended learning? A cost-benefit analysis. *Internet and Higher Education, 18*, 61–68.

Valiathan, P. (2002). Blended learning models. *Learning Circuits , 3*(8), 50–59.

Zacharis, N. Z. (2015, October). A multivariate approach to predicting student outcomes in web-enabled blended learning courses. *Internet and Higher Education, 27*, 44–53.

I

NEW ISSUES AND APPROACHES

2

THREE MODELS FOR BLENDING CLASSES IN A MULTISECTION COURSE

Bonnie Ferri, Joyelle Harris, and Aldo Ferri

MIX Taxonomy Classification: The courses are blended. Content is delivered through technology with MOOC videos. Instructors in each section also deliver content and examples in class. Students practice applying content both in class, where they receive feedback from the instructor, and through homework, which is completed in an online system that provides instant feedback.

Research Method Classification: The research method is a descriptive design. Though data was collected for multiple courses, direct comparisons between courses was not appropriate. The chapter examines various metrics that are germane to students (e.g., student performance), instructors (e.g., freedom), and department goals (e.g., student retention). Descriptive statistics are used to generalize across multiple sections of the courses.

Courses with high enrollments often appear in the first two years of the college curriculum and present great challenges to students and instructors alike. In many colleges and universities, introductory courses like chemistry and physics are often taught in large lecture halls with enrollments of 100–300 students. Though efficient from a teaching perspective, large lecture courses suffer from a climate during the lecture period that is not generally conducive to two-way student-instructor interaction, leading to a suboptimal in-class social climate (Mulryan-Kyne, 2010). As a result, students often disengage during the lecture. Recitation sections are often added to large lecture courses to give students better access to an instructor, feedback on problem solving, and more opportunities to ask questions. An alternative delivery method for large lecture courses is to teach multiple sections of the same course with each section being smaller in size, on the order of 25–50 students, thus giving improved student-instructor interactions when compared to the large lecture format. However, courses taught across multiple sections often suffer from consistency problems, both in coverage of course material and in grading (Yalcin et al., 2015).

Teaching a multiple-section course in a blended format can provide an opportunity to compromise between the advantages afforded by the single large lecture section and by the multiple smaller-sized sections (Perrin et al., 2009). As discussed in this chapter, both consistency and good student-instructor interactions can be maintained. The basic premise is that a large part of the common, fundamental lecture material would be video-recorded and made available for all sections of the course. Several short videos would replace one 50-minute lecture. Ideally, the videos should be recorded in short segments of 6–8 minutes and include pop-up formative quizzes that require student interaction (Guo, Kim, and Rubin, 2014). The advantage of the videos compared to a large lecture hall is that students can pause and rewind the video and watch it at customizable speeds, from half speed to double speed. Having watched videos online, students would then attend regular-sized classes to gain depth in the material or to work collaboratively on problems.

This chapter examines three different models of implementing blended learning across multiple-section courses via the use of case studies. The goal is to introduce evaluation criteria and give guidelines for determining which model might work best for a given department or faculty. The first case study presents a *centralized model* of course design, where all sections of the course share resources and learning materials and where summative assessments are common among the sections. A *coordinated model* allows more flexibility among the instructors who synchronize their schedule of topics and share some summative assessments but differ in depth and presentation of some course topics and major summative assessments. The final model considered is *distributed*, where faculty have access to the same course resources but conduct their classes without coordination.

EVALUATION CRITERIA

Many different criteria can be used to evaluate the appropriateness of a model for a specific school or situation. Some criteria are student-centered, such as student performance on assessment. Others might be classified as instructor-centered, such as academic freedom, while still others might be department-centered, such as retention rate.

Student-Centered Criteria

Student performance is one of the most important criteria used when evaluating different teaching methods. Performance can be divided into subtopics such as measurable gains in basic skills and knowledge, problem-solving ability, analysis, and synthesis. In other words, student performance can be evaluated for the various levels of Bloom's taxonomy (Bloom and Krathwohl, 1956; Krathwohl, 2002). Other possible taxonomies can also be used to target and classify types of learning and types of knowledge acquired by students, for example (Shavelson et al., 2005).

Another set of student-centered criteria revolves around student attitude, including confidence in the course topics, appreciation of the material, and motivation. Whereas performance criteria, such as exams and homework, can usually be measured quantitatively, attitude is usually assessed from student surveys. End-of-term surveys can ask students to rate their level of understanding of specific topics in the course as a proxy for confidence in the material. Survey questions that measure the desire to take additional (elective) courses on the topic, or to seek employment related to the topic, or that simply ask if they like the material, all relate to appreciation. The level of a student's motivation can be related to their perception of the value of the course and to their perceived probability of success or *expectancy* (Vroom, 1964). Motivation might be measured more accurately by surveys taken during the term with questions aimed individually at value and at expectancy. Course effects that might influence expectancy include the approachability of the instructor and the level of organization of the course. A poorly organized course might increase student uncertainty, for example.

The final set of criteria revolves around student effort, including how hard students must work and how much time they must study. To take this one step further, efficiency in the learning process might be considered. Efficiency can be defined as the student learning gains divided by the student workload, which can be defined as the amount of time students spend per week on the course. Student effort is hard to measure quantitatively, although it can be estimated by student responses on surveys.

Instructor-Centered Criteria

If student performance was the only criterion in judging an educational method, then one-to-one tutoring should be used since it yields the greatest student performance. This paradigm is commonly described as the "Bloom's 2 Sigma Problem" (Bloom, 1984). However, costs of instruction as well as the potential impacts on academic freedom need to be considered for the evaluation. As with the student metrics, specific instructor metrics can be defined in the categories of performance, attitude, and effort (or costs). An instructor's performance is typically evaluated based on teaching ratings from student surveys taken at the end of the term. In addition to questions that ask about the effectiveness in teaching, students can evaluate the instructor performance in terms of their ability to motivate students, the quality of the course resources, and the percent of coverage of the course syllabus. Quantitatively, the instructor can measure the average gains in student performance over the span of the term to achieve a better indicator of the instructor's performance.

Instructor attitude encompasses several factors, including the instructor's comfort level in teaching a course using a specific approach and their confidence that the method will be successful. Implementing blended learning can be challenging for instructors accustomed to lecture-style teaching. Blended learning is more flexible than flipped classes in that there are many more variables in the types of activities done in the classroom, in how these activities are conducted, and in how much time is devoted to each. As a result, it can be intimidating to instructors new to the pedagogy and difficult for them to implement the first time without support from a mentor or instructional specialist. In contrast, traditional lecturing is more linear with fewer variables in the classroom and is more familiar to most faculty. Therefore, blended learning is a more robust method for most new instructors to implement, but its added flexibility means it has the potential to greatly outperform classes that rely entirely on traditional face-to-face (F2F) lectures. Instructor costs include their workload, the amount of time they spend on the course per week, and how difficult they find teaching the course a specific way.

Department-Centered Criteria

A department has program-level criteria, such as yearly retention rates, four-year graduation rate (the percent of students who complete the program in four years), accreditation issues, and general student opinion of the department. These criteria can be related back to individual courses through the DFW rate, consistency among sections, student preparation for subsequent courses, and student attitude toward the courses. The DFW rate is the percent of students who earn a D or F or withdraw from the course. A high DFW rate means that students are less successful in completing the program and may not remain in the program or may take longer to graduate. Inconsistency among sections has some direct impact on student attitudes toward particular courses, but it also impacts the consistency of student preparation for subsequent courses. A course might have a systemic problem if it is taught in such a way that instructors typically do not cover all the material in the course, thereby giving rise to problems in subsequent courses.

Additional department-centered criteria include the ease of finding suitable instructors for a course and financial costs. A course that is well organized with abundant resources may mean that the pool of instructors who can teach the course is large, including possibly the use of advanced graduate students (who cost less than full professors). The departmental costs are also related to the DFW rate in the course. A high DFW rate means that more students will need to repeat a course, which increases the teaching load for the department.

CASE STUDIES OF THE THREE BLENDED COURSE MODELS

Three case studies are described below that demonstrate three models of blended learning across sections and include instructor suggestions on how to implement them effectively. The cases are similar in that they all involve large-enrollment courses that were required, the videos used in the courses were developed for use in massive open online courses (MOOCs), and some hands-on experimental activities were used in the classroom.

Additional resources and support were needed in all three of these cases for the design and production of the MOOCs and for the design and development of the hands-on experiments used in the classrooms. The Center for 21st Century Universities (C21U) at Georgia Tech provided financial support for developing the MOOCs, and Georgia Tech Professional Education filmed and produced the MOOCs. The faculty who developed the MOOCs were also given advice and guidance by educational researchers and instructional designers. These MOOCs were used to blend the three courses discussed below, but there was no institutional support for the process of developing a blended format for these courses. The community of educational scholars coalesced by C21U, however, provided an informal support mechanism for discussion of techniques, strategies, and handling problems.

Blending these three courses meant that there was more time during the class period to introduce meaningful and engaging activities, including hands-on experiments. The experiments used in all courses were developed under two NSF grants.[1] The objectives of those grants were to develop portable, inexpensive experimental platforms so that students can enhance the learning of fundamental concepts with hands-on experiments done anytime and anywhere, including at their desks in a lecture-based course.

Case Study 1: Centralized Model

In the *centralized model* of blended course design, the course resources, course schedule, overall assessments, and grading policies are common across the sections. The decisions on course content and schedule might be determined by an individual or a group, but it is essential that all instructors abide by those decisions. Exams are given at a time when all the students can take them, and each exam question is graded by a single instructor for all students across all sections. The main benefit of the centralized model is consistency among sections in topic coverage, course resources, test coverage, and summative assessments. From the students' perspective, consistency gives them a sense of fairness—no one has an "easy" versus a "hard" instructor. Also, students all have the same degree of exposure to material that might be needed in subsequent courses. The consistency is a benefit from the department's perspective, too—instructors in subsequent courses can better predict the incoming level of knowledge/skills of the students, so they can plan their courses accordingly. The students' sense of fairness over courses impacts their overall impression of the department. The common course resources/schedule means that it is easier for the department to assign new instructors to the course because these instructors do not need to prepare as much.

The case study described here is Circuits and Electronics, a two-hour junior-level semester course required of aerospace engineering, biomedical engineering, mechanical engineering, and materials science engineering students at Georgia Tech but not electrical or computer engineering (ECE) students. The material is challenging to teach because the coverage is broad but not as deep as the equivalent course taught to ECE students. Prior to 2013, Circuits and Electronics was taught in multiple sections of 40–50 students, with each section taught primarily by advanced PhD students. In a typical fall or spring offering of the course, 500 students take the class, spread over 11 to 13 sections. Both student instructors and full-time faculty who taught the course had difficulty pacing themselves properly to finish all the topics in the course. In fact, a survey of the instructors found that the coverage was approximately 75% of the course, with a maximum mismatch of 50%—that is, two instructors in the survey each skipped 25% of the material, but the skipped material was completely different in the two sections. In addition to inconsistency in coverage, the grading policies were very different, resulting in average class GPAs that varied from section to section with the minimum and maximum class GPAs over a multiyear period of 2.35 and 3.95, respectively, and a standard deviation of 0.28 across the sections.

The desire for consistency across sections coupled with a desire to introduce experiential learning and increase student engagement in the course led to the decision to convert the course into a blended model, where all students watch the same lectures online. Circuits and Electronics was reformatted from a traditional lecture-based course taught in multiple independent sections to a blended course starting in the summer of 2013 and continuing to the present. Since consistency was such a large factor, the centralized model of blending was chosen. To achieve student engagement, the in-class time is spent in more interactive activities, with collaborations between students and small-group interaction with the instructor. The course was made more experiential by adding seven in-class hands-on labs. The labs are done by students at their desks in pairs using student-owned devices. Research on the impact of the labs shows that students perform better and have more confidence on topics that are reinforced by the labs than on topics unrelated to the labs (Ferri et al., 2016). Thus, the addition of the labs, made possible by blending the course, has improved student performance.

The online content in the blended version of the course is delivered in three MOOCs: *Linear Circuits 1: DC Analysis, Linear Circuits 2: AC Analysis,* and *Introduction to Electronics.* All three MOOCs are offered on the Coursera platform (coursera.org). All sections use the same online lectures, and there are common homework assignments and common tests across the sections. Like the single large lecture format, the Circuits and Electronics delivery method has the advantage of consistency in the lectures and assignments, but the students are able to watch the lecture videos online at their own pace and on their own time. These videos are broken into six- to ten-minute lengths to accommodate the average attention span and can be accessed through desktop and portable computers as well as through a variety of mobile devices. To facilitate active note taking and to keep students focused, electronic copies of partial slides are provided online so that students can fill in details as they watch the videos. In addition, there are short pop-up quizzes every two or three minutes during the videos. Students need to click on either the answer or the "skip" button to proceed, giving them timely feedback on their understanding of the basic concepts.

Many of the features built into these online videos can be duplicated in a large lecture format—for example, clicker questions can substitute for the in-video quizzes and the PowerPoint slides can be made more active by providing partial slides and having the instructor write on the slides during the lecture. A live lecture gives students the ability to stop the professor in real time to ask for clarification or more depth. However, very few students will stop the instructor with questions in a large lecture hall; hence, this benefit of a live lecture is not realized in actual situations.

Each semester, this course has a lead instructor who is experienced at blending classes, and section instructors who conduct the classes. The role of the lead instructor is to coordinate the other instructors and to mentor the ones who are new to blending classes. To help both the students and the instructors keep the same pace throughout the course, several instructional tools are utilized: online lectures and homework, a weekly course schedule, common in-class structure, common labs, common exams, and weekly coordination meetings. Each tool is described below.

Online Lectures and Homework Organization of the online material is critical to synchronization across sections and to improved student expectancy. The online lectures and homework within the MOOCs are labeled by module and lesson number. Students are responsible for watching the assigned lessons prior to attending each class. Each module within the MOOCs contains video lectures followed by online homework that tests the concepts covered in the associated video lectures. As an example of the organizational structure, consider the sample outline below taken from Linear Circuits 1: DC Analysis. For example, students can watch lesson 2.1 and then solve homework problems 2-1-1 and 2-1-2 via the online platform.

Module 2 Resistive Circuits
Lesson 2.1 Kirchhoff's Voltage Law
Problem 2–1-1
Problem 2–1-2
Lesson 2.2 Kirchhoff's Current Law
Problem 2–2-1
Problem 2–2-2
Problem 2–2-3

The greatest advantages of the online homework platform are automatic grading, immediate feedback, and multiple attempts. Automatic grading drastically decreases the instructor workload and incentivizes instructors to use the common platform. Immediate feedback increases student engagement and learning (Chen et al., 2010; Bartsch and Murphy, 2011) because they can readily identify gaps in their knowledge. When allowed multiple attempts, students are encouraged to bridge their knowledge gaps in order to get full credit for the homework problems.

Course Schedule The course schedule specifies content that students should study prior to each class, topics the instructor will discuss in class, which in-class lab experiments will be conducted, and dates for the common exams. The sample weekly schedule below shows three weeks in one semester of Circuits and Electronics. (Note that each section meets twice per week, so the schedule is divided into content for "Class 1" and "Class 2" because the actual class days differ among the sections.)

Week 1 (January 9)
   Class 1: Course Introduction
   Class 2: All lessons in Module 1 and Lessons 2.1–2.2
Week 2 (January 16)
   Class 1: Lessons 2.3–2.6
   Class 2: Lessons 2.7–2.10 and Lab 1
Week 3 (January 23)
   Class 1: Lessons 2.11–2.13
   Class 2: Lessons 2.14–2.15 and Lab 2

The synchronization among sections means that any student in any section can go to any of the instructors' office hours. With each instructor having three scheduled office hours per week, having 11 different instructors means that there are 33 scheduled instructor office hours per week, making this centralized model much more accommodating for the students than typical uncoordinated courses.

Common Class Structure One of the greatest challenges of implementing a blended course is determining the best use of class time. Therefore, the structure of the class time has been refined through an iterative feedback process over the course of several semesters (Ferri and Ferri, 2016b), culminating in a format where class days include a short quiz, a minilecture, worksheet problems, and homework problems if time permits. On days in which students conduct hands-on experiments, the class begins with a minilecture and then students build their circuits. Below is a sample timeline of a typical 50-minute class day and a detailed description of each class activity.

- Quiz (2–5 minutes)
- Minilecture (10–15 minutes)
- Worksheets (20–25 minutes)
- Homework (5 minutes, as time permits)

Students are responsible for watching the video lectures prior to attending class. A short quiz is given at the beginning of class that covers content from the video. Quizzes are designed to be a reward for those who come to class prepared and a warning to those who do not. Students use clickers to answer quiz questions and receive their quiz grade immediately after all quizzes are submitted. The instructor then solves the quiz problem, and students ask questions about any concepts that were not understood.

After the quiz, the instructor gives a minilecture for 10–15 minutes by solving more complex examples than those provided in the video lectures. With the centralized model of a blended course, all important lecture material should be common; therefore, all lecture material is placed online in the videos. While the videos are designed to introduce individual concepts that are applied to simple problems, the minilectures allow instructors to show students how to combine the concepts to solve more complicated problems. Positive feedback from students indicates that the minilectures improve their understanding of the concepts and are an excellent use of class time.

Following the minilecture, students solve worksheet problems for 20–25 minutes and use personal response devices to enter their answers throughout the problem-solving session. The worksheets require students to implement the tools they learned by watching the videos and minilectures. After a worksheet problem is presented, students must solve the problem individually and submit an answer. Then they work in groups to solve the same problem and submit an answer. Both answers count toward their worksheet grade, and the instructor paces the room to help the groups. This hybrid structure encourages each student to attempt the problem and also allows students to help each other arrive at the correct answer. As a result, students remain engaged throughout the entire problem-solving session of the class. Toward the end of the semester, the worksheets become more open-ended, requiring higher-level reflection on how to apply the concepts to real-world problems.

Instructors use the last five minutes of class time to answer brief questions about the homework problems.

Common Labs There is a different class structure on days in which students complete lab experiments. There are no quizzes and the instructor gives a five-minute minilecture about the lab exercise, including advising students about common pitfalls and providing details to help students successfully complete the experiment.

To complete the lab exercises, students use their laptops and the National Instruments myDAQ. The myDAQ provides a voltage source, and the software enables the laptop to function as a digital multimeter and function generator. Students also purchase lab parts kits, which include electronic components, wires, and a breadboard. By using laptops, myDAQs, and parts kits, the classroom becomes a pop-up laboratory for electronic experimentation. The lab sheets are instructional guides that walk students through the steps in creating a physical circuit from a circuit diagram, using lab equipment to take electrical measurements, and comparing those measurements to theoretical values.

In addition to measurements and calculations, each lab sheet contains one or two free-response questions that enforce reflection on and interpretation of the concepts covered in the experiment. Students are allowed (but not required) to work in pairs to complete the lab exercises.

Because the hands-on labs require a deeper level of engagement than worksheets, the section instructor plus two instructors from other sections are in the classroom to assist students. Thus, in weeks with labs, each instructor is in four classes (as opposed to two in a normal week).

Common Exams The three exams in the course are common across all sections, and each question is graded by one person across all sections. The common exam provides a metric for gauging consistent instruction and learning across all sections. There is a systematic process to create each exam: four instructors each agree to write one exam question about a particular concept. Each instructor presents his or her exam question to the full group of instructors. The remaining instructors solve the exam problem to determine: (1) Is the question clearly stated? (2) Is the question fair and reasonable given the resources available to the students? (3) Does the question adequately test the intended concepts? (4) Should students have the ability to solve the problem within the allotted time? Each exam question is edited based on the instructors' feedback in order to create the common exam. Finally, the instructor who creates the question also grades that question for every student across all sections (450–500 students), which creates consistency in the grading. Due to the common exam and grading structure, most of the section instructors only create and grade one exam problem for the entire semester.

Grading The course grading policy is the same across all sections based on in-class quizzes (5%), in-class worksheets (5%), online homework (15%), in-class labs (15%), and three exams (20% each). The exams, labs, and homework are common among sections while the quizzes and worksheets are instructor-dependent. There is an archive of old worksheets that instructors might choose to use for their section. An individual test might be curved across all sections if it was determined that it was particularly hard, but the end-of-course grades are not curved (i.e., 90–100 is an A, 80–89 is a B, etc.).

Weekly Coordination Meetings The lead instructor for the course has weekly meetings with the section instructors to coordinate each element of the course and to discuss problems that the individual instructors might be facing. During the first meeting of the semester, the workload is assigned. Specifically, the instructors choose the exam for which they will write test questions, and instructors select several sections in which they proctor labs. Subsequent weekly meetings are dictated by the weekly schedule. The coordination meetings are also used to iterate through the exam creation process described in the previous section.

Discussion of Centralized Model Evaluation Criteria

One of the prime drivers to change the format of this course from the traditional lecture format to a centralized blended model was based on *department-centered* evaluation metrics, with the goal of improving course coverage and consistency across sections. The results show that these goals were achieved. Not only was syllabus course coverage 100% for all of the sections in the blended format, student performance on common tests was very consistent across the sections. This is especially impressive considering that the entirety of the in-class time was spent with different instructors for each section.

To examine the consistency more carefully, consider the test averages. Recall that the tests are common across all 11 sections and that each test problem is graded by one person across all sections. After all the exams are graded, the average exam grade is determined for each section. Then statistics are computed across the section averages to ensure that students are receiving a consistent learning experience across sections. Table 2.1 shows these statistics for two semesters. While there is a range in performance across the sections, as seen by the low and the high section averages, the standard deviation across sections is remarkably small considering that there are 11 sections with a total course enrollment of 450–500 students spread across the sections. The small

Table 2.1
Exam Statistics Performed on Section Test Averages

	Spring 2016			Fall 2016		
	Test 1	Test 2	Final	Test 1	Test 2	Final
Average	77.5	82.5	78.8	76.2	89.8	81.1
Standard deviation	2.84	1.92	1.99	2.08	2.6	2.84
Low–High	72–82	80–86	77–82	73–80	83–92	74–86

standard deviation shows that this course format enables multiple instructors to provide a common learning experience for the students.

Since the different sections are taught on different days and at different times, there is some variation in performance across sections that will result from self-selection of students for particular sections. For example, a Monday/Wednesday 8:00 a.m. section might attract a different set of students than does a Tuesday/Thursday 6:00 p.m. section. This effect was examined by doing a circuits concept inventory (CCI) on the students both at the beginning of the term (pretest) and at the end of the term (posttest). The results for fall 2013, when only nine sections were being taught, are shown in figure 2.1. The pretest shows that there was a difference in scores among sections and that the gain across all sections was relatively similar (Ferri et al., 2014).

Other drivers for change in the course format (from traditional lecture to blended) were based on *student-centered metrics:* performance and attitude. In particular, experiential learning and student engagement afforded by the blended class format were important factors. As mentioned previously, a study on the effect of the in-class labs shows significant improvement in performance and student confidence on concepts that relate to the labs versus concepts that are unrelated.

The DFW rates, another department-centered metric for the course, falls in the range of 12% to 14%, which is comparable to other required junior-level courses in the department.

While student attitude toward the course varies with the skill of the section instructor, which is true for all courses, two common patterns of student

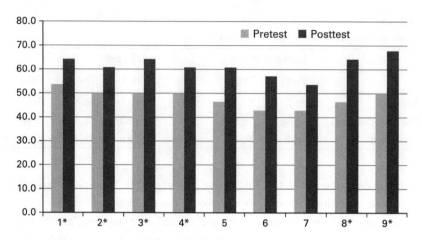

Figure 2.1

* = significant

CCI pretest and posttest medians by course section (Ferri et al., 2014). 1(N = 38); 2(N = 23); 3(N = 31); 4(N = 40); 5(N = 36); 6(N = 39); 7(N = 18); 8(N = 34); 9(N = 27).

attitude emerge. This particular model of the course is an aggressive form of course blending: to achieve consistency across sections, all important concepts and methodologies are covered in the online videos, leaving class-time mini-lectures for additional, more complex examples rather than any new material. Some of the best students in the class feel that they should not have to come to class except on lab days, because they are able to learn the material from the online lectures (since those lectures are so complete). Some of the lowest-performing students feel too much material is taught online, and they struggle with understanding the content in that format. Both of these sets of student complaints are valid and would be motivation, in a single-section course, for moving some of the more difficult content from online to an in-class supplemental lecture format. This is a case where a decision was made that the improved consistency in coverage and quality across sections was worth the trade-off. Recall that the complete synchronization among the sections meant that any student could go to any of the instructor office hours, giving struggling students more resources for help.

There are pros and cons to this model when considering *instructor-centered criteria*. There is clearly less instructor academic freedom and a great deal of instructor coordination time and effort that need to be invested. For new instructors or for instructors who are new to blended learning, this model provides an apprenticeship opportunity where they can work with an experienced lead course instructor who coordinates the course and mentors the section instructors on the blended classroom approach. In fact, since almost all of the section instructors are PhD students, teaching the courses is marketed to graduate students who are interested in academic careers as an opportunity to gain experience in several new pedagogical methods.

Case Study 2: Coordinated Model

The *coordinated model* requires strong collaboration among instructors for the development of instructional materials, student assessment methods, ordering and scheduling of topics, test schedules, and course format. Collaboration means extra instructor effort in planning the course and may require compromises among the instructors on matters such as the ordering and relative importance of topics. Thus, a coordinated model means that some of the instructors' academic freedom is lost. On the other hand, the compromises may result in a better course format and schedule for the students because of the collaborative effort among the instructors. Other benefits of a coordinated model mean that the instructors can share the load for developing new course resources, thereby reducing their individual efforts despite the extra effort needed for planning and coordination. Instructors also have shared experiences with the blending process and can discuss specific problems and solutions, which has benefits similar to those that students gain by working in study groups. From a departmental perspective, coordination means that there is some consistency across sections on the course breadth and depth of coverage and general student experiences with the course. While instructors need not discuss their course grades, the close coordination opens the door for the instructors to compare grades to make sure that the section GPAs are comparable. From the department and student perspectives, some consistency in grading across sections is desirable, though some differences may be expected based on the differences among students who registered for the different sections.

The case study of the coordinated blending model described below is Circuit Analysis, a required course taught at the sophomore level to students majoring in electrical and computer engineering. There are typically three to four sections of the course taught each term, usually by different instructors, with each section enrolling 40–50 students. This case study considers two instructors who taught this course in a coordinated manner twice. Circuit Analysis covers almost the same topics as Circuits and Electronics but covers them in greater depth because it is aimed at electrical and computer engineering majors and because it is a three-credit-hour semester class as opposed to a two-credit-hour semester course. (Note that students cannot get credit for both classes.) However, the similarity of the subject matter meant that the same videos used for Circuits and Electronics could be used for Circuit Analysis, but they played a different role. Whereas the videos contained all of the pertinent knowledge and skills needed in Circuits and Electronics, the same videos were used in Circuit Analysis as a means to cover introductory material and give simple examples. As in Circuits and Electronics, classroom time in Circuit Analysis was devoted to gaining experience solving more problems, often more complex problems, and to doing hands-on labs. The number of hands-on labs in Circuit Analysis was 50% higher than in Circuits and Electronics—nine versus six 50-minute labs. In addition, Circuit Analysis had supplemental lectures on topics not covered in Circuits and Electronics or in the MOOCs. These lectures were typically on more complex methods that would typically generate more questions from students than the lecture topics covered online.

For the first offering of Circuit Analysis in this new format, a lot of time was spent developing resources for the course, such as the in-class labs, worksheets, and two-minute quizzes given at the beginning of class. Coordination between the instructors started several weeks before the semester began by working together to come up with a common syllabus for the course that detailed the weekly schedule of topics and videos assigned, course policies, test schedule, and weekly lab topics. The only difference between these syllabi was the relative weighting of grades between the different course components:

lab worksheets, in-class quizzes, online homework, supplemental homework, and tests. Both instructors needed to compromise the way they taught the material in the past, especially with regard to the order of topics and relative time spent on individual topics, in order to be highly coordinated with each other. The format of the class was the same between the sections, starting with a very short quiz on the online material, followed by supplemental lectures including extra problems worked at the board and extra worksheets and in-class labs.

Throughout the term, the instructors shared the worksheets, supplemental homework assignments, and exams to make sure that they were covering the topics at the same depth and that the level of difficulty for the exams was approximately the same. They shared a few common worksheets and homework assignments; most were different yet comparable.

Because of the time-intensive nature of creating labs, the nine in-class labs in the course were common between the sections. These labs included modified versions of the labs used in Circuits and Electronics plus three additional labs. The development of these labs started several weeks before the semester began and continued throughout the term, always staying one or two weeks ahead of schedule in the development versus implementation of the labs. Lab development was facilitated by having two instructors involved since they could subdivide duties and also review and test the procedures developed by the other person.

Discussion of Coordinated Model Evaluation Criteria In terms of student performance on exams, both sections met the desired expectations of the instructors. Another performance metric correlated with student attitude is a survey of self-perceived competence in the subject matter. Students were given a survey at the end of the course and asked to rate their level of understanding of the individual topics in the course, with 4 being "solid understanding," 3 being "moderate understanding," 2 being "minimal understanding," and 1 being "no understanding." Figure 2.2 shows the results of this survey for one of the blended sections compared to the average of the two traditional sections during the first semester of this case study. The figure shows the topic number

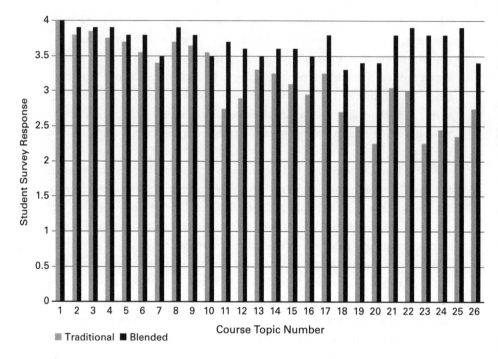

Figure 2.2

Results of a student survey of self-perceived competence on course topics, numbered in the order in which they were covered in the course

chronologically, starting with Topic 1 being the first topic in the course and Topic 26 being the last. This survey of self-perceived competence is related to student confidence in the subject matter. The uptick in the ratings for Topics 21–22 in all the sections is due to the fact that those topics are covered in another course as well.

The figure shows a general drop-off in confidence near the end of the term for the traditionally taught sections, while the blended section shows more consistency in confidence among the different topics. One thought is the blended sections kept on their weekly schedule due to their coordination and synchronization, while for traditional, uncoordinated sections, it is common for typical instructors to fall behind in a course and rush the material at the end. This would explain the drop-off in confidence regarding the later material in the traditional sections. For consistency, only the sections taught by instructors who were experienced in that particular delivery method are shown in figure 2.2. However, the confidence ratings for the section taught by the instructor new to the format of blending classes (not shown) were higher and more uniform than those of the traditional lecture sections.

When comparing the sections using instructor-centric criteria, it is clear that the resource development took much longer for the blended courses than for the traditional courses. Furthermore, coordination efforts took additional time, but that additional collaboration improved the resources and timing of the schedule, which ultimately benefited the students.

In the first offering of Circuit Analysis in this format, coordination was the priority without consideration for instructor mentoring, which was *definitely a lost opportunity*. Blending a course well takes practice. Mentoring could play a significant role in improving instructor confidence and performance. In the second offering of the course in this format, several changes were made. One is that the instructor who was experienced in blending classes mentored the instructor who was newer to that method on how to manage the in-class time. This resulted in a higher comfort level for the instructor and for the students in that section. Also, the videos were revised and re-recorded for the second offering of the course. This revision was done through coordination among the instructors, and both instructors recorded modules of videos. Many instructors prefer to use their own videos than those of a colleague, yet this takes a great deal of time. With coordination, no single instructor has to develop the entire set of videos, yet they benefit from the collaboration among the instructors on the general content and flow of the videos.

From a department-centered viewpoint, the main advantage of this model is that coordination among the sections did help to increase consistency among the sections. Because there was still a great deal of instructor flexibility, this model is not as consistent as the centralized model of blending that is performed in Circuits and Electronics.

Additional observations about the length of class time can be made based on the two semesters of this case study. During one semester, Instructor

A's section met twice per week for 75 minutes each period while Instructor B's section met three times per week for 50 minutes each period. In the other semester, they switched roles with Instructor B meeting twice per week and Instructor A meeting three times per week. Both instructors felt that the 50-minute time period was too short to run the blended class effectively using the format described, and so the class periods seemed "rushed." Alternatively, both instructors felt that the pace of the class when implemented in a 75-minute class period was very good. Both instructors additionally felt that they had to give up an activity for the 50-minute class. One instructor gave up the daily quizzes, while the other gave up much of the worksheet activity.

Case Study 3: Distributed Model

The *distributed model* is one where the online resources, such as videos, may be shared but the individual section instructors retain complete control of the course format, weekly schedule, assessment methods, and determination of in-class activities. The distributed model is closest to the traditional format in which engineering lecture classes are taught. When compared to the two other models, this model affords the instructor the greatest flexibility and freedom in the course in order to adjust to the needs of individual students. The loss of coordination might lead to inconsistency among sections in terms of topics covered and the amount of time spent on each topic.

The case study considered here is Dynamics of Rigid Bodies, a sophomore-level required course in mechanical engineering. Four or five sections of the course are typically taught each semester, with each section having enrollments ranging from 35 to 70. In any particular semester, one or two of the sections are taught in a blended mode using the same video lectures, which were developed by one of the instructors. Similar to the circuits classes described above, the video lectures for Dynamics of Rigid Bodies were developed as part of two MOOCs: *Engineering Systems in Motion: Dynamics of Particles and Bodies in 2D Motion*, and *Advanced Engineering Systems in Motion: Dynamics of Three Dimensional (3D) Motion* (developed by Wayne Whiteman, 2014, on the Coursera platform). The two MOOCs constitute about 80 videos of 6 to 10 minutes each designed to cover all of the material in Dynamics of Rigid Bodies. The existence of the MOOC provides a tremendous advantage in developing a flipped or blended class.

Especially in the distributed model, it is difficult for a single instructor to justify the amount of time and effort to create a library of well-produced online videos. As mentioned earlier, there is a surprising amount of reticence among some veteran faculty members to use videos that they themselves did not develop; other instructors view the use of the online videos as they would view a textbook. In the latter case, the videos and textbook serve as basic resources, allowing students to learn material on their own prior to coming to class. Indeed, some instructors of Dynamics of Rigid Bodies continue to teach using traditional lectures but make the MOOC videos available to their students as an additional resource.

In the distributed model of course delivery, there is an official syllabus that lists topics that must be covered, but the syllabus does not specify the emphasis or the time that should be devoted to each topic. The phenomenon seen in figure 2.2, where there was a declining confidence level as the semester progressed for the traditional lecture classes, is a common pitfall for instructors who vary their schedule to suit student needs. In other cases, some instructors skip topics in an effort to squeeze all of the material into one semester. For example, in Dynamics of Rigid Bodies, some instructors may only cover work-energy methods in the context of two-dimensional problems, while other instructors may elect to cover work-energy concepts in both planar and three-dimensional systems. In this sense, it is helpful if the library of videos covers more than the minimum number of concepts, so that instructors can select which to assign to students and can choose the order and emphases to be placed on the various topics. The in-class time freed up by the online videos is used by each instructor in different ways: possible in-class activities include supplemental lectures, team assignments and/or worksheets, in-class quizzes, instructor-led demos, and student hands-on activities. Further information about the blended version of Dynamics of Rigid Bodies, including a description of the hands-on learning activities, can be found in Ferri and Ferri (2016a). There was no coordination on tests, homework, quizzes, or worksheets among the various sections. This format provided the most flexibility among instructors and required the least coordination. Each instructor made up his or her tests and assignments. The disadvantage was that this model could result in the least consistency across sections.

Discussion of the Distributed Model Evaluation Criteria   The distributed model of delivery has several features that bear mentioning. From an instructor-centered perspective, the independence of the sections gives added flexibility to the instructor. However, the effective blending of online material requires a surprising amount of effort, especially for a veteran instructor who is adopting a blended format for the first time. If they didn't develop the videos, instructors *must watch the videos themselves* prior to assigning them so that the online material can be tightly integrated with the in-class activities. This contrasts with the level of prep time when reviewing a textbook, which instructors can skim. Poor integration of the online material with the in-class activities may cause more confusion and frustration for students and result in a learning experience that is worse than traditional lecturing. Thus, the distributed model allows instructors to tailor the level of blending to their own teaching style and doesn't coerce them into going outside their comfort zone. It also avoids issues of academic freedom, which have been addressed by the American Association of University Professors (Flaherty, 2013).

From a student-centered perspective, not all in-class activities are equal in the value that they add to the online material. The use of evidence-based learning strategies such as active learning, hands-on learning, and problem-based learning are excellent ways to complement online lectures with guided learning periods that make students *want to attend class.* If individual sections of a course have different in-class activities and are conducted using different formats, then many students would prefer the flexibility to choose a section based on their own preferences.

From a departmental perspective, there is no additional work required for scheduling these distributed blending sections compared to those taught using the traditional lecture style. Furthermore, allowing complete instructor flexibility means that there is virtually no pushback from the faculty about added work required for coordination. On the other hand, as mentioned above, the loss of consistency across sections can impact the student preparation for subsequent courses.

CONCLUSIONS

Each of the three models of blending across multiple-section courses has advantages and disadvantages. The centralized model yields the strongest consistency across sections. It also works well when there are a significant number of instructors who are not skilled in blended learning, because of the centralized decisions on course format, resources, and scheduling and the fact that the instructors must meet weekly with a lead instructor, who will help mentor them and coordinate their efforts. A case study where it has been shown to work well is in a very high-volume course taught by advanced graduate students to undergraduates from another major. One benefit from a student perspective is that the strong synchronization among sections means that there are far more instructor office hours that students might attend each week. The lack of flexibility in schedule and coverage of the centralized model, though, means that an instructor cannot adapt to the needs of a particular section. Also, since all the important concepts are taught online to achieve consistency, weaker students may have trouble following the material while the strongest students feel that the in-class component does not add much value over watching the videos.

The distributed model gives the most instructor flexibility but also requires the most individual instructor effort and time, a pro and a con in terms of instructor-centered metrics. The added flexibility in the schedule and course in the distributed model can be a benefit for improving student performance by adapting to the needs of a particular class if the instructor is skilled at blended learning. Due to the overhead needed to make online videos, the distributed model has a strong barrier to implementation, unless the videos are already available.

The coordinated model is a compromise between the two extremes, allowing for some sharing of materials and resources among the instructors. Also, the instructor coordination means that the resulting basic schedule and resources reflect a consensus among faculty, possibly providing a better-thought-out plan than could be achieved by the distributed model. The classroom flexibility afforded by the instructors in the coordinated model means that more of the difficult, high-level material can be covered in the classroom, leaving the low-level conceptual material for the online coverage. Thus, the weak students are not disadvantaged by the online material and the strong students feel that there is still some value added by coming to class. Although the individual section instructors may allow some variation in the schedule throughout the term, the coordination means that they are less likely to suffer from the phenomenon displayed in figure 2.2, where the course-topic confidence dipped toward the end of the term due to the instructors' poor time management during the term. It can be concluded that from a student-centered perspective, the coordinated model provides a little more robustness against instructors' inexperience level in blending, as well as some flexibility to adapt to the learning needs of a particular section.

Notes

1. NSF DUE 0618645 and TUES 1226065. Further efforts supported by NSF IUSE 1626362.

References

Bartsch, R. A., & Murphy, W. (2011). Examining the effects of an electronic classroom response system on student engagement and performance. *Journal of Educational Computing Research, 44,* 25–33.

Bloom, B. S. (1984). The search for methods of group instruction as effective as one-to-one tutoring. *Educational Leadership, 41*(8), 4–17.

Bloom, B. S., & Krathwohl, D. R. (1956). *Taxonomy of educational objectives: The classification of educational goals, by a committee of college and university examiners. Handbook I: Cognitive domain.* New York: Longmans, Green.

Chen, J. C., Whittinghill, D. C., & Kadlowec, J. A. (2010). Classes that click: Fast, rich feedback to enhance students' learning and satisfaction. *Journal of Engineering Education, 99*(2), 158–169.

Ferri, A. A., & Ferri, B. H. (2016a). *Blended learning in a rigid-body dynamics course using on-line lectures and hands-on experiments.* Paper presented at the 123rd ASEE Annual Conference & Exposition, New Orleans.

Ferri, B. H., & Ferri, A. A. (2016b). A controls approach to improve classroom learning using cognitive learning theory and course analytics. In American Automatic Control Council (Ed.), *Proceedings of the American Control Conference* (pp. 7321–7328). Piscataway, NJ: IEEE.

Ferri, B. H., Ferri, A. A., Majerich, D. M., & Madden, A. G. (2016). Effects of in-class hands-on laboratories in a large enrollment, multiple section blended linear circuits course. *Advances in Engineering Education, 5*(3), 1–27.

Ferri, B. H., Majerich, D. M., Parrish, N. V., & Ferri, A. A. (2014, June). *Use of a MOOC platform to blend a linear circuits course for non-majors.* Paper presented at the 121st ASEE Annual Conference & Exposition, Indianapolis.

Flaherty, C. (2013, November 8). AAUP asserts that instructors should control classroom curricular decisions. *Inside Higher Ed.* https://www.insidehighered.com.

Guo, P. J., Kim, J., & Rubin, R. (2014). How video production affects student engagement: An empirical study of MOOC videos. In *Proceedings of the First (2014) ACM Conference on Learning @ Scale* (pp. 41–50). New York: ACM.

Krathwohl, D. R. (2002). A revision of Bloom's taxonomy: An overview. *Theory into Practice, 41*(4), 212–218.

Mulryan-Kyne, C. (2010). Teaching large classes at college and university level: Challenges and opportunities. *Teaching in Higher Education, 15*(2), 175–185.

Perrin, K., Rusnak, L., Zha, S., Lewis, D., & Srinivasan, S. (2009). Using blended learning to ensure consistency and quality in multiple course sections. *Journal of the Research Center for Educational Technology, 5*(1), 42–48.

Shavelson, R. J., Ruiz-Primo, M. A., & Wiley, E. W. (2005). Windows into the mind. *Higher Education, 49*(4), 413–430.

Vroom, V. H. (1964). *Work and motivation.* New York: Wiley.

Yalcin, M. A., Gardner, E., Anderson, L. B., Kirby-Straker, R., Wolvin, A. D., & Bederson, B. B. (2015). *Analysis of consistency in large multi-section courses using exploration of linked visual data summaries.* PeerJ PrePrints.

3

PRELIMINARY EVIDENCE FOR THE BENEFITS OF ONLINE EDUCATION AND BLENDED LEARNING IN A LARGE ARTIFICIAL INTELLIGENCE CLASS

Ashok Goel

MIX Taxonomy Classification: This course is blended. For the students who meet face to face, the content is delivered both online before class and through lecture during class. Students test their knowledge with an online tool before coming to class, where they work on group projects and discuss concepts while receiving feedback from the instructional team. The students also have online discussions that are monitored by the instructional team.

Research Method Classification: The research method used here is a quasi-experimental design. One group was online only and one group was blended. These two groups were separated by section but had the same instructor. The blended group, in addition to having the online lectures and discussions, also had in-class lectures, activities, and discussions. The students' demographic information, performance, and retention were measured and presented through descriptive statistics.

BACKGROUND, MOTIVATIONS, AND GOALS

In January 2014, Georgia Institute of Technology launched its Online Master of Science in Computer Science[1] program, a fully accredited Georgia Tech graduate degree offered to selected students from around the world. The semester-long online courses are developed and taught by Georgia Tech faculty and offered through the Udacity platform,[2] often in parallel with in-person classes for residential students. The goal of the Online MS in CS (OMSCS) program is to offer the same courses and specializations online that are offered through the equivalent on-campus MS in CS program (Joyner, Goel, and Isbell, 2016). In fall 2017, the Online MS in CS program enrolled an order of magnitude more students (approximately 5,800) than the equivalent residential program (approximately 350) with almost an order of magnitude lower cost (approximately $7,000) than the residential program (approximately $30,000). More than four hundred students already have completed the online program, and the diploma awarded to them does not mention word *online* at all. By now the Online MS in CS program is perceived to be a success both internally and externally (Carey, 2016; Goodman, Melkers, and Pallais, 2016).

Prior to the launch of the Online MS in CS program, there was much debate within the Georgia Tech community about the program's goals and prospects. In faculty meetings as well as informal discussions, many colleagues skeptical of the proposed online program asserted that learning is largely a social process and that the online medium does not allow the same kind and degree of social interactivity that residential instruction affords (Daniel, 2012). They observed that the quality of learning in many massive open online courses (MOOCs) is questionable and that the student retention rate as measured by course completion is typically less than 50% and often less than 10% (Yuan and Powell, 2013). The critics also pointed out that studies of learning in MOOCs have recommended enhancing interaction between the teacher and the students as well as among the students (Hollands and Tirthali, 2014). Although this debate has abated a little with the perceived success of the Online MS in CS program, it has not completely dissipated. Several learning scientists and engineers at Georgia Tech, including specialists in computer science education, continue to seek hard evidence for the effectiveness of learning in the online program and to construct alternative explanations for its success.

Soon after the launch of the Online MS in CS program, several instructors of the online classes came to recognize that the video lessons they had prepared for the online program could also be useful for the residential classes they teach. Thus, some of them have been experimenting with various versions of flipped classes and blended learning (Bonk and Graham, 2006; Garrison and Vaughan, 2008) in their current residential courses, though the experiments remain largely informal and undocumented. The expectation in these experiments has been that flipped classes and blended learning will help enhance the quality of learning in the residential classes as measured by learning outcomes. However, empirical evidence in support of this hypothesis in the given context has not been easy to obtain because of the informal nature of the experiments.

This chapter describes one course—Knowledge-Based Artificial Intelligence—that we have been teaching in the fall semester of each year for more than a decade. In 2014, when we developed an online version of the Knowledge-Based AI (KBAI) course for the Online MS in CS program, we expected that the performance of the online class might not be up to the level of the residential class because of the limitations of the medium, including the lack of social interaction, as briefly discussed above. However, in a quasi-experimental study in fall 2014, we found that the online students performed on par with or slightly better than the residential students on the writing and programming assessments. This finding provided preliminary evidence in support of the quality of learning as measured by learning outcomes on a set of assessments in the online KBAI course.

In fall 2015 and again in fall 2016, we used the video lessons we had developed for the online KBAI class to support blended learning in the residential class. Our expectation was that blended learning will help improve the performance of the residential students as measured by learning outcomes on a set of assessments. When we repeated the quasi-experimental study in 2015 and 2016, we found that the residential students now performed about as well as the online students on the same assessments. This provides preliminary evidence in support of using blended learning in the residential section of the KBAI class. In this chapter, we describe these experiments and potential explanations and discuss their implications.

THE ONLINE KNOWLEDGE-BASED ARTIFICIAL INTELLIGENCE CLASS

In previous work, we described the design of the semester-long online KBAI course in detail (Goel and Joyner, 2016). Broadly speaking, this course adopts a cognitive systems view of AI (Goel and Davies, 2011; Langley, 2011, 2012). Thus, the course discusses AI techniques inspired by human cognition on the one hand, and AI hypotheses and models of human cognition on the other. On the one hand, the course materials for the online KBAI class are closely based on the residential course the instructor has been teaching for more than a decade;[3] on the other, we developed almost all materials for the online class from scratch. For example, we developed the videos for the KBAI course in a special studio, not by taping the lectures in the residential class. Similarly, we developed the script for each video lesson, and each slide in the script, especially for the online KBAI class. Georgia Tech provided significant resources for the development of the online KBAI course. For example, it provided significant time on the part of an instructional designer (David Joyner), as well as the time of a videographer and video editor. It also provided the instructor with a modest stipend.

The course consists of 26 video lessons developed by the instructor and the instructional designer that help teach the course material, a digital forum[4] in which students post questions and answers as well as participate in discussions, a learning management system through which students submit assignments and receive grades,[5] a proprietary peer feedback tool developed at Georgia Tech where students read and submit feedback on each other's assignments, a proprietary autograder tool developed by Georgia Tech and Udacity that helps grade the source code of programming projects, and a library of classic AI programs written in Python (Connelly and Goel, 2013). All KBAI video lessons[6] are freely available from Udacity. The course is administered by the instructor assisted by a small team of graduate teaching assistants (TAs). The teaching assistants typically answer questions and facilitate discussions on the digital forum and grade assignments, projects, and examinations. A typical offering of the course may have 200 to 400 students. The number of TAs varies accordingly; there are typically one head TA for each offering and an additional teaching assistant for every 50 students in the class. Thus, a class of 200 students may have five teaching assistants including the head TA. Since spring 2016, the teaching team has also included an AI teaching assistant named Jill Watson that answers routine, frequently asked questions on the discussion forum (Goel and Polepeddi, 2017; Maderer, 2016).

The pedagogy of the online KBAI course is organized around a small set of learning goals and outcomes, and the assessments are specifically designed around the desired outcomes (Goel and Joyner, 2016). All instruction and class activities are based on one of ten key strategies from the learning sciences, or a combination of more than one (e.g., Bransford, Brown, and Cocking, 2000; Clark and Mayer, 2016): *learning by example, learning by doing, authentic practices, project-based learning, personalized learning, collaborative learning, peer-to-peer learning, learning by teaching, learning by reflection,* and *immersion in a community of practice.* For example, the design and programming projects in the class are based on real AI research and involve the writing of reflective design reports, thus promoting learning by doing, project-based learning, authentic practices, and learning by reflection (Goel et al., 2013). As another example of a learning strategy, we not only strongly encourage participation on the online discussion forum by the online students as well as the teaching staff, we also use peers as reviewers of students' assignments, reports, and examinations as well as TAs as metareviewers (Joyner et al., 2016). This affords immersion in a community of practice, peer-to-peer learning, collaborative construction of knowledge, and learning by teaching. As yet another example of a learning strategy in the KBAI class, we have developed and deployed about a hundred microexercises accompanied by *nanotutors* for teaching a variety of KBAI domain concepts and methods (Goel and Joyner, 2017). A nanotutor is a small, focused AI agent embedded in the video lessons that models students' reasoning on a particular problem, where the problem engages a domain concept or method to be learned. Given a student's answer to the problem, the nanotutor first classifies the answer as correct or incorrect, and then explains why the answer is (in)correct. Together the microexercises and nanotutors support learning by example, learning by doing, personalized learning, and learning by reflection.

Table 3.1

Student responses to questions comparing the online KBAI class to other classes. Answers on the 7-point Likert scale questions ranged from "significantly worse than" (1) to "significantly better than" (7). The final question ranged from "bad" (1) to "excellent" (7). (Adapted from Goel and Joyner, 2016.)

Prompt	1	2	3	4	5	6	7
On a scale of 1 to 7, how would you rate the quality of the video lessons and exercises in KBAI compared to other OMS courses you've taken?	0%	1%	2%	15%	24%	23%	14%
On a scale of 1 to 7, how would you rate the quality of the video lessons and exercises in KBAI compared to other non-OMS online classes you've taken?	0%	2%	1%	7%	13%	30%	29%
On a scale of 1 to 7, how would you rate the quality of the lectures in KBAI compared to any other college courses you've taken, including courses in person?	0%	1%	2%	10%	25%	44%	16%
On a scale of 1 to 7, how would you rate the quality of the KBAI course as a whole, including the assignments, projects, and forum discussions, compared to other OMS courses you've taken?	0%	1%	1%	9%	24%	23%	20%
On a scale of 1 to 7, how would you rate the quality of the KBAI course as a whole, including the assignments, projects, and forum discussions, compared to other non-OMS online courses you've taken?	0%	0%	2%	4%	11%	40%	24%
On a scale of 1 to 7, how would you rate the quality of the KBAI course as a whole, including the assignments, projects, and forum discussions, compared to any other college courses you've taken, including courses in person?	0%	0%	6%	9%	22%	39%	22%
On a scale of 1 to 7, how would you rate the overall quality of CS7637: Knowledge-Based AI?	0%	0%	1%	0%	16%	31%	52%

We adopted the methodology of design-based research (Brown, 1992; Collins, 1992) in developing the online KBAI course. Thus, we introduce educational interventions, conduct detailed formative assessments, reflect on the course evaluations, and repeat the cycle on an ongoing basis. Since fall 2014, we have offered the online KBAI course each fall, summer, and spring term (except summer 2017). Initial enrollment in the class has ranged from about 200 to 400 students each term, so that by now about 2,000 online students have enrolled in the course. For the most part, student feedback on the online KBAI course has been quite positive (Goel and Joyner, 2016). Table 3.1 summarizes the student responses to questions on a survey the course instructors conducted at the end of the course. Note that >50% of the students in the fall 2014 offering of the class give it a score of 7 ("excellent") on a 7-point Likert scale and another >30% give it a score of 6. The student reviews of the 26 video lessons too have been positive. Almost 30% of the students rate the videos as 7 ("significantly better than other online courses") on the 7-point Likert scale and another 30% rate them as 6. Ou et al. (2016) analyzed the videos in terms of design of constructivist learning environments (Clark and Mayer, 2016; Jonassen, 1999).

COMPARISON OF LEARNING IN THE ONLINE AND RESIDENTIAL KNOWLEDGE-BASED AI CLASSES IN FALL 2014

In addition to offering the online KBAI class each term since fall 2014, in the fall terms of 2014, 2015, and 2016 we offered the same course to residential students at both the graduate and undergraduate levels. This allowed us to compare the performance of the online students with that of the residential students. However, it is useful to separate the comparison in fall 2014 from the comparisons in fall 2015 and fall 2016, because while in fall 2014 the residential section followed the traditional format of lectures and discussions, in fall 2015 and again in fall 2016 the residential section used blended learning. Indeed, it was the success of the online course in fall 2014 that led us to experiment with blended learning in the residential classes in fall 2015 and fall 2016.

In the following paragraphs, we compare learning in the online and residential sections of the KBAI course in fall 2014 to analyze the effectiveness of online education using the traditional residential section as the benchmark. This comparison is important in establishing the effectiveness of learning in the Online MS in CS program, even if only partially and implicitly. Later in this chapter, we will use the learning in the residential and online courses in fall 2014 to assess learning in the residential course using blended learning in fall 2015 and fall 2016.

To conduct the quasi-experimental study (Shadish, Cook, and Campbell, 2002) comparing the learning in the online and residential sections of the KBAI class in fall 2014, we used exactly the same course syllabus, structure, pace, and assessment in both sections. Both sections used the same set of tools for learning management, online discussion, and peer feedback. All assignments, projects, and examinations from the two sections were distributed randomly among the teaching assistants, and the teaching assistants graded the assignments, projects, and examinations "blindly"—that is, they did not know if the student was in the online or the residential section. The only major difference between the teaching in the two sections was that while the online students had access to the 26 video lessons, in the residential section we had face-to-face lectures and discussions. The lectures and discussions were equivalent to those the instructor has used while teaching this course for the past 10 years. The medium of instruction and discussion was the independent variable in the study.

It is important to repeat that the 26 video lessons also contain about 150 microexercises; thus, the online students were asked not only to watch the videos but also to complete the microexercises. The quasi-experimental study had two dependent variables: student retention and student performance on course assignments, projects, and exams. The online KBAI class in fall 2014 started with 196 students. At the end of the semester, 170 students were enrolled in the class and received a grade for it, a completion rate of about 87%. This is a high rate compared to other Online MS in CS classes (and much higher than most MOOCs; Yuan and Powell, 2013). In fall 2014, the residential offering of the KBAI class had a completion rate of 88%. *Thus, the retention rate in the online section of the KBAI class was about the same as in the residential section.*

In fall 2014, both sections had to complete eight written assignments, four projects, and two examinations. *As table 3.2 indicates, the online KBAI students outperformed residential students on every assessment in the class as well as in the class as a whole.* Thus, in terms of duplicating the learning seen in the residential KBAI class in the past, the online offering of the KBAI class appears successful: students in the online section performed as well as or better than students in the residential class. In fact, some of the projects submitted by the online students were of such high quality that they led to a research publication in an AI conference (Joyner et al., 2015).

Table 3.2

Average grades on each assessment for the online and residential sections of the KBAI class in fall 2014. (Adapted from Goel and Joyner, 2016.)

Item	Maximum points	Online mean	Residential mean	Online – residential
Assignment 1	4	3.90	3.52	0.38
Assignment 2	4	3.94	3.70	0.24
Assignment 3	4	3.95	3.52	0.42
Assignment 4	4	3.92	3.83	0.09
Assignment 5	4	3.89	3.75	0.14
Assignment 6	4	3.86	3.62	0.24
Assignment 7	4	3.91	3.77	0.14
Assignment 8	4	3.97	3.90	0.08
Project 1	100	94.47	92.61	1.86
Project 2	100	92.74	89.64	3.10
Project 3	100	93.10	92.17	0.92
Project 4	100	92.0	88.5	3.53
Midterm	100	70.2	70.0	0.20
Final exam	75	93.76	93.48	0.29
Final grade	100	92.32	91.31	-1.01

The results in table 3.2 seem a little surprising at first: given that learning is largely a social process, and instructor-student interaction as well as interaction among the students in the online section are modest compared to their counterparts in the residential section, we would have expected the residential students to do better on the assessments. One explanation for the superior performance of students in the online KBAI class is that online students make more extensive use of the discussion forum. Once the online class actually started, we soon realized that while the video lessons were like an interactive textbook, the discussion forum was the virtual classroom for the online section. Through extensive interaction among themselves and to a lesser degree with the teaching staff in this virtual classroom, the online students were able to partially compensate for the lack of social interaction in a physical classroom.

Another explanation for the superior performance of the online section compared to the residential section may lie in the student demographics. Table 3.3 compares the student demographics between the two sections. As in Christensen et al.'s (2013) study of the demographics of students who take MOOCs, most Online MS in CS students are young, male, domestic, employed, and highly educated. However, compared to the students in the residential section, the students in the online section of the KBAI class were older, more educated, and had significantly more programming experience. In fact, we found a strong correlation between prior programming experience and performance in the KBAI course in both the online and residential sections.

Table 3.3 also indicates that the online and residential students may have different motivations for taking the KBAI course. When asked to select the reason for taking it at the start of the class, while the residential students selected "The course is required to complete their degree" more often than any other reason, the online students selected "The topic is interesting" most often. This is a little different from Christensen et al.'s study: they found that most MOOC students are motivated by better employment opportunities. Of course, these three explanations are not mutually exclusive; on the contrary, the three explanations likely complement one another to give a fuller account of the superior student performance in the online KBAI class.

Table 3.3
Student demographics in the online and residential (graduate) sections of the KBAI class in fall 2014

	Online	Residential
Age	<24: 15% 25–34: 47% >35: 39%	<24: 82% 25–34: 17% >35: 1%
Gender	Female: 10% Male: 90%	Female: 24% Male: 76%
Highest level of prior education	Bachelor's: 87% Master's: 11% Doctoral: 2%	Bachelor's: 94% Master's: 6% Doctoral: 0%
International or domestic	International: 13% Domestic: 87%	International: 68% Domestic: 32%
Employment status	Full time: 90% Part time: 5% None: 5%	Full time: 5% Part time: 15% None: 80%
Years of programming experience	<4: 16% 4–8: 29% 9–13: 21% 14–18: 20% >18: 14%	<4: 28% 4–8: 62% 9–13: 9% 14–18: 1% >18: 0%
Top reasons for enrollment in CS7637	The topic is interesting; AI is a useful career skill; AI will complement existing CS knowledge.	The course is required to complete their degree; the topic is interesting; AI will complement existing CS knowledge.

EXPERIMENT IN BLENDED LEARNING IN THE KNOWLEDGE-BASED AI CLASS IN FALL 2015

In fall 2015, we again offered both the online and residential sections of the KBAI class. The general design of the pedagogy in the two sections was similar to the designs described in the second and third sections of the chapter, respectively. However, we made one important change: in the residential section we used blended learning instead of the traditional classroom instruction involving lectures and discussions. Although Georgia Tech provided significant resources and modest incentives for the development of the online KBAI course as noted above, it provided few resources and no incentives for the development of blended learning in the residential KBAI class. The instructor developed the blended course mostly on his own initiative, through his own efforts, and on his own time.

For our blended KBAI class, we made the 26 video lessons developed for the online students available to the residential students as well. Note that the video lessons also contained ~150 microexercises, which amounts to about one exercise for every eight minutes of video on average. Each video lesson also contained a reflection exercise at the end asking students to summarize the main lessons they had learned. We asked the residential students to complete all videos and exercises relevant to a given topic prior to the class on the topic. Thus the students not only had to watch the videos but also to reach a level of competency prior to the class. However, we did not monitor the performance of the students on the exercises embedded in the videos.

We used the class time itself for several purposes: (1) using slides derived from the videos to go over the most salient aspects of the lesson; (2) working in small teams on open-ended exercises; and (3) engaging in general discussions on the topic of the day as well as on AI as a whole. To address the classroom exercises, students worked in self-selected teams of three to four; the self-selection was typically based on physical proximity in the classroom and this often resulted in the same teams. As the student teams worked on a problem, some of the teaching assistants and the instructor moved from team to team, answering any and all questions to the extent possible. Finally, the problem was discussed by the class as a whole, which developed a solution starting from the solutions student teams had proposed. This strategy supports the social construction of knowledge (Papert and Harel, 1991). There was no direct equivalent of these classroom team activities in the online class.

We term the KBAI class in fall 2015 blended learning instead of just flipped classroom because of the use of technology to support learning beyond the videos the students watched before coming to class. In particular, we made extensive use of the Piazza digital discussion forum for sustained conversations and collaborative learning throughout the semester. However, the Piazza discussion forum for the online class was much more active than for the residential class, and we observed significantly more spontaneous student-led social construction of knowledge in the discussion forum of the online class than the residential class.

We also repeated the quasi-experimental study comparing the effectiveness of learning in the two sections as measured by a common set of assessments. The design of the study closely followed the experiment in fall 2014 as described in the third section of the chapter with one important difference: based on the student feedback from fall 2014, in fall 2015 we reduced the number of assignments from eight to six and reduced the number of projects from four to three. Table 3.4 summarizes the performance of students in the two sections: the residential students performed as well as the online students on all assessments except one; on three projects, the performance of the residential students was significantly better than that of the online students. Table 3.5 summarizes the demographics of students in the online and residential

Table 3.4

Average grades on each assignment in the online and residential sections of the KBAI class in fall 2015

Item	Max	Online (mean)	Online (SD)	Residential (mean)	Residential (SD)	Residential – online (Mean)
Assignment 1	40	35.30	5.62	36.24	2.82	0.94
Assignment 2	40	36.09	4.20	36.90	2.69	0.81
Assignment 3	40	36.54	3.69	36.90	7.42	0.36
Assignment 4	40	36.77	3.75	36.22	8.53	-0.55
Assignment 5	40	34.74	8.79	37.07	2.60	2.33
Assignment 6	40	35.20	7.54	37.12	2.20	1.92
Project 1	100	84.22	15.53	88.37	10.81	4.15
Project 2	100	72.86	20.17	79.27	13.21	6.41
Project 3	100	64.63	18.63	72.91	12.16	8.28
Midterm	100	95.44	10.33	98.22	2.39	2.78
Final exam	100	78.13	19.36	85.85	5.22	7.72
Final grade	100	82.82	5.62	86.66	6.25	3.85

Table 3.5
Student demographics in the online and residential sections of the KBAI class in fall 2015

	Online fall 2015	Residential fall 2015
Age	<24: 15% 25–34: 44% >35: 41%	<24: 83% 25–34: 14% >35: 3%
Gender	Female: 13% Male: 87%	Female: 24% Male: 76%
Highest level of prior education	Bachelor's: 79% Master's: 17% Doctoral: 4%	Bachelor's: 89% Master's: 11% Doctoral: 0%
International or domestic	International: 42% Domestic: 58%	International: 62% Domestic: 38%
Years of programming experience	<4: 22% 4–10: 43% 10–15: 18% >15: 17%	<4: 27% 4–10: 67% 10–15: 5% >15: 1%
Top reasons for enrollment in CS7637	The topic is interesting; AI is a useful career skill; AI will complement existing CS knowledge.	Interested in AI and KBAI; the course is required to complete their degree; the topic is interesting.

sections of the KBAI class in fall 2015. We also found that student retention in the online class in fall 2015 was comparable to that in the residential class in fall 2015 as well as the online KBAI class in fall 2014.

These comparative results from fall 2015 (summarized in table 3.4) stand in marked contrast to those from fall 2014 (summarized in table 3.3): they indicate that blended learning helped improve the performance of the residential students in fall 2015 relative to the residential students in fall 2014. A potential explanation for the improvement in the performance of residential students pertains to the changing demographics of students in the residential and online sections of the KBAI class. On the one hand, while the online section in fall 2014 consisted of 87% domestic and 13% international students, the online section in fall 2015 had 58% domestic and 42% international students. On the other hand, while in fall 2014 the residential students, when asked to select the reason for taking the KBAI course, chose "The course is required to complete their degree" most often, in fall 2015 they chose "Interested in AI and KBAI" most often. We do not yet fully understand the implications (if any) of either factor for the student performance assessments of learning.

Two additional aspects of blended learning in the KBAI class are noteworthy. First, in both fall 2014 and fall 2015, the residential section of the class met in large lecture halls on Monday, Wednesday, and Friday from 9:00 to 10:00 a.m. The physical arrangement of student seating in the lecture halls was not conducive to blended learning in fall 2015, and especially not for student work in small teams or interaction between the instruction and the student teams. Second, while we have not done a formal analysis of class attendance, based on informal attendance records it seemed that on a typical day in fall 2014, 60%–70% of the students enrolled in the course attended the class. But it seemed as if in fall 2015 and fall 2016, no more than 40%–50% of the enrolled students were present on a typical day. This reduction in class attendance might be because once all students had access to the video lessons, some may have felt less compelled to attend the actual class. This implies that the benefits of blended learning were limited to only about half of the class.

EXPERIMENT IN BLENDED LEARNING IN THE KNOWLEDGE-BASED AI CLASS IN FALL 2016

In fall 2016, we again offered both the online and residential sections of the KBAI class and repeated the quasi-experimental study. The general design of the pedagogy as well as the procedures followed by the two sections were as described for fall 2015. Thus, we again made the 26 video lessons with the ~150 microexercises available to the residential students at the start of the term. Further, we again used the class time to go over the most salient aspects of the video lessons, working in small teams on open-ended exercises and having general discussions about the topic of the day as well as AI as a whole. We did make three major changes in both the online and residential sections. First, we provided edited transcripts of the videos in the form of an ebook. Second,

Table 3.6

Average grades on each assignment for the residential and online sections of the KBAI class in fall 2016

Item	Max	Online (mean)	Online (SD)	Residential (mean)	Residential (SD)	Residential – online (mean)
Assignment 1	40	34.15	3.99	33.59	3.60	-0.56
Assignment 2	40	34.09	4.35	33.24	4.89	-0.85
Assignment 3	40	35.19	3.01	34.78	3.43	-0.41
Project 1	100	81.37	18.58	81.01	14.90	-0.36
Project 2	100	70.67	22.23	71.11	19.00	0.44
Project 3	100	65.85	22.21	64.96	19.20	-0.89
Midterm	25	22.24	2.21	21.79	3.17	-0.45
Final exam	25	22.19	1.89	22.40	1.87	0.21
Final grade	100	81.06	12.33	79.93	11.47	-1.13

in order to reduce the students' workload, we reduced the number of written assignments from six in fall 2015 to three in fall 2016. Third, we introduced the AI teaching assistant called Jill Watson to answer routine, frequently asked questions on the Piazza discussion forum.

We also made two changes to the pedagogy of blended learning in the residential class. First, early in the term we formed small teams of three to four students through random assignment, while making sure that we had good mixes of undergraduate and graduate students as well as male and female students on each team. This was in contrast to the formation of teams based on seating in fall 2015. Second, we used the strategy of think-pair-share (Lyman, 1992). In this technique, students first work on a problem by themselves for a specific time. Then they join their team, share and explain their solution, and listen to the solutions of the other team members. Finally, the whole class discusses the solutions, with the instructor acting as a facilitator.

As in fall 2015, again in fall 2016 the physical classroom in the style of a large lecture hall was not conducive to student-teacher interaction or teamwork. This negatively influenced opportunities for collaborative and active

Table 3.7
Student demographics in the online and residential sections of the KBAI class in fall 2016

	Online fall 2016	Residential fall 2016
Age	<24: 18.2% 25–34: 54.7% >35: 27%	<24: 87.2% 25–34: 10.4% >35: 2.3%
Gender	Female: 12% Male: 88%	Female: 27.9% Male: 82.1%
Highest level of prior education	Bachelor's: 79% Master's: 16.4% Doctoral: 4.3%	Bachelor's: 43% Master's: 8.1% Doctoral: 1%
International or domestic	International: 13.6% Domestic: 86.4%	No satisfactory results for this
Years of programming experience	<4: 25% 4–10: 49% 10–15: 14.2% >15: 10.6%	<4: 36% 4–10: 62.7% 10–15: 1% >15: 0%

learning. Further, as in fall 2015, we estimate that in fall 2016 only about half of the students enrolled in the class physically attended the class on a typical day. We expect that the low attendance partially masks the benefits of blended learning.

Table 3.6 summarizes the results of student performance on the learning assessments in both the online and residential sections in fall 2016. These results are very similar to those from fall 2015 (table 3.4). We also found that the student retention in the online class in fall 2016 was again comparable to that in the residential class in fall 2016 as well as the online classes in fall 2014 and fall 2015. Table 3.7 summarizes the student demographics in the residential and online sections in fall 2016. This summary is very similar to that in fall 2014 (table 3.3), except that due to a glitch in administering the survey, we could not collect reliable data on the nationality of students in the residential section. Together these tables appear to confirm the benefits to performance of blended learning. They also appear to indicate that benefits persist irrespective of minor changes in student demographics.

As in fall 2014 and fall 2015, in fall 2016 the residential section of the KBAI class met in large lecture halls on Monday, Wednesday, and Friday from 9:00 to 10:00 a.m. As in fall 2015, in fall 2016 no more than 40%–50% of the enrolled students were present on a typical day. Again, this poor attendance could be because the students had access to the video lessons, so that some of them may have felt less need to attend class.

COMPARISON OF RESIDENTIAL KNOWLEDGE-BASED AI CLASSES IN FALL 2014, FALL 2015, AND FALL 2016

While in fall 2014 the residential section of the KBAI class used the traditional format of lectures and discussions, in fall 2015 and again in fall 2016 it used the pedagogy of blended learning. Thus a direct comparison of student performance in fall 2014, fall 2015, and fall 2016 on the learning assessments in the KBAI class may provide evidence for the impact of blended learning. Unfortunately, many of the learning assessments across the three years were quite different and thus do not provide a sound basis for comparison of student performance. In particular, the midterm and final examinations, as well as the written assignments, varied quite a lot over the years. In fact, the number of assignments decreased from eight in fall 2014 to just three in fall 2016.

The design and programming projects in fall 2014, fall 2015, and fall 2016 might provide some basis for comparing student performance. While the number of projects also decreased from four in fall 2014 to three in fall 2015 and fall 2016, the projects were fundamentally the same across the three years. However, the projects are also the farthest away from classroom activities and thus least likely to manifest any impact of blended learning in the KBAI class. As mentioned earlier, the design and programming projects in the class are based on real AI research and promote project-based learning and authentic scientific practices (Goel et al., 2013), and thus form a thread of activities fairly distinct from classroom activities. A definitive demonstration of the impact of blended learning in the residential section of the KBAI class requires controlled A/B experimentation.

CONCLUSIONS

The novel and bold Georgia Tech Online MS in CS program is perceived to be a success in terms of enrollment and cost both internally and externally. However, questions about the quality of learning in the online program persist in part because of the lack of empirical data. Our quasi-experimental study in the KBAI class in fall 2014 provides preliminary evidence that the student learning in the online section of the KBAI class as measured by learning assessments is at least as effective as that in the residential section. The study also found that student retention in the online KBAI class was comparable to that in the residential class. If these results hold for other Online MS in CS courses, it may indicate that the learning in the Online MS in CS program as a whole as measured by learning assessments is as effective as in the residential MS in CS program.

While the pedagogy of blended learning is gaining in popularity (Bonk and Graham, 2006; Garrison and Vaughan, 2008), questions about the design of blended classes and the effectiveness of blended learning persist (Dziuban et al., 2016; Vaughan et al., 2013). Our quasi-experimental studies in the KBAI class in fall 2015 and again in fall 2016 provide preliminary evidence that student performance on learning assessments using the pedagogy of blended learning is at least equivalent to the traditional pedagogy of classroom lectures. Our experiments in the KBAI class in fall 2015 and fall 2016 also affirm one of the side benefits of developing an online course: the educational materials developed for the online course can be also be used to promote blended learning in residential classes.

Our experiments with online education and blended learning in the KBAI class have led us to a few lessons. First, scientists and engineers often tend to look for analytic models for designing blended learning classes. However, despite significant research on blended learning, there is at present no good analytic model for designing blended classes. This is not surprising: good analytic models for designing any kind of educational class are difficult to build because of the large number of interacting variables of many different kinds.

Second, the literature on the learning sciences in general (e.g., Bransford, Brown, and Cocking, 2000; Clark and Mayer, 2016; Jonassen, 1999) and blended learning in particular (such as Dziuban et al., 2016; Vaughan et al., 2013) provides ample guidelines for designing blended classes. These guidelines are a good place to start in thinking about the development of a blended learning class.

Third, in practice, the design of blended classes often is based on precedents. Thus, we were inspired to develop the online KBAI class in part by a similar AI course[7] developed by Sebastian Thrun and Peter Norvig at Stanford University in 2011. Indeed, we watched some of the videos from their AI class before developing the video lessons for our class.

Fourth, although guidelines and precedents for developing blended classes do exist, the absence of an analytic model implies that the development of a blended class will include a lot of exploration and experimentation, reflection, and revision. Although we have described results only from fall 2014, fall 2015, and fall 2016 in this chapter, at the time of this writing we are still experimenting with both the online and residential sections of the KBAI class.

Fifth, while past precedents are useful in developing new blended classes, they also impose strong biases on the design that may not be relevant to the goals and context of the new class and may even get in the way. Thus, it is important to use precedents mostly as inspirations, not as templates to be rigidly followed. While we were inspired in part by Thrun and Norvig's online AI course, we designed the videos for the KBAI class for our own purposes. As just one example, we introduced ~100 nanotutors into the KBAI videos, which turned out to be quite successful (Ou et al., 2016).

Sixth, there is a general tendency to use extant technologies in developing online and blended courses such as video lessons, interactive books, discussion forums, and autograders. However, online and blended classes also provide ample opportunities to develop new technologies. Thus, the needs of the online class inspired us to develop an AI agent for answering simple questions in the class discussion forum. We have also used the AI agent to answer questions in the blended class.

Finally, given that the development of online education and blended learning entails exploration and experimentation, there are bound to be failures, surprises, and new insights; it is important to be open to them. One of the most important insights in these experiments was the centrality of the discussion forum to both online education and blended learning. Like most first-time developers of an online course, we assumed that the development of the video lessons was the critical part of the course and thus devoted a lot of attention and resources to them. However, once the course actually started, we soon realized that the discussion forum was the "beating heart" of the class: the discussion forum acted as the virtual classroom, the place where students interacted with one another and with the teaching staff and collaboratively constructed knowledge and understanding (Joyner, Goel, and Isbell, 2016). We also came to realize the discussion forum needed as much as attention as the video lessons. We have found the same is also true for blended learning: while online educational materials such as videos and books are important, the critical question really is how to make use of them to promote active learning in the class.

ACKNOWLEDGMENTS

I am grateful to David Joyner for his help in developing the online KBAI course. I thank the dozens of TAs and the thousands of students in the online and residential sections of the KBAI class since fall 2014 for participating in the experiments described in this chapter. I am grateful to Parul Awasthy for constructing tables 3.4 and 3.5, to Shruti Bhati for constructing tables 3.6 and 3.7, and to Bobbie Eicher for some of the analysis of these tables. The second and third sections of the chapter, including tables 3.1, 3.2, and 3.3, are adapted from Goel and Joyner (2016).

Notes

1. http://www.omscs.gatech.edu/.

2. https://www.udacity.com/courses/georgia-tech-masters-in-cs.

3. https://www.cc.gatech.edu/classes/AY2014/cs7637_fall/.

4. https://piazza.com.

5. The Sakai Project. (2014). Sakai 10. https://sakaiproject.org/sakai-10.

6. https://www.udacity.com/course/knowledge-based-ai-cognitive-systems--ud409.

7. https://www.udacity.com/course/intro-to-artificial-intelligence--cs271.

References

Bonk, C. J., & Graham, C. R. (2012). *The handbook of blended learning: Global perspectives, local designs*. San Francisco: Wiley.

Bransford, J., Brown, A., & Cocking, R. (2000). *How people learn: Mind, brain, experience, and school*. Washington, DC: National Research Council.

Brown, A. (1992). Design experiments: Theoretical and methodological challenges in creating complex interventions in classroom settings. *Journal of the Learning Sciences*, 2(2), 141–178.

Carey, K. (2016, September 29). An online education breakthrough? A master's degree for a mere $7,000. *New York Times*. http://www.nytimes.com/2016/09/29/upshot/an-online-education-breakthrough-a-masters-degree-for-a-mere-7000.html.

Christensen, G., Steinmetz, A., Alcorn, B., Bennett, A., Woods, D., & Emanuel, E. (2013). The MOOC phenomenon: Who takes massive open online courses and why? Available at SSRN: http://dx.doi.org/ 10.2139/ssrn.2350964.

Clark, R., & Mayer, R. (2016). *E-Learning and the science of instruction: Proven guidelines for consumers and designers of multimedia learning* (4th ed.). Hoboken, NJ: Wiley.

Collins, A. (1992). Toward a design science of education. In E. Scanlon & T. O'Shea (Eds.), *New Directions in Educational Technology* (pp. 15–22). New York: Springer-Verlag.

Connelly, D., & Goel, A. (2013). *Paradigms of AI programming in Python*. Paper presented at the Fourth Symposium on Educational Advances in AI (EAAI-2013), Bellevue, WA.

Daniel, J. (2012). Making sense of MOOCs: Musings in a maze of myth, paradox and possibility. *Journal of Interactive Media in Education*, 2012(3).

Dziuban, C. D., Picciano, A. G., Graham, C. R., & Moskal, P. D. (2016). *Conducting research in online and blended learning environments: New pedagogical frontiers*. New York: Routledge/Taylor & Francis.

Garrison, D. R., & Vaughan, N. D. (2008). *Blended learning in higher education: Framework, principles, and guidelines.* Hoboken, NJ: Wiley.

Goel, A., & Davies, J. (2011). Artificial intelligence. In R. Sternberg & S. Kauffman (Eds.), *Handbook of intelligence* (pp. 468–484). Cambridge: Cambridge University Press.

Goel, A., & Joyner, D. (2016). An experiment in teaching cognitive systems online. *International Journal for the Scholarship of Technology Enhanced Learning, 1(1)*, 3–23.

Goel, A., & Joyner, D. (2017). Using AI to teach AI. *AI Magazine, 38(2)*, 48–59. https://aaai.org/ojs/index.php/aimagazine/article/view/2732/0.

Goel, A., Kunda, M., Joyner, D., & Vattam, S. (2013). *Learning about representational modality: Design and programming projects for knowledge-based AI.* Paper presented at the Fourth AAAI Symposium on Educational Advances in Artificial Intelligence, Quebec City, Canada.

Goel, A., & Polepeddi, L. (2017, June). *Jill Watson: A virtual teaching assistant for online education.* Paper presented at the Learning Engineering for Online Learning Workshop, Harvard University, June 2017. Available as Georgia Tech Technical Report (http://hdl.handle.net/1853/59104).

Goodman, J., Melkers, J., & Pallais, A. (2016). *Does online delivery increase access to education?* Harvard University Kennedy School Faculty Research Working Paper Series RWP16-035.

Hollands, F., & Tirthali, D. (2014). *MOOCs: Expectations and reality.* New York: *Center for Benefit-Cost Studies of Education,* Teachers College, Columbia University.

Jonassen, D. H. (1999). Designing constructivist learning environments. In C. M. Reigeluth (Ed.), *Instructional design theories and models: A new paradigm of instructional theory* (Vol. 2, pp. 215–239). New York: Routledge.

Joyner, D., Ashby, W., Irish, L., Lam, Y., Langston, J., Lupiani, I., et al. (2016). Graders as meta-reviewers: Simultaneously scaling and improving expert evaluation for large online classrooms. In *Proceedings of the Third (2016) ACM Conference on Learning @ Scale* (pp. 399–408). New York: ACM.

Joyner, D., Bedwell, D., Graham, C., Lemmon, W., Martinez, O., & Goel, A. (2015). Using human computation to acquire novel methods for addressing visual analogy problems on intelligence tests. Paper presented at the Sixth International Conference on Computational Creativity, Park City, UT, June 2015.

Joyner, D., Goel, A., & Isbell, C. (2016). The unexpected pedagogical benefits of making higher education accessible. In *Proceedings of the Third (2016) ACM Conference on Learning @ Scale* (pp. 117–120). New York: ACM.

Langley, P. (2011). Artificial Intelligence and cognitive systems. *AISB Quarterly, 133,* 1–4.

Langley, P. (2012). The cognitive systems paradigm. *Advances in Cognitive Systems, 1,* 3–13.

Lyman, F. (1992). Think-pair-share, thinktrix, thinklinks, and weird facts: An interactive system for cooperative thinking. In N. Davidson & T. Worsham (Eds.), *Enhancing thinking through cooperative learning* (pp. 169–181). New York: Teachers College Press.

Maderer, J. (2016, May 9). Artificial intelligence course creates an AI teaching assistant. Georgia Institute of Technology news release. http://www.news.gatech.edu/2016/05/09/artificial-intelligence-course-creates-ai-teaching-assistant.

Ou, C., Goel, A., Joyner, D., & Haynes, D. (2016). Designing videos with pedagogical strategies: Online students' perceptions of their effectiveness. In *Proceedings of the Third (2016) ACM Conference on Learning @ Scale* (pp. 141–144). New York: ACM.

Papert, S., & Harel, I. (1991). *Constructionism.* New York: Ablex.

Shadish, W. R., Cook, T. D., & Campbell, D. T. (2002). *Experimental and quasi-experimental designs for generalized causal inference (2nd ed.).* Independence, KY: Cengage.

Vaughan, N., Cleveland-Innes, M., & Garrison, D. (2013). *Teaching in blended learning environments: Creating and sustaining communities of inquiry.* Athabasca: Athabasca University Press.

Yuan, L., & Powell, S. (2013). *MOOCs and open education: Implications for higher education.* Bolton, UK: University of Bolton, Centre for Educational Technology, Interoperability and Standards & JISC. Retrieved from http://publications.cetis.ac.uk/wp-content/uploads/2013/03/MOOCs-and-Open-Education.pdf.

4

BUILDING PURPOSEFUL ONLINE LEARNING: OUTCOMES FROM BLENDING CS1301

David Joyner

MIX Taxonomy Classification: This course was blended—at least for some students. The required parts of the course were delivered entirely online. The online components included content delivery and content application with feedback through Vocareum and McGraw-Hill's adaptive Smartbook. The optional parts of the class provided in-person content delivery and feedback during content application. During recitation, teaching assistants provided lectures and guidance on activities. For additional guidance on activities, the students could go to the help desk or the instructor's office hours.

Research Method Classification: The research method was a quasi-experimental design. The two experimental groups, students who took the face-to-face class and students who took the blended class, took the class during the same semester, though the instructors differed. Student performance was measured through a standardized computer science assessment. Student perceptions, demographic information, and expectations for the course were measured through surveys.

INTRODUCTION

In theory, blended learning refers to any pedagogical approaches on the spectrum between traditional face-to-face instruction and purely online instruction.

In practice, blended learning usually refers to a specific pedagogical approach where technology-based online instruction is used to replace in-classroom instruction, and the in-classroom instruction is then modified to focus on practice, collaboration, and reinforcement. A key characteristic here is that mandatory class attendance and participation have not vanished, but rather class time has been modified to take better advantage of the opportunities of synchronous, co-located meetings.

However, blended learning may take on other forms as well, at different points along the spectrum from pure traditional instruction to completely online instruction. Large universities, for example, often have enormous core classes taken by hundreds or thousands of undergraduate students per semester. Their admission numbers may even be throttled by how many students they can offer these core classes to in a single semester. In these instances, these large core classes may be offered online. Unlike the blended learning approach described above, these classes may not have a synchronous co-located component at all: all class instruction and work may be completed in the online environment.

Unlike purely online instruction, however, this approach still embodies many of the characteristics of traditional face-to-face instruction. Although there are no scheduled synchronous co-located meeting times, the students are still geographically close to one another, which may support greater collaboration and community support. As residents of the university, these students also have access to university resources, like tutoring services and office hours. As full-time students, they also embody a persona more like traditional on-campus students than online students.

Thus, this version of blended learning exists at a different place on the spectrum between traditional and online learning: the students and the resources available to them are largely traditional, but the classroom is online. The enrollment bottleneck is thus resolved because there are no mandatory synchronous co-located activities that press for lecture hall space. Course creators can take advantage of the opportunities provided by online instruction like personalized feedback, individualized pacing, and adaptive instruction without sacrificing the community, social, and human support characteristic of traditional education.

Georgia Tech's CS1301

This version of blended learning is the basis of Georgia Tech's online version of CS1301. CS1301 is one of three Introduction to Computing classes offered by Georgia Tech. It is primarily taken by computer science majors, although it also draws students from business administration, industrial systems engineering, and the sciences. Additionally, any student can take the class for their core computer science credit, although other majors typically take CS1371: Computing for Engineers or CS1315: Introduction to Media Computation.

The course assumes no prior computer science experience and requires no prior math background beyond high school algebra. It takes students from the basics of procedural programming through variables, control structures, data structures, and the basics of objects and algorithms. The course is taught in Python 3.

In the traditional version of CS1301, students attend two or three lectures a week, totaling three hours of lecture time. Students also have 90-minute once-weekly recitation sections, but these are strictly optional, and attendance is typically sparse. Students enrolled in the class also have access to a help desk, effectively the equivalent of office hours, for the class: typically help is available any time during normal hours on weekdays from one of the class's many teaching assistants. The course enrolls nearly 1,000 students per year (spread across three semesters), and it is a bottleneck on the number of students that may be admitted to the computer science program at Georgia Tech.

CS1301 Goes Online

To resolve this bottleneck, Georgia Tech moved to create an online section of CS1301. Absent any synchronous co-located meetings, the size of this section would be limited only by grading capacity, which typically has been higher than the available lecture hall space. Students in this section would continue to have access to optional recitations and the help desk, as well as office hours with the course instructor.

Thus, CS1301 online (colloquially and henceforth referred to as CS1301x, given that it is hosted on edX) falls closer to the online side of the blended spectrum. It blends pure online instruction with a more traditional on-campus student body bolstered by traditional in-person student services. In this evaluation, we report on the design and structure of CS1301x, emphasizing how it was designed to take unique advantage of the online medium to compensate for features lost in the removal of a traditional lecture. We then report on the inaugural semester of the course and how it was delivered. Finally, we report on the results of this design and delivery, including a demographic comparison of enrollees in the online and traditional versions, a comparison of their learning outcomes, and a comparison of the student experience as evaluated through mid- and end-of-term surveys.

It is important to note that CS1301x has also been offered on edx.org as a MOOC, open to the public; however, this report focuses solely on the design, delivery, and evaluation of the course with traditional students at Georgia Tech.

COURSE DESIGN

The course design refers to the content of the course constructed prior to student enrollment. This emphasizes the portions of the course that, ideally, are durable and reusable semester after semester, including videos, books, practice problems, homework assignments, and automated evaluation tools. In contrast, course delivery emphasizes the portions of the course that cannot be preproduced or reused, such as office hours, recitations, forum and chat interactions, and grading.

To describe the design of the course, we will start by providing a brief background on the technological infrastructure. Then we will describe the structure of the course, the design of the videos, and the design of the assessments and exercises, emphasizing the design principles that guided all three.

Technological Infrastructure

CS1301x consists primarily of four integrated pieces. First, edX: the course as a whole is presented on the edX platform, and edX is the container or launcher for all components of the course. Students never directly access any tool except through edX. edX organizes the course into units, chapters, and lessons, and each lesson consists of multiple videos, text blocks, and interactive exercises. edX also computes student grades and presents them on the progress page, shown in figure 4.1.

Second, the course also has a virtual textbook built on McGraw-Hill's Smartbook platform. The textbook contains questions (multiple choice and fill in the blank) that students complete for course credit, as shown in figure 4.2. Each learning objective in the Smartbook is connected to multiple questions, so if students initially miss a question, they may demonstrate understanding of that learning objective through a different question. The Smartbook is launched from the end of each chapter in the edX course. Approximately 1,000 problems are available in the Smartbook, although most students will not see all of them.

Third, living coding examples are injected into the course material in edX through Vocareum, as shown in figure 4.3. These problems let students write code within the browser, run it to see the results, and submit it against test cases for grading. After submission, students are given case-by-case results for revision and resubmission. All coding exercises give students an

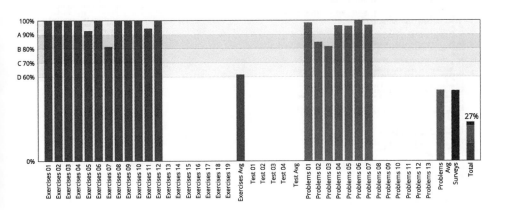

Figure 4.1
The progress diagram for a student approximately midway through CS1301x

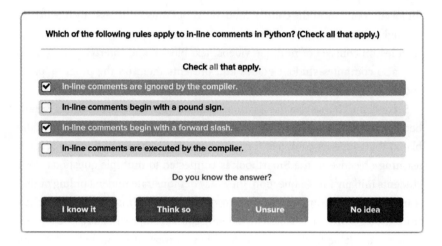

Figure 4.2
A question asked through the Smartbook interface

Coding Problem 3.5.3 (External resource) (3.0 points possible)

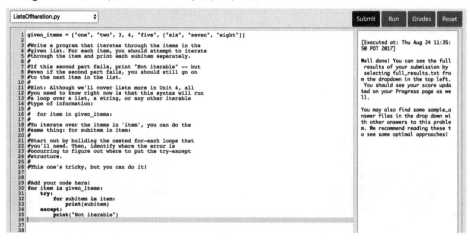

Figure 4.3
A coding problem in Vocareum

unlimited number of attempts, and they are encouraged to iterate, debug, and test. Custom feedback is also available after submission on some common errors, and work is underway to add in additional intelligent debugging help, as well as feedback on style and approach.

Fourth, a requirement of canceling scheduled lecture time for the class was the ability to allow students flexibility in when and where they take exams. Toward this end, a digital proctoring solution, Proctortrack by Verificient, is used to proctor students on their own computers during tests. Proctortrack takes several sources of data (screenshots, webcam recordings, audio recordings, and more) to ensure the students' identity and detect collaboration using AI. Because Proctortrack runs on students' own computers, the actual structure of the test is familiar: on the tests, students complete the same types of edX and Vocareum exercises noted above. These four tools make up the bulk of the student experience in CS1301x, although a handful of other tools are used as well: Qualtrics and Sakai for administering course surveys and Piazza for course discussions.

Course Structure

CS1301x is organized into five units totaling nineteen chapters, taking students from the basics of computing through debugging, variables and data types, operators, control structures, data structures, objects, and algorithms. Each chapter of the course is made up of a series of videos, text blocks, and interactive exercises, some of which involve live coding. Most chapters in the course are further supplemented by a problem set of more challenging questions. Both the in-chapter exercises and the problem set are counted in students' grades. The overall structure of the course is built around three main design principles: congruency, modularity, and personalization.

Congruency Congruency refers to presenting the same material in different media or formats. Our prior experiences with the Georgia Tech Online Master of Science in Computer Science program (OMSCS) (Joyner, 2017) noted that different methods of presentation are better suited for different content, situations, and individual preferences. Students would, for example, use video transcripts as more easily perused representations of the course material, but video transcripts are not congruent with course material because they lack the visual examples. Other times, textbooks are used, but a textbook rarely follows the identical organizational scheme and structure as the course that is using it, requiring more than novice-level knowledge to find the mappings between lecture material and readings.

To support multiple study habits while preserving accessibility for novices, the video course and textbook in CS1301x are constructed congruently. Both follow the same overall structure, with a 1:1 mapping between course videos and textbook sections. The examples, visuals, and explanations across both are the same, allowing students to alternate between them. Anecdotally, we find that students consume video lectures initially for overall subject knowledge and follow up with the textbook for a more easily perusable presentation of the course. From the perspective of the blended classroom, this also blurs the lines between lecture content and readings: like reading content in a traditional class, the lecture content is persistently available and can be consumed at the student's own pace. Additionally, the connections between the lecture and reading content are clearer due to their shared examples and structure.

Modularity   Modularity refers to limiting the interdependencies between videos, lessons, and chapters within the course to allow for easy insertion, deletion, or revision of new or existing course material. In computer science, this is a difficult challenge over the scope of an entire course because topics regularly build on one another; however, CS1301x leverages modularity in other ways. The course design splits the material itself into three categories: fundamentals, language, and domain. Fundamentals cover the principles of computing that are general to all programming languages. Language covers the implementation of those principles within a certain programming language (currently Python). Domain covers the application of those principles in that language to a certain problem domain (currently computer graphics). These three types of content are interleaved within each chapter.

Because of this modular structure, content can be more flexibly revised to incorporate student feedback, introduce new information, or provide further instruction. For example, based on initial feedback from the inaugural semester, additional material was planned to explicitly teach common design patterns within loops and to more directly correct commonly observed misconceptions around Boolean logic. These insertions can range from new sections to entire new chapters without disrupting the overall course structure. More importantly, this modularity also supports the adaptation of the course to new languages or new domain areas without necessitating a complete re-creation of the course from scratch.

Personalization The modularity of the course design supports revision of the course material, but it also supports the course's push for personalization. Personalization, for our purposes, is the alteration of course content based on student preferences; adaptivity is the alteration of course content based on student abilities. The increasingly interdisciplinary nature of computer science creates a demand for this type of personalization. At Georgia Tech, for instance, there are three Introduction to Computing classes to tailor the instruction to the demands of different majors. For example, engineers (taking CS1371: Computing for Engineers) have a different set of use cases for computing than computer science, business, science, or liberal arts majors, and yet all do have strong use cases for learning computer science.

This modular design, then, allows the course to be personalized to individual students without creating entirely new courses. An accounting major, for example, could take the core Introduction to Computing material with Python, supplemented by domain material in finance rather than computer graphics. An engineer might take only the fundamentals of the class, while learning it instead in Matlab with an application to engineering problems. These alternate language and domain pathways have not yet been created, but leaving room for them in the design of the course was one of the fundamental determinants of course structure.

Video Design

Although we resist the common perception that online courses are "video" courses, video does comprise a significant portion of development and student learning time. In total, CS1301x has approximately 500 videos, averaging around 3 minutes each in length. Roughly 20% of the videos in the course are "head-shots," where the instructor appears on camera accompanied by some graphics or text, while 80% of the videos utilize "screen capture." Typically, headshots cover fundamental material, or serve as bookends introducing and concluding a lesson otherwise recorded using screen capture.

Independence Video independence follows the same pattern as the modularity described above, but with a differing emphasis; whereas modularity focuses on the ability to make changes or create branches in the overall course struc-ture, video independence refers to the ability to make smaller-scale revisions or improvements to individual videos. From a student perspective, this would also allow a student to understand a particular video even if they had skipped the prior videos, so long as they understand the prerequisite content.

Toward this end, each video is individually scripted to be internally indepen-dent; if a student enters the video without watching any prior course material, then the video will still be internally complete so long as they have the content prerequisites necessary for the topic to be covered. For example, if a lesson uses a recurrent example, the example is briefly reintroduced in each video where it comes up a new time. In this way, a student who is skipping around in the course material will not suffer from lack of context, and if revisions are necessary we need not worry about how much of an impact a revision will have on other sections of the course.

Simplicity In selecting a way to present code visually, we surveyed several other online computer science courses. We found that many courses record an authentic programming context, which has significant benefits for authentic-ity. However, we also observed two problems with this approach: first, authen-tic programming environments often dedicate significant screen real estate to information or actions unnecessary in a teaching environment; and second, instructors are forced to simultaneously think about the screen contents, the operations in the development environment, and the narration to students, which presents a significant cognitive load.

To alleviate both issues, the visual style chosen for CS1301x emphasized pre-prepared visuals in a simple canvas rather than live coding in an authentic environment. This presented two initial advantages: it allowed instructors to separate the tasks of preparing visual contents and recording audio narration, simplifying each; and it maximized the screen real estate dedicated to actual contents, allowing larger font sizes, clearer syntax coloring, and a large canvas for writing, as shown in figure 4.4.

Flexibility In some courses surveyed, a third disadvantage of the authentic programming context arose: instructors were often forced to use vague methods for highlighting certain portions of code or drawing relationships between different parts. The move to pre-prepared visuals supported an additional advantage of the presentation style: the ability to draw on top of existing code.

This ability creates enormous flexibility around the way visuals can be used. Throughout the course, red lines are drawn to mark when individual lines of

A Function with Multiple Parameters (3.4.4.3)

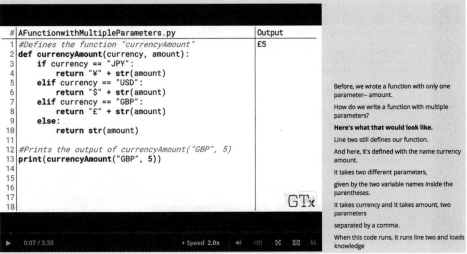

Figure 4.4
A visual from CS1301x

code are run. When a certain complex line is resolved down to simpler lines (such as print(5 + 3) resolving to print(8)), each subsequent stage of evaluation is crossed out and the new one is written in. Lines are drawn connecting print statements to the output window, or connecting the values of variables to where they were assigned, as shown in figure 4.5. While balancing these handwritten portions of the visuals with verbal narration increases cognitive load, the mechanism presents enough extra flexibility and expressiveness to compensate.

Exercise Design

As noted above, we push back against the perception that online courses are primarily video courses. Our emphasis is on the ability to embed feedback and interaction directly into the instruction, such that receiving the instructional material inherently involves demonstrating understanding. This close tie between individualized assessment and instruction provides one of the

A Function with Multiple Parameters (3.4.4.3)

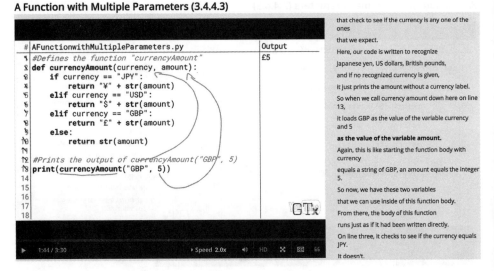

Figure 4.5
A visual from CS1301x with handwritten lines connecting code to output

greatest opportunities for online education. Toward that end, we emphasize three principles in the design of the course's exercises: integration, iteration, and adaptivity.

Integration   As alluded to above, both online and traditional course design often separate out instruction and assessment. In person, long lectures are often followed up by take-home assignments or tests at a later date. Online, instruction and assessment are often presented in different areas of a course's user interface, or assignments are presented that are dependent on consuming entire large sections of instructional material. Even blended or flipped classrooms enforce this dichotomy: even if assessment is during lecture periods and instruction happens at home, a separation still exists.

CS1301x instead pushes for a heavy integration of interactive exercises directly into the course material. Short videos are used so that interactivity can be rapidly interspersed between instruction. Most short videos in the course are followed by at least one exercise (either multiple choice/fill in the blank through edX or live coding through Vocareum), and feedback is always built live into the exercise for students to immediately assess their ability and understanding. In a more traditional blended or flipped classroom, this embedded formative assessment could become a powerful tool to ensure students complete required at-home work prior to attending a flipped class session.

Iteration   One of the instructional emphases of CS1301x is on the overall coding workflow: not on syntax and program flow, but on writing, debugging, and revising a program. Toward that end, the major learning goal emphasizes iteration: students should learn to iterate over their programs, and so they should also be tested on iteration in the assessments. As such, all programming exercises in the course allow unlimited attempts until the students have completed the problem. After every attempt, they receive individual feedback on how their program performed and are encouraged to revise and reattempt it. In this way, testing against the automated evaluator is identical to testing against test cases in a true software development environment. This even remains true during tests, ensuring that students are tested on the same knowledge the course material aims to communicate.

Adding onto this explicit feedback, students also receive implicit feedback in the form of exemplary answers presented after they have already come to their own answers. In this way, students may discern personal feedback not only on whether their solution works, but also on how far it was from some exemplary ideal solution. The same sort of iteration also exists in the edX and Smartbook exercises: for most, students receive individual feedback on their answers and can try again if the initial answer is incorrect. This is particularly powerful in the Smartbook, where missing a question leads to a different question on the same topic rather than rote repetition of the same question's answer.

Adaptivity As noted above, we differentiate personalization and adaptivity as preference versus ability; students may personalize the course to their own tastes, but the course may also adapt to students' ability. At present, this adaptivity comes in two forms. First, the Smartbook itself is adaptive in that students' performance on the Smartbook exercises changes the presentation of text within the textbook. Areas in which students have already demonstrated competence are shown in one style, while areas where students may need to focus more are shown differently. Struggles with the exercises cause the Smartbook to point students directly back to the corresponding sections as well, minimizing the amount of search students must do to correct their understanding.

Second, the integrated assessment throughout the course material gives students the ability to self-adapt the material to their current understanding. By being equipped with an explicit, immediate opportunity to test their current knowledge, they receive the information necessary to decide whether to move on or to continue focusing on the current material. Plans for the future involve making this more fundamental and inherent in the system by generating explicit recommendations or even locking material until prior competency has been demonstrated.

COURSE DELIVERY

As noted above, course design and production refer to the creation of persistent course materials, reusable semester after semester. Course delivery refers to the specific instantiation of the course in one semester. Generally, details of course delivery are more easily altered than details of course design. At the time of writing, the summer semester of the course has begun, and so this section will also briefly describe the changes made for the shorter semester.

Course Structure and Calendar

Student grades in CS1301 were based on four components: nineteen exercise sets (20%), thirteen problem sets (25%), tests (50%), and surveys (5%). Exercise sets were the assessments embedded in instructional material, and problem sets were the assessments provided at the end of most of the course's chapters. Surveys included a precourse test and postcourse test, a precourse survey and postcourse survey, and two midsemester surveys. Tests were each 90-minute proctored exams featuring both multiple-choice/fill-in-the-blank problems and live programming problems, all graded live during the exam.

During the spring 2017 semester, students had effectively 15 weeks to complete the course; the course exam took place in week 16, but no other assessments or instruction could be issued during that week. To complete the course, students completed one or two chapters and one problem set per week. All assignments were due on Friday at midnight, with a grace period until Sunday at midnight; the grace period was effectively to set up a time where students could not rely on teaching assistants to answer questions, but were still permitted to continue their own work.

Each Monday morning, the gradebook was exported, and the instructor emailed students showing signs of struggling, typically symbolized by low grades on the preceding week's problem set. These emails usually offered support and requested feedback. Most student replies to these emails noted reasons outside the class (e.g., athletic competitions, health issues, other classes) as the reason for the struggles, not difficulties with the course material itself.

The four tests corresponded to units 2, 3, 4, and 5 of the course, with the fourth test partially cumulative over the semester as well. Tests were given two Thursdays after the end of a unit—for example, the last lesson of unit 2 was due on Friday February 3, and its test was Thursday February 16. This was designed to give students plenty of time to ask questions after finishing a unit, as well as to avoid unit tests coinciding with weeks where additional chapters were assigned.

The summer 2017 semester was shorter and students completed the material in 10 weeks instead of 15. To compensate, the schedule for summer broke the one-chapter-per-week structure, and instead allocated a number of days to each chapter determined by the observed difficulty the previous semester. For example, chapter 2.1 (procedural programming), a short chapter, was given a single day, while chapter 3.3 (loops), the toughest chapter, was given a full week. Grace periods were extended to run until the corresponding unit test, and unit tests were kept two weeks after the deadline for the final chapter in the unit.

Student Support

As noted previously, although all instruction and assessment for this course are online, the course is blended in the sense that (1) the students are on-campus students, and (2) the students have access to traditional on-campus resources. For CS1301x, the primary forms of this are office hours (also referred to as the help desk) and recitations.

The help desk for CS1301 is open each day from 9:00 a.m. to 5:00 p.m. Individual teaching assistants sign up for three help desk hours per week, during which they are on hand to answer questions, and the number of TAs available to the sections is enough to keep the help desk open during normal weekday hours. The help desk is shared between the online and traditional sections, and no records were kept as to how many students were attending from each section, nor were the sections asked during the surveys. So, no information is available as to how many students in the online section utilized the help desk.

There was also a once-a-week 90-minute recitation specifically for students in the online section. This recitation met on Thursdays but did not meet during testing weeks, so that students could instead use that place and time for their exam if they did not have access to another quiet place. Recitations typically involved the teaching assistants presenting on the week's material, giving worksheets for extra practice, and answering student questions. At the beginning of the semester, roughly one-third of students in the online section attended these recitations, but by the end of the semester, only 5% were typically present.

In addition, the instructor and teaching assistants held "Slack office hours." Slack office hours used the popular organizational chat tool Slack and allowed students to message instructors or teaching assistants directly. The instructor offered three hours of Slack office hours per week, although in practice students sent along questions at other times as well. The instructor and teaching assistants also answered questions on the class Piazza forum.

During the summer of 2017, these services generally remained in place. However, half of the students in the summer 2017 section were off campus for the summer and could not attend recitation at all. Additionally, almost no students posted on Piazza or sent questions via Slack for the summer semester.

Examinations

Four exams were given during the semester, each worth 12.5% of the student's average. The first three covered units 2, 3, and 4 respectively; the fourth test was half-cumulative, half-specific to unit 5. Students completed the tests on their own computers and could start the test at any time during the Thursday the test was offered. They would have 90 minutes after starting the exam. Afterward, their proctoring data would be uploaded and analyzed, and a report generated on any suspicious activity.

Each test consisted of both edX multiple-choice/fill-in-the-blank problems and live Vocareum programming problems. All were graded automatically and students were able to check their course Progress page midexam to see how they were progressing. Because students had access to a live debugger on the test, all programming problems were graded all-or-nothing with no partial credit; this connects with the stated goal of teaching the programming flow and echoes the desire to test students on their ability to execute that programming flow.

COURSE RESULTS

During the spring 2017 semester, both the traditional on-campus section and the online sections of CS1301 were offered. The two classes do not follow the same pacing or structure, but both cover the same concepts. As such, this evaluation of the inaugural semester focuses on the data points shared between the two: the precourse test and survey, and the postcourse test and survey. From these, we glean information about the differing demographics between the sections, the students' learning outcomes, and the student experience.

It is worth noting that during the spring semester, the majority of students in CS1301 are typically not computer science majors; most come from industrial and systems engineering, while others come from business administration, the sciences, or the liberal arts.

Demographic Information

Because both the online and the traditional sections draw from the same student body (Georgia Tech undergraduate students) and count for the same transcript credit, we hypothesized that there generally would be little difference between students in the sections. Others disagreed. Some hypothesized that the online section would draw students with more prior experience who were comfortable in a more independent environment; some hypothesized that the online section would draw less dedicated students who would anticipate an easier course load from the online section; and some hypothesized that the online section would draw a more male audience.

In the precourse survey, students were asked several questions to address these points, including their age, gender, prior computer science experience, and anticipated workload. A total of 382 students completed this survey, 327 from the traditional section and 55 from the online section. The full results of the survey are shown in table 4.1.

Table 4.1
Results of the demographic survey

	Online	Traditional
Gender	Female: 49% Male: 49%	Female: 54% Male: 46%
Age	18–20: 67% 21–25: 24% 26–30: 4% 31+: 6%	18–20: 95% 21–25: 3% 26–30: 1% 31+: 0%
Race/ ethnicity	White: 57% Black or African American: 13% Hispanic, Latino, or Spanish origin: 4% Asian: 23% Other: 4%	White: 61% Black or African American: 5% Hispanic, Latino, or Spanish origin: 6% Asian: 24% Other: 5%
Target industry	Engineering: 33% Business/financial: 25% Computing/math: 7% Healthcare: 7% Other: 27%	Engineering: 48% Business/financial: 19% Computing/math: 5% Healthcare: 6% Other: 21%
Reason for selecting section	I can do the work at any time: 84% I can do the work from anywhere: 78% I prefer self-paced learning: 58% In-person wouldn't fit schedule: 49% Prefer to communicate online: 4%	Prefer more structured schedule: 75% Prefer live lectures: 74% Prefer to communicate in person: 59% Unaware of online section: 40% Online was full: 6%
Prior programming experience	In-person programming course: 31% Online programming course: 7% Self-taught programming: 20% No prior experience: 49%	In-person programming course: 20% Online programming course: 6% Self-taught: 9% No prior experience: 65%
Estimated hours of work per week	<5: 19% 5–7: 52% 8–10: 22% 11–13: 0% 14+: 7%	<5: 7% 5–7: 35% 8–10: 40% 11–13: 10% 14+: 8%
Likelihood to switch to CS	Not at all likely: 68% Somewhat likely: 17% Very likely: 8% Unsure: 8%	Not at all likely: 66% Somewhat likely: 20% Very likely: 5% Unsure: 10%
Likelihood to pursue CS minor	Not at all likely: 45% Somewhat likely: 17% Very likely: 32% Unsure: 6%	Not at all likely: 34% Somewhat likely: 36% Very likely: 17% Unsure: 13%

This survey produced some interesting takeaways, although the statistical conclusions carry the caveat that repeated testing may suggest relationships that actually arose by coincidence. First, there was no statistically significant difference ($\chi^2 = 0.472$) in the gender ratio between the online and traditional classes. However, there was a statistically significant difference ($\chi^2 = 5.205$, $p < 0.05$) in the ratio of black or African American students. Most significantly, 34% of students in the online section reported an age of 21 or older, compared to only 4% of residential students ($\chi^2 = 55.409$, $p < 0.0001$), despite drawing from the same student body.

Student interests between the sections differed significantly as well, with statistically fewer students in the online section projecting a future in engineering compared to the residential section ($\chi^2 = 4.256$, $p < 0.05$). While the ratio of students considering a switch to computer science (major or minor) was similar across the sections, students in the online section were more certain; however, this was largely due to their higher age and lacking time to add a minor or change a major.

Most significantly, there was data supporting the hypothesis that the online section would draw lazier students as well as the hypothesis that it would draw more experienced students. A statistically significant difference existed in expected workload ($\chi^2 = 15.890$, $p < 0.0001$), with 29% more online students expecting to spend 7 hours or fewer per week on the course. A statistically significant difference also existed in prior computer science experience between the sections ($\chi^2 = 5.140$, $p < 0.05$), with 16% more online students having prior experience. It is worth noting, however, that anecdotally, several students in the online section reflected (in the free-response survey questions, on Piazza, or in private correspondence) that their "prior computer science experience" was either failing or dropping the same course in a previous semester, and so prior experience should not be misconstrued as prior expertise. Further supporting this, there did not appear to be a strong relationship between prior experience and projected workload.

As noted above, the risks introduced by repeated testing mean these differences should be taken with skepticism; specifically, we hypothesize that the different racial and ethnic distributions are likely coincidental. The differences in age and anticipated workload, however, are too significant to dismiss.

Learning Outcomes

Students in both sections completed the Second CS1 Assessment (Parker, Guzdial, and Engleman, 2016), a standardized and validated replication of a prior validated assessment, FCS1 (Tew and Guzdial, 2010), at the beginning and end of the course. Completion of the test was counted toward students' grades, but performance on the test did not factor into credit. Students completed the test on their own time in a web browser and could take as much time as they wanted to on it.

Table 4.2 reports the results for the pre-test and post-test. Note that only students who completed a test are included; if a student abandoned a test halfway through, their score is not included in the average. "Paired pretests" and "paired posttests" refer to averaging only tests from students who also completed the other test (to look at the change in score).

Students in the online section begin and end the course with higher scores on the SCS1 test, but neither those differences nor the difference in change in scores is statistically significant. We therefore conclude that in spring 2017, there was no evidence that students in the online section were disadvantaged by their participation in the new version of the course compared to students in the traditional section.

Table 4.2

Pretest and posttest averages for students in the traditional and online sections of CS1301 in spring 2017

	Traditional	Online	Δ	t
Pretests completed	269	55	—	—
Posttests completed	227	46	—	—
Complete pretest/posttest pairs	193	45	—	—
Average score for *all pretests*	6.78	7.36	+ 0.58	1.14 ($p > .05$)
Average score for *all posttests*	9.73	10.78	+ 1.05	1.47 ($p > .05$)
Average score for *paired pretests*	6.80	7.78	+ 0.98	1.78 ($p > .05$)
Average score for *paired posttests*	9.71	10.84	+ 1.13	1.54 ($p > .05$)
Change in score for tests in pairs	+ 2.91	+ 3.07	+ 0.16	0.21 ($p > .05$)

Some hypothesized, similar to the previous hypothesis about students with prior experience enrolling in the course, that students with prior experience would be more likely to succeed in the course. To examine that, we also isolated pretest and posttest scores and changes based on prior experience (table 4.3).

As before, there are no statistically significant differences between the traditional and online sections across any of these metrics (table 4.4).

Table 4.3

Results only for students *with* prior experience in computer science

	Traditional	Online	Δ	t
Pretests completed	91	26	—	—
Posttests completed	70	23	—	—
Complete pretest/posttest pairs	64	23	—	—
Average score for *all pretests*	8.54	9.42	+ 0.88	0.98 ($p > .05$)
Average score for *all posttests*	10.90	11.91	+ 1.01	0.93 ($p > .05$)
Average score for *paired pretests*	8.52	9.61	+ 1.09	1.17 ($p > .05$)
Average score for *paired posttests*	11.11	11.91	+ 0.80	0.73 ($p > .05$)
Change in score for tests in pairs	+ 2.59	+ 2.30	- 0.29	0.23 ($p > .05$)

Table 4.4

Results only for students *without* prior experience in computer science

	Traditional	Online	Δ	t
Pretests completed	157	26	—	—
Posttests completed	121	21	—	—
Complete pretest/posttest pairs	110	20	—	—
Average score for *all pretests*	5.90	5.65	- 0.25	0.46 ($p > .05$)
Average score for *all posttests*	9.10	9.86	+ 0.76	0.93 ($p > .05$)
Average score for *paired pretests*	5.98	5.95	- 0.03	0.05 ($p > .05$)
Average score for *paired posttests*	9.11	9.95	+ 0.84	0.79 ($p > .05$)
Change in score for tests in pairs	+ 3.13	+ 4.00	+ 0.87	0.80 ($p > .05$)

It may be worth noting that the difference between sections was greater for students without prior experience. These students benefited more from the online section than students with prior experience did. Thus, no evidence was found to support the hypothesis that students without prior experience performed better in the traditional section.

Student Experience

In the end-of-course survey, students from both sections were asked several multiple-choice and free-response questions. Table 4.5 compares their perceptions (using a 7-point scale) of the pace, rigor, and quality of the course.

Generally, students across both sections rated the pace and rigor approximately evenly, although students in the online section rated the course as being of higher quality in general.

Table 4.5
Student responses to Likert-scale questions on course pace, rigor, and quality.

Question	Options	Traditional	Online
How would you rate the pace of CS1301?	(Way too slow) 1	0%	0%
	2	0%	8%
	3	5%	0%
	(About right) 4	56%	57%
	5	28%	26%
	6	10%	9%
	(Way too fast) 7	2%	0%
How would you rate the rigor of CS1301?	(Way too easy) 1	0%	0%
	2	0%	4%
	3	9%	11%
	(About right) 4	36%	30%
	5	31%	32%
	6	22%	15%
	(Way too hard) 7	2%	8%
How would you rate the overall quality of CS1301?	(Bad) 1	0%	0%
	2	1%	0%
	3	8%	4%
	(Fair) 4	20%	2%
	5	31%	23%
	6	27%	36%
	(Excellent) 7	13%	36%

Students were also asked several questions about their experience with specific pieces of each course, such as the lectures, homework, textbooks, forums, and tests. For each of these questions, they were asked to rate on a scale of 1 to 7 (from "strongly disagree" to "strongly agree") the extent to which they agreed that the piece was "valuable in helping them learn the material." For brevity, table 4.6 displays the "disagree," "neither," or "agree" values for each set of responses. Numbers in parentheses are the number of responses that are "strongly" in the given category, the most extreme value.

Notable differences existed in perceptions of the lectures, recitations, textbooks, and Piazza. Online students valued the lectures and Piazza forums most highly, while traditional students preferred the recitations and textbook. It is worth noting that the textbook used by the traditional version is a free,

Table 4.6
Student responses to Likert-scale questions on whether each of the listed components "were valuable in helping me to learn the material."

Component	Options	Traditional	Online
Lectures	Disagree	(3%) 20%	(2%) 2%
	Neither agree nor disagree	8%	6%
	Agree	(20%) 72%	(43%) 92%
Recitations	Disagree	(3%) 25%	(8%) 15%
	Neither agree nor disagree	16%	55%
	Agree	(13%) 59%	(11%) 30%
Textbook	Disagree	(4%) 23%	(19%) 34%
	Neither agree nor disagree	14%	23%
	Agree	(14%) 62%	(19%) 44%
Homework	Disagree	(1%) 6%	(2%) 2%
	Neither agree nor disagree	5%	6%
	Agree	(42%) 89%	(60%) 92%
Tests	Disagree	(2%) 18%	(2%) 19%
	Neither agree nor disagree	18%	13%
	Agree	(14%) 64%	(15%) 68%
Piazza	Disagree	(6%) 19%	(2%) 2%
	Neither agree nor disagree	20%	8%
	Agree	(24%) 61%	(35%) 91%

interactive textbook that includes many of the same features of the online course's lectures (such as in-browser coding), and so the comparisons may not be one to one. It is also worth noting that online students' relative ambivalence toward recitations mirrored attendance patterns: very few students in the online section attended recitations. Anecdotally, many students noted that they took the online section because of the flexibility it granted to coordinate with health issues or work schedules, both of which would similarly preclude attending recitations.

Finally, a few other miscellaneous comparisons were derived based on responses to the survey and enrollment patterns (see table 4.7).

The online section compared very favorably with other online courses: 35% of the students labeled it "enormously better," 82% believed it was some degree of "better," and 94% believed it was at least as good. Online students

Table 4.7
Student responses to Likert-scale questions regarding the quality and their confidence in their performance in the course.

Question	Options	Traditional	Online
How would you rate the quality of CS1301 compared to other college classes you have taken?	(Not nearly as good) 1	1%	0%
	2	3%	0%
	3	9%	6%
	(About the same) 4	25%	12%
	5	30%	16%
	6	24%	31%
	(Enormously better) 7	9%	35%
How confident are you in your performance in CS1301?	Very unconfident	4%	6%
	Somewhat unconfident	15%	21%
	Neither confident nor unconfident	12%	9%
	Somewhat confident	44%	34%
	Very confident	26%	30%
Approximately how many hours per week did you spend working on the course?	<5 hours	10%	13%
	5-7 hours	32%	40%
	8-10 hours	33%	37%
	11-13 hours	18%	8%
	14+ hours	7%	2%
Withdrawal rate	—	14%	2%

were more likely to be certain in their confidence, likely due to the course's instant and concrete grading. Online students also reported significantly less time spent per week: 90% reported less than 10 hours and 53% reported less than 7 hours per week, compared to 75% and 42% respectively in the traditional section.

Free-response questions were only analyzed from the online course. The most common points of praise were: the responsiveness of the instructor and teaching assistants; the course structure; the flexibility of the online medium; and the student community that formed around the class. The first and last of these points are especially notable given the common fear that online courses diminish student-student and student-teacher interaction.

CONCLUSION

Blended learning typically refers to a mix of classroom and online instruction, but the needle between the extremes may hover closer to the online side. In this model, we have applied purely online instruction to a traditional student body. The students match the demographics of traditional students and have access to normal student services, but the instruction and assessment are purely online.

To take advantage of this arrangement, we were careful in developing the course material to leverage the unique advantages of an online environment. With respect to the course design, the course's emphasis on congruency, modularity, and personalization all present potential benefits problematic or incompatible with typical large synchronous classrooms. The emphasis on high-fidelity, well-produced, targeted course videos provides a resource akin to a strong multimedia textbook, merging the benefits of at-home study and multimodal lecture. The integration of opportunities for assessment within the course material gives students ample opportunity to participate in more active learning, as well as to gain insights into their own understanding and adapt their studies accordingly. In these ways, the design of the course takes advantage of the online medium to compensate for what may be lost in the transition to asynchronous video instruction.

Based on a first evaluation, the results are promising. Students in this online section showed no signs of being disadvantaged by this model but reported higher levels of satisfaction with the course material. An argument could be made that students in the inaugural semester learned more efficiently, as the same learning gains required a smaller amount of self-reported work per week. Thus, the early results from this alternate form of blended learning are encouraging.

Ongoing Work

Ongoing work on CS1301x covers several areas. First, the analysis presented here covers only a fraction of the data generated so far. Current research directions are examining the breadth of student approaches to course exercises; the pattern and trajectories of student submissions as they debug and iterate on exercises; the interaction patterns with course material; and demographic and geographic effects on the previous variables. Follow-up studies have replicated these initial results, finding no overall differences in learning outcomes between the course versions (Joyner 2018a), although some evidence suggests students with prior failures in a CS class achieve greater learning outcomes in the online version (Joyner 2018b).

Second, informed by the above analysis, the course is under constant improvement. Based on the experience of the first semester, a new suite of more sophisticated, consistent autograders was deployed, giving students more complete feedback on their submissions. All problems were also equipped with exemplary answers to provide implicit feedback to students on completing exercises in the course. More ambitiously, new developments and collaborations are being pursued to provide more intelligent and comprehensive feedback to students on the course exercises, from debugging help based on prior students' submissions to style help based on the Python style guide.

Third, the course is being expanded to realize the goal of the design principle of personalization. New content, currently in the domain area, is being produced to target problems in engineering, accounting, and data science, giving students more leeway to get exactly what they want out of the course. The ultimate goal of these pursuits is a "Choose Your Own Adventure"–style computing course, where students choose the programming language and domain, and perhaps ultimately their instructor and spoken language as well.

Finally, the course is also expanding to realize the other part of its original vision: the goal is for the course to not only be used by students in residence at Georgia Tech, but also to be used by future students to earn college credit prior to arriving on campus. The self-paced, autograded nature of the course means it could be straightforwardly integrated into existing curricula in high schools or taken independently, and the proctored tests provide sufficient integrity to grant a path to real course credit to students completing the online course even without admission to Georgia Tech. The course was first used for dual enrollment high school students in Spring 2018, with plans to do so again in the future.

References

Joyner, D. (2017). Scaling expert feedback: Two case studies. In *Proceedings of the Fourth (2017) ACM Conference on Learning @ Scale* (pp. 71–80). New York: ACM.

Joyner, D. (2018a). Toward CS1 at Scale: Building and Testing a MOOC-for-Credit Candidate. In *Proceedings of the Fifth ACM Conference on Learning @ Scale.* New York: ACM.

Joyner, D. (2018b). Intelligent Evaluation and Feedback in Support of a Credit-Bearing MOOC. In *Artificial Intelligence in Education, AIED 2018, Lecture Notes in Computer Science 10948.* Cham, Switzerland: Springer.

Parker, M. C., Guzdial, M., & Engleman, S. (2016). Replication, validation, and use of a language independent CS1 knowledge assessment. In *Proceedings of the 2016 ACM Conference on International Computing Education Research* (pp. 93–101). New York: ACM.

Tew, A. E., & Guzdial, M. (2010). Developing a validated assessment of fundamental CS1 concepts. In *Proceedings of the 41st ACM Technical Symposium on Computer Science Education* (pp. 97–101). New York: ACM.

5

AN INNOVATIVE, BLENDED, PROJECT-BASED HEALTH INFORMATICS COURSE

Mark L. Braunstein, Cheryl Hiddleson, Timothy G. Buchman,
Mohammad M. Ghassemi, Shamim Nemati, Paula Braun, and
Alyson B. Goodman

MIX Taxonomy Classification: This course is blended. For the students who meet face to face, the content is primarily delivered online through the MOOC. The students also have guest lectures from healthcare industry mentors who provide the projects. Much class time is devoted to working on projects and receiving feedback from the instructor and mentors. For students who are only in the MOOC, the course is not blended because it does not include a face-to-face component. They receive content for and feedback on their project online only.

Research Method Classification: The research method is a descriptive design. A survey of the online-only students captured their perceptions of the course. Descriptive statistics are used to summarize their experience.

INTRODUCTION

Despite being far more expensive than that of other advanced, industrialized countries and arguably delivering the world's best high-technology care, the US healthcare system has long suffered from a number of significant problems. Experts generally agree that the US system far too often fails to provide optimal evidence-based care, is inefficient and wasteful, and, for many patients, is unsafe. The Institute of Medicine (IOM, now the Academy of Medicine) of the National Academies of Science led in identifying these problems and declared "a chasm" between the healthcare system we have and the one we need (Richardson, et al, 2001). To enable progress, it proposed the development of an informatics-powered "learning healthcare system" in which analysis of aggregated digital data from actual patient care would provide new knowledge, such as information on the safest, most cost-effective treatments, and use it to provide guidance to providers as they treat new patients (Smith, et al, 2012).

In keeping with the IOM's vision, Georgia Tech designed its CS 6440: Introduction to Health Informatics graduate seminar as the first to train computer science and engineering students in the latest technologies designed to facilitate a learning healthcare system. It uses a massive open online course (MOOC) to provide those students with a basic healthcare and health informatics background. The class time this frees up gives students the opportunity to work with domain experts on problems they choose using two cutting-edge health informatics technologies—Fast Healthcare Interoperability Resources (FHIR®) (Bender and Sartipi, 2013) and SMART® on FHIR, the FHIR-based healthcare app platform (Mandel, et al 2016). Kenneth Mandl is professor of biomedical informatics and pediatrics at Harvard Medical School and director of the Computational Health Informatics Program at Boston Children's Hospital. His team developed SMART on FHIR and, in a personal communication, he says of this course: "Georgia Tech's innovative Introduction to Health Informatics graduate seminar is the first course I know of that brought FHIR and SMART on FHIR to the core of the curriculum, turning its students into innovators of modular apps that can run across healthcare." As we will now discuss, the current course design has led to a significant increase in enrollment and has successfully brought domain experts together with our students to tackle real-world problems. Some of these efforts are on a path to clinical use and possible commercialization.

First, this chapter outlines the course. Forty-two on-campus students took Introduction to Health Informatics in the spring 2016 semester, the first semester the blended course was offered. One hundred seventy-nine remote students took it in the fall that year as an elective in Georgia Tech's Online Master of Science in Computer Science program (OMSCS). Students in both versions of the course viewed a 10-week Udacity MOOC as "homework." On-campus students gain important additional real-world background through lectures from the healthcare and health informatics industries and from Georgia Tech faculty working in health informatics and related fields. OMSCS students have access to recordings of similar past lectures. In both versions of the course students form teams of four to six members to develop FHIR apps in response to the challenges posed by clinicians and researchers, most of whom are from local healthcare systems or the Centers for Disease Control and Prevention (CDC) located in Atlanta.

The apps might respond to challenges to offer decision support to a provider in a specific clinical scenario; they might provide patients with personalized education or support using information from their electronic record; or they might support population/public health–level surveillance, data aggregation, and reporting. Teams are often multidisciplinary and might include students with strong programming skills, students with an interest in human-computer interaction, and students from a related discipline, such as biomedical or industrial and systems engineering or bioinformatics.

Second, this chapter describes the transformative potential for this type of learning. When both versions of the course are taught during the same semester (as was the case in the spring of 2016), students can form cross-course teams. These have the potential advantage that on-campus students may have more time to devote to the course, while OMSCS students are older and have more real-world experience, including possible experience in the healthcare or health informatics industries.

Finally, this chapter describes future directions. Managing a project-based course has its own special challenges that include assessing individual performance and managing inevitable issues with team coordination and individual contributions. These challenges are potentially greater in an online course, where direct instructor supervision and assessment are more difficult. The results of a survey of the 179 fall 2016 OMSCS students focused on the team-project component of the course and suggested the need for further refinement. It is one of the inputs guiding a MOOC redesign and the development of a novel course platform by a team of former course TAs.

INTRODUCTION TO HEALTH INFORMATICS: COURSE DESIGN EVOLUTION

Introduction to Health Informatics is designed as an entry-level graduate seminar for Georgia Tech students with no background in either healthcare or health informatics. Current and planned additional courses will eventually lead to a graduate certificate and possibly a master of computer science degree program in health informatics. The didactic component of the course consists of four sections:

The US healthcare system and federal health IT programs and policies
- The chronic disease challenge
- Current versus innovative system designs
- Federal efforts to spur adoption of digital records and data sharing

Core technologies
- Healthcare data, messaging, document, and interoperability standards
- Health information exchange
- Privacy, security, and trust

Real-world systems
- Electronic records for providers
- Tools for patient empowerment
- Population/public health

Data aggregation and analysis
- Federated research technologies and networks
- Analytic techniques
- Examples of the applications of analytics

The course originated in 2008 in a traditional on-campus lecture format supplemented by a few guest speakers from the local healthcare and health informatics industries. In the spring of 2011, the six students in the class formed three 2-student teams and entered an NHIN-CONNECT Code-a-Thon Challenge. The challenge consisted of usefully visualizing the data represented in a Continuity of Care Document (CCD), which is a summary patient record represented in an XML-based standard. The instructor was so impressed with the students' work (they won all three prizes) and the accelerated learning that took place that he restructured the course around a predefined CCD-based programming challenge.

Introduction to Health Informatics was one of Georgia Tech's early Udacity MOOCs. A major motivation for the MOOC was that students often complained that it was difficult to coordinate out-of-class schedules to work on their team projects. In the spring of 2014, the instructor "flipped" the course, requiring the MOOC as homework. The revised syllabus opened up a number of class sessions for project work on days and times when all students were certain to be available.

A second advantage of making more in-class time available was the opportunity to increase the number of guest lecturers from the healthcare and health informatics industries. This exposure to "real-world" applications of the concepts and technologies presented in class is very appealing to career- and engineering-oriented Georgia Tech students. Despite having had no prior background in the field, each year a few students seek internships in health informatics or jobs in the field after graduation.

Another consideration for a flipped course was to allow time for student teams to develop their own project concepts rather than working on a single assigned challenge. The multidisciplinary nature of the students meant that their core interests and capabilities ranged from effective user-interface design for patient-facing apps that might provide instruction or support, to applying machine learning to guide clinical decision making by physicians based on individual patient considerations (e.g., precision medicine).

The final unanticipated advantage was the opportunity for prospective project mentors to come to early class sessions and propose their challenge to the students. At present, enrollment in the on-campus course is reliably at its 60-student limit and each mentor has half a class session. Thus, with 10–12 project teams available and two 90-minute class sessions per week, mentor presentations consume most of the first month of the semester.

The Course Infrastructure

FHIR: The field of health informatics is rapidly shifting to a modern approach based on internet technologies. Health Level 7 (HL7) is the global health data standards body. Fast Healthcare Interoperability Resources (FHIR) is HL7's latest and potentially most impactful standard. FHIR began in 2011 with a "fresh look" at how healthcare could standardize and share data. It uses the same web technologies[1] common in other industries to represent and access data from electronic records and other clinical systems and tools. Because of the technologies it uses, FHIR is ideal for mobile and web applications. It also provides a facile and approachable development platform that most Georgia Tech students are already familiar with and is therefore ideal for a one-semester course.

FHIR App Platform: SMART on FHIR is an FHIR-based app platform that adds tools necessary to ensure data security and manage patient privacy.[2] It also provides apps with a "launch context" so that busy providers do not need to reenter data already available in the patient's chart. Finally, if properly integrated into an electronic record, SMART on FHIR apps become a relatively seamless part of the care provider's workflow and clinical process, a very attractive feature to busy clinicians.

Tech on FHIR: In January 2015, Georgia Tech's Interoperability and Integration Innovation Lab (I3L) launched the beta version of the first FHIR server (Tech on FHIR, now renamed OMOPonFHIR - https://github.com/gt-health/GT-FHIR2) for educational support on any campus. By spring 2015, the server supported most of the key clinical data documented by physicians and other providers in the course of routine care.

Access to Patient Data: A number of public FHIR servers are available for experimentation. Prospective FHIR developers often create the make-believe data contained in those resources and it is typically limited in scope and quality. Something that more closely mimics actual patient data is desirable for student projects.

Approval for student use of actual patient data is time consuming and this usage is potentially problematic, even if all the fields that could identify the patient are removed (i.e., deidentified health data). To get around these issues Georgia Tech licensed a synthetic dataset representing 10,000 "typical" US multiple chronic disease patients from ExactData (http://www.exactdata .net/). We mapped that dataset to the OMOP v5 Clinical Data Model (CDM) (Hripschak, G, et al, 2015) and subsequently mapped the CMS Synthetic public use files (SynPUF) (https://www.cms.gov/Research-Statistics-Data-and -Systems/Downloadable-Public-Use-Files/SynPUFs/DE_Syn_PUF.html) and the MIMIC III ICU dataset (Johnson et al., 2016) to the OMOP CDM so the data could be accessed via FHIR's REST API.

FHIR-Based Team Projects

With the availability of Tech on FHIR, the spring 2015 class projects were, for the first time, required to involve the use of FHIR. Forty-two students formed nine teams and developed apps of their own choice and design that targeted healthcare providers or patients, often with a theme of bringing data together and usefully displaying it. One particularly outstanding project aggregated data at a population level and provided a number of innovative visualizations of that data. Two teams worked with personnel from the American Cancer Society (ACS), whose headquarters is near Georgia Tech, to turn a cancer survivorship plan into an interactive tool. This positive experience working with an outside project mentor informed the next stage in the evolution of the course, into its current mentor-driven project model.

By spring 2016 interest in FHIR was noticeably more widespread both nationally and in the local healthcare community. With the very positive educational experience of having students work with actual domain experts at the ACS on a problem of importance to *them*, the instructor reached out to Emory and CDC faculty researchers whose work seemed well suited to the kind of apps student teams might develop using FHIR. Mentors came to class early in the term and presented a challenge amenable to solution with one or more FHIR apps that they would be willing to mentor a student team to develop over the semester.

In the section that follows, mentors describe three of these projects. The first two provide advice to physicians making care decisions (clinical decision support or CDS). The third uses a suite of FHIR apps to create a coordinated, communitywide approach to the management of pediatric obesity. First, it is useful to mention again that the time required for project presentations and app development almost certainly could not have been available without the use of a flipped classroom. This is particularly true for students who come to the course with little or no domain expertise. The ability of these students to master the domain knowledge and specialized health informatics technologies and deliver projects that are so valued by expert mentors within the constraints of a one-semester course testifies to the value of the flipped course paradigm.

The project details may be primarily of interest to instructors teaching health informatics or related fields. A basic understanding of the nature, scope, and complexity of the projects and the work completed by the students should help other readers put the material relating to challenges in teaching a project-based, flipped or online course into perspective within their own subject area. These case studies are also suggestive of the role that modern programming tools and approaches can play in making a rich project experience feasible even within the context of a single semester course taken by students with limited background or experience in the course domain.

CLINICALLY INSIGHTFUL EICU DATA VISUALIZATION

Case Study Led by Cheryl Hiddleson and Timothy G. Buchman

Imagine, for a moment, that you are looking at the dashboard of your automobile. You can see your speed and your direction. You can see the pressure in each of your tires. You can see the fuel gauge, the water temperature, the oil pressure. You can look in the rearview mirror to see what lies behind and through the windshield to see what lies ahead. You can see all this at a glance.

Now imagine, for a moment, that you have installed an unusual dashboard. It allows you to see only two or three of the readouts at a time. Perhaps your speed and the oil pressure. A few moments later, the pressure in the right-rear tire and the water pressure. A moment later you know the direction of travel and whether the battery is charged. After months or years, you would somehow learn to drive the car. It would command your full attention ... and you would probably not easily notice the leak in the left-front tire.

This is how doctors and nurses care for patients. Scary stuff.

Now imagine that you had 20 older cars. Each with its own dashboard. Each periodically flickering data at irregular intervals. It would be difficult to tell the difference between common random variation and impending failure. It would be difficult to tell which car needs attention right this moment—until it stopped moving or the tire went completely flat.

This is how doctors and nurses care for patients in intensive-care units. Scarier still.

We wanted "better."

We asked the six on-campus students on our team to start simple: a single data type, like snapshots of the battery voltage. In our case, a single blood chemistry measurement—creatinine. Creatinine is a waste product of muscle metabolism. Muscles produce it. Kidneys excrete it. When the muscles produce less, the creatinine level falls. When the kidneys are injured, the creatinine level rises. When kidney function first begins to improve creatinine levels can continue to increase, but at a slower rate. Doctors order creatinine "snapshots." The specimens are timestamped. The laboratories submit the result and the timestamp to a database. As is illustrated in figure 5.1, simply plotting creatinine levels versus time does not clearly convey the early improvements in kidney function that can signal the need to change treatment strategy.

We have the database. We asked for real-time alerting and intuitive displays highlighting renal function, including the signs of deterioration from the patient's usual state as early as possible.

To do that, the students needed to understand the mathematical physiology of kidney function. We gave them a reference (Hübler and Buchman, 2007).

They wondered, what can we do with a time series? Anyone can plot values versus time. Plotting hundreds of time series might not be the best idea. What else might be informative?

They looked at the equation and saw the terms. They realized that there was physiological significance in the first derivative. They warmed to the idea of displaying the data not as a time series, but rather as a representation of the trajectory of creatinine levels versus time—a phase plot (Δ[Creatinine]/Δt versus [Creatinine]) as shown in figure 5.1.

Then they had to make it work, eavesdropping on the clinical data system (figure 5.2) and listening for new (creatinine) entries among all the other data flowing past (figure 5.3). They detected it "in flight" but did not disturb it in its travels. They tagged it, verified it, sent it on to a buffer. They built a front end, not just a visualization tool. It is a learning visualization tool, one that would enable clinicians to mark the "patterns that matter" so that, in time, the system would learn which patterns to bring to the attention of the clinicians.

Which of those older cars needs attention "right now"?

They made the system scalable (to thousands of different data types) and diffusible (so it can easily be ported to other medical centers).

The students did it.

There is work to be done. It is still a prototype. One data type, a limited number of displays, and the learning architecture and decisional principles are just now being built. It is not just learning, not just supervised learning, but in fact supervised learning informed by physiological models and clinical actions.

If the students do this right, they invent a completely new style of 'computed' clinical decision support, one that is meaningful at the bedside because it allows us to provide the right care, right now, to every patient, every time. There are no more flickering dashboards. Instead, this is a first step toward a "GPS for the sickest patients" (figure 5.4).

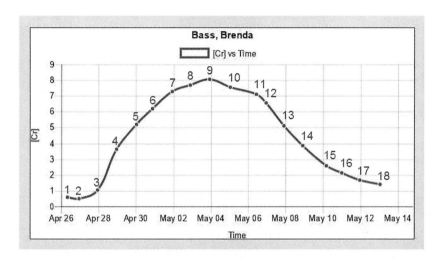

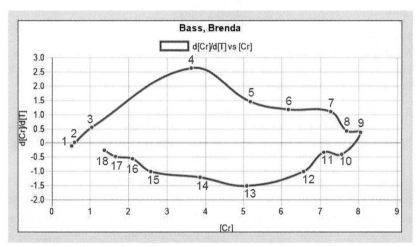

Figure 5.1

The FHIR app created this pair of plots. The numbers along the plots correspond in time. In both plots, creatinine increases over time through point 9 and then begins to decrease. On the left is a traditional plot of creatinine versus time. On the right is a novel phase plot of creatinine level (*x*-axis) versus the first derivative of creatinine level divided by the first derivative of time. The phase plot makes it far more obvious that the rate of creatinine increase is decreasing after point 4. This signals the onset of renal function improvement much more clearly than can be appreciated in the traditional plot.

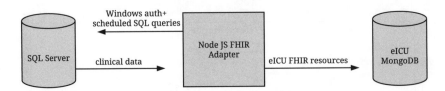

Figure 5.2
A visualization of the eICU FHIR adapter architecture. Clinical data (on the left) is pulled at regular intervals, formatted into FHIR resources, and placed in an eICU-specific data mart (on the right).

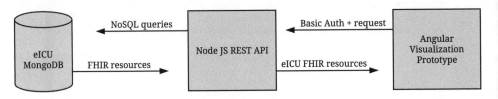

Figure 5.3
A visualization of the eICU REST API architecture. Resources stored in the data mart (on the left) are requested by front-end applications (on the right). The REST API queries the data mart and responds with JSON FHIR resources.

Here are some of the challenges we met, and how we overcame them. First, IT resources/additions had to be made available to the clinical systems. Second, there were all sorts of legal issues and agreements. We had to organize several meetings to determine the correct path to follow that would allow the students to gain access to the data we wanted them to acquire and process. Once the permissions were obtained, we arranged training for the students in the clinical data environment. This involved collaborating with the vendor's database experts to ensure the students were proficient in accessing the needed data without disturbing clinical processes. We also had to have several meetings with legal teams to develop an affiliation agreement between Emory University and Georgia Tech to ensure the project would be applied to the students' coursework.

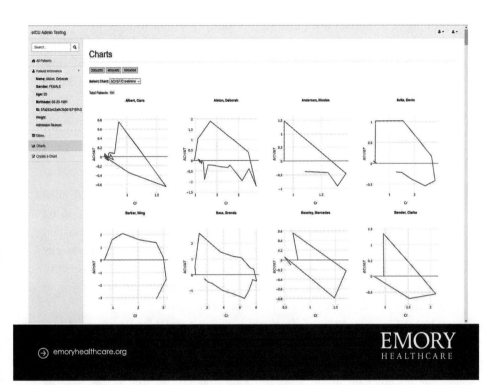

Figure 5.4
A dashboard from the eICU Visualization prototype graphing Δ[Creatinine]/Δt versus
[Creatinine] for several patients using FHIR resources requested from the eICU FHIR
adapter. (Courtesy of Tim Buchman and Cheryl Hiddleson.)

BUILDING A HEPARIN-DOSING APPLICATION: CASE STUDY LED BY
MOHAMMAD M. GHASSEMI AND SHAMIM NEMATI

Overview

This project required seven on-campus students to participate in end-to-end
development of an application intended to help intensive-care clinicians dose a
commonly prescribed anticoagulant, heparin. Accomplishing this goal required
students to overcome three central challenges, all of which provided practical

training in important computer science skills. These challenges were (1) the extraction of data from a large retrospective clinical archive, (2) the training and implementation of machine learning algorithms that utilized information extracted from the database, and (3) the development of a web-based user interface that allows clinical staff to estimate a dose of the medication. Here we will discuss our approach to overcoming each of these challenges in the context of MOOCs.

Challenge 1: Database Technology

The project required students to implement a previously published algorithm that estimates an optimal initial dose of unfractionated heparin, using retrospective clinical data (Ghassemi et al., 2014). To learn the association between medication dose, patient covariates (such as age, gender, and severity of illness), and patient response, the students had to first extract retrospective data from the publicly accessible Multiparameter Intelligent Monitoring in Intensive Care database (MIMIC) (Johnson et al., 2016).

MIMIC is a repository of structured (e.g., heart rate, blood pressure, demographics) and unstructured electronic health record data (e.g., clinical notes) from over 50,000 unique intensive-care-unit stays at the Beth Israel Deaconess Medical Center in Boston in 2001–2012. Although the MIMIC database has been purged of all private health information (medical record numbers, patient names, phone numbers, etc.), it may still be possible to reidentify patients based on the available data (age and length of stay and illness, for instance). Consequently, the use of MIMIC requires all users to be trained in the ethical utilization of retrospective human subjects' data. Hence, we asked the students to participate in the required online Collaborative Institutional Training Initiative (CITI) courses prior to gaining access to the data. Following completion of the required training, we referred the students to online documentation that contained guidance on the schema of the database in addition to an online "cookbook" containing example SQL queries for MIMIC. Following their exposure to training materials, we asked the students to read a paper related to the heparin project (Ghassemi et al., 2014).

Specific Challenges and Opportunities

Unlike reading textbooks, reading and understanding academic journal articles is a skill that requires practice. By asking students to implement an algorithm described in a previously published academic journal article, we helped train them in this important skill set. We found that the students struggled to understand many of the concepts in the journal article describing the heparin-dosing algorithm. We addressed this by arranging regular conference calls, where students could ask questions about the approach.

MIMIC is an excellent tool for researchers as well as for student instruction, as it constitutes a real-world "big data" set. Because the data is raw, it is also subject to many imperfections including missing values, erroneous entries, and a complex database schema. Ironically, these imperfections in the data make it an ideal learning tool for students aiming to develop skills to work with real-world datasets.

Challenges 2 and 3: Algorithm Implementation and User Interface Design

Following extraction of the data from MIMIC, students were asked to implement the heparin-dosing algorithm described in Ghassemi et al. (2014) in an open-source programming language of their choice (e.g., Python, C, Java, JavaScript). The estimation algorithm consists of two steps. In the first step, students trained a multinomial logistic regression model (MNR). In the second step, students utilized the trained MNR to identify a dose that maximized the probability of a therapeutic patient outcome, given covariates. Following training on the algorithm, the students implemented an online user interface similar to that of Rowley and Ghassemi (2015) (see figure 5.5).

Specific Challenges and Opportunities

The paper by Ghassemi et al. (2014) describes a means to estimate an optimal heparin dose using multinomial logistic regression. Unfortunately, there is a large variance in the familiarity of students with the basic statistical concepts of regression and classification, which can lead to apprehension and mistakes during implementation. We addressed this by instructing students to read chapter 1 of a freely accessible online textbook (Nielsen, 2015) that describes

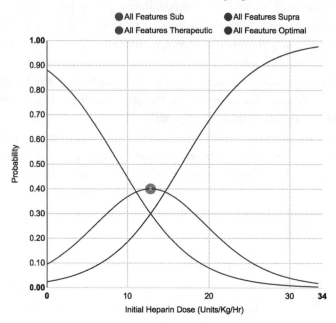

Outcome Probabilities for Varying Doses

● All Features Sub   ● All Features Supra
● All Features Therapeutic   ● All Feauture Optimal

Dashed lines represent results from the weight-only based model.
As the infusion rate increases, the probability of a sub-therapeutic PTT (less than 60 seconds) in 6 hours time decreases, and the probability of supra-therapeutic PTT (greater than 100 seconds) increases. The dose which minimizes the sum of the sub-therapeuditc and supra-therapeutic probabilities is the optimal dose.

Figure 5.5

The illustrative user interface for computer-aided heparin dosing provided to students logistic regression, and we scheduled follow-up calls to ensure appropriate comprehension of the material. We also provided a MATLAB-based implementation of the algorithm to the students as a reference.

Many computer science students have limited experience building front-end applications. We found that students often did not know where to start with the deployment of a web application and with the connection of the algorithmic back end to the user interface. To address this, we gave them access to a simple website template that contained JavaScript functionality and user forms.

Conclusion

In the absence of face-to-face instruction, students benefit immensely from templates and tutorials that allow them to learn by example, at their own pace. Importantly, we found that regular communication with students was essential to help clarify misunderstandings and allow for the timely completion of project milestones.

PEDIATRIC OBESITY MANAGEMENT: CASE STUDY LED BY PAULA BRAUN AND ALYSON B. GOODMAN

The prevalence of childhood obesity has risen dramatically over recent decades, with approximately 12 million US children currently having obesity; low-income children and those in the southeast US are at disproportionately high risk. The US Preventive Services Task Force recommends screening all children aged 6–18 years for obesity, and providers should offer or refer children who have obesity and their families to comprehensive pediatric weight management programs. The American Academy of Pediatrics also recommends that primary-care providers universally assess children for obesity risk to improve early identification of overweight or obesity, medical risks, and unhealthy eating and physical activity habits; healthcare practitioners should provide obesity prevention messages for most children and suggest weight control interventions for those with excess weight.

The goals of CDC's Division of Nutrition, Physical Activity, and Obesity for this project were to

• Assess the feasibility of using Fast Healthcare Interoperability Resources (FHIR) to promote an evidence-based, family- and community-centered care model to help screen all children for healthy weight and behaviors to identify children at risk for overweight or obesity.

• Promote improvements in weight status and in healthy behaviors.

• Link clinical and community programs to help remove barriers to improving behaviors among high-risk populations.

• Facilitate use of clinical data for evaluation or surveillance purposes. We were particularly interested in solutions that were open to innovation and could potentially scale nationwide.

The CDC aims to improve child obesity primary prevention (preventing overweight and obesity) and secondary prevention (preventing negative health outcomes associated with overweight and obesity). Electronic health records (EHRs) can be a valuable resource for supporting high-quality, evidence-based child obesity–related clinical care, coordination, and quality improvement activities. Further, community programs aimed at facilitating healthy weight among children need data to evaluate their activities' impact, and local, state, and tribal public health agencies need healthy weight–related data to provide communities, states, and regions with surveillance data to inform progress toward meeting child healthy weight population goals.

We began this project with a hypothetical question: What would we do if we could easily integrate patient, clinician, and community asset data? We then explored the SMART on FHIR Growth Chart app, developed for Boston Children's Hospital, which plots a child's growth over time on appropriate growth charts (Boston Children's Hospital, 2017). Our vision was to expand the app to help establish patient-centered health goals for at-risk children, support clinical quality improvement through automated decision supports, strengthen clinical-community linkages, and respond to the public health need for healthy weight surveillance and research.

To address the inherent complexity of the project, we divided it into four separate applications:

- **Patient-facing application**: Healthy weight requires a lifestyle that includes healthy behaviors, such as healthful eating and regular physical activity. Unfortunately, practitioners typically do not have enough time to capture information on healthy behaviors during a short clinical encounter. The patient- (or parent-) facing application helps address that by facilitating a collection of answers to key behavioral questions from patients/parents that support best practices in counseling patients and families on improving healthy habits. Any questionnaire presented on this type of app (in the waiting room, for example) would need to be thoroughly tested to ensure data usefulness, acceptability, and quality.
- **Physician-facing application**: This application provides clinical decision support: it collects and plots children's anthropometric (i.e., height, weight, and BMI) data on appropriate growth charts, displays healthy weight behavior information collected in the patient app, prompts patient-centered healthy behavior goal setting, allows physicians to order labs electronically, and facilitates e-referrals to clinical and community resources.
- **Care-coordinator application**: This application receives e-referrals from the physician app—for example, a referral for nutrition and physical activity resources. It creates a list and map of community resources near where the patient lives, such as a farmer's market, boys' and girls' club, playground, or after-school programs. It helps facilitate the process of scheduling appointments with these community resources if appropriate.
- **Analytics and reporting application**: This application allows the healthcare provider or entity to use their own data for quality improvement and to share data with public health for surveillance purposes.

We worked under agile design principles: start small, fail fast, and focus on users' needs. The teams held weekly calls with the CDC and some interviewed prospective users, such as care coordinators at a local pediatric healthcare organization. The Georgia Tech students mapped key healthy weight data elements to existing FHIR resources, identified gaps, and proposed solutions.

Our project was the only project in the class that required four teams of students, each building separate applications, to work together and develop

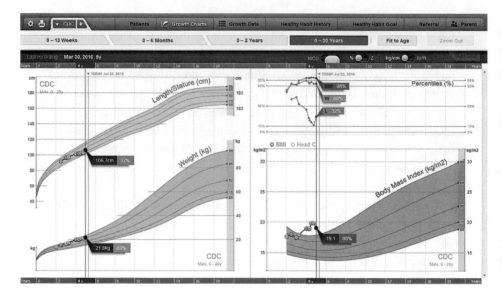

Figure 5.6
Mock-up solution for physician-facing app. Data collected at home and in the office is combined to plot the child's growth against standards.

strategies for the entire suite of applications to communicate with one another. This was an important learning experience, both for the students and for the CDC, as we begin to understand how emerging technologies, like FHIR, can help coordinate and strengthen community-centered care.

In the end, the students took our original functional requirements and added their own creativity. For example, the patient-facing app helped users identify healthy food choices.

We worked with two 4-member teams of students. The on-campus team consisted of full-time students and the online team consisted of working professionals who brought a high level of experience and professionalism to the project.

On the last day of class, the on-campus student teams presented their final projects at Georgia Tech. The audience included representatives from health insurance companies, hospital systems, private industry, public health, the

Figure 5.7
The care-coordinator app uses GPS data to suggest community resources near each family's home.

CDC, and other state and local agencies. All of the students who participated agreed to open-source their code so that anyone could use, build on, or contribute in any way. This openness and transparency helped spawn several follow-on projects, including a pilot project between Georgia Tech, Emory University, Children's Healthcare of Atlanta, the Georgia Department of Public Health Women's, Infants, and Children (WIC) program, and the CDC to improve data exchange between pediatricians and WIC nutritionists. A group of the online students were so dedicated to the project that they have continued working with the CDC and other stakeholders on the technical development of these applications.

The content of this chapter expresses the opinions of its authors and does not necessarily represent the views of the Centers for Disease Control and Prevention.

FALL 2016 OMSCS COURSE AND STUDENT SURVEY

Further Evolution of the Course Structure

Health informatics is a rapidly evolving field. A substantial update to the MOOC video lectures was planned for the summer of 2016. This was to include substantial new coverage of FHIR in response to student requests for more help in learning the technology. Many new public tools and APIs have become available so the update plan included new exercises and activities to give students hands-on experience with both FHIR and other tools that would potentially be useful for their projects. Due to resource and scheduling limitations, only the expanded coverage of FHIR was complete in time for the fall 2016 OMSCS course. Given the class size, there was substantial scaling up to nearly 30 projects proposed to the 179 OMSCS students by over 20 prospective mentors. It is significant that some mentors from the spring course proposed new projects, and in some cases, mentors who had proposed one project proposed others as well despite the increased time commitment this entails on their part.

Scaling a course virtually always presents challenges, but a project-based course such as Introduction to Health Informatics arguably presents special challenges with respect to course management and evaluation. To help manage at scale, mentors used a standard, structured form to present their projects. This form served for screening of the projects for practicality and assigning them in logical groups to each of four teaching assistants (TAs). This was a first step toward an organizational approach that would improve the productivity of the individual TAs and help support future scaling of the course.

Ultimately, evaluation may be the limiting challenge in scaling a MOOC-based course. Partially as a result, peer evaluation is potentially an important component of the course. It also has the potential for expanded learning by giving students the opportunity to see other projects and providing hopefully thoughtful feedback to other teams.

In spring 2016, we experimented with an early version of the peer feedback tool developed at Georgia Tech, but various technical issues kept the results from being particularly useful (Perez, 2017). In fall 2016, we used an enhanced version of the tool that we feel helped with evaluating student participation in the course and simulated audience participation for presentations (the on-campus students actually present their projects to a live audience, including people from the local healthcare industry). Furthermore, it helped to give students a more rounded evaluation of their progress in the course, because other students gave them feedback in addition to the TAs, mentors, and instructors. On the other hand, the tool still has some technical shortcomings that had a negative impact on the course. Ultimately, once these issues are resolved, we feel that peer feedback could be a major benefit to the course.

Student Survey

A project-based course introduces special challenges. In team projects, students must cooperate and coordinate their efforts. Assessing individual performance within the context of a team is challenging. A large-scale, online course format could potentially magnify these challenges. Understanding and overcoming these challenges is critical for further scaling a course of this type. To help with that, the 179 fall 2016 OMSCS students received a survey about the team-project component of the course. Fifty-eight (32.4%) responded. As anticipated, most students come to the course with limited or no domain experience: 34 (58.6%) had no background prior to taking the course. Seven (12.1%) reported a little experience; ten (17.2%) reported some experience; and six (10%) reported a lot of experience. The final responding student works professionally in healthcare. Overall, despite their limited healthcare backgrounds, 36 responding students (62%) found the project very or extremely beneficial while nine students (15.5%) reported little or no benefit.

Does a healthcare background increase the usefulness of the team project to students? The data shown in figure 5.8 suggests that it does, but the effect is not strong. Thus 71% of students with some or a lot of healthcare background ($n = 34$) found the project extremely or very useful, versus 53% of students ($n = 17$) with no background. Half of the students with no healthcare background found it only somewhat or less useful versus 27% of the students with a stronger background.

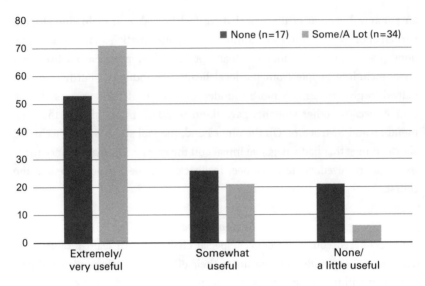

Figure 5.8
Project usefulness by healthcare background

Do team projects work well remotely with students spread across geography and time zones? To get a sense for this, we asked the students if everyone contributed equally. Thirty-five responding students (60%) said they did, but this leaves 40% who said they did not, suggesting that this is a problem. It is not clear from this survey if the remote OMSCS format exacerbates the problem (which does occur with on-campus teams), but that would be an interesting future comparison to make.

Were the team members coordinated? Like equal contribution, team coordination can be problematic, no matter the course format. Twenty-eight responding students (48%) reported their team worked well together and another 15 (26%) reported issues but nothing major. At the other end of the spectrum, 10 students (17%) reported that a subset of the team did all the work. Interestingly, three students reported that their team never "gelled" but everyone did some of the work. Two students who responded overall did not answer this question. No students reported the final choice that "we had some issues but were able to overcome them."

How did the teams coordinate their efforts? Students could report the use of more than one approach. Unsurprisingly, all but seven students reported using a web collaboration technology such as Google Hangouts or Microsoft Skype. Twenty-five respondents reported using conference calling and all but 14 respondents reported using email. Although Piazza is the "official" course discussion/collaboration tool and each team had a forum for their use, only 12 students reported using Piazza.

Did the teams actually function as teams with work assigned according to each individual's skill set? It is difficult to be certain of this from the survey, but interestingly, and probably unsurprisingly for a Georgia Tech computer science course, all but 13 students reported doing some coding. Twenty-eight students reported working on workflow/process design and 21 provided user interface design suggestions, while 19 served as "domain experts."

Given the students' lack of domain expertise, the instructor struggles with when to introduce the projects. By scheduling earlier, teams have more time but most students lack the needed background. The projects were introduced a month into the course and 60% of the students felt that was about right. Almost all of the remaining students (19) would have preferred that the projects start earlier.

Finally, when asked about the educational value of the team projects, only 9 students (16%) found that they had no value or only a little value, while 29 students (50%) found them a very or extremely valuable educational experience. However, the correlation of these responses with the students' healthcare backgrounds (figure 5.9) is relatively neutral. This question was intentionally somewhat duplicative of the earlier question about the benefits of the projects and the two were placed far apart in the survey as a "sanity check" on this important issue. It is not clear how to interpret the difference.

Asked how likely they are to recommend this course to a friend, 40% were very or extremely likely, 36% were somewhat likely, and 24% ($n = 14$) were not likely to recommend it. The latter group of students reported a wide variety of reasons from difficulty working with their mentor to technical issues to the timing of the project to team issues. No more than four students reported a particular issue.

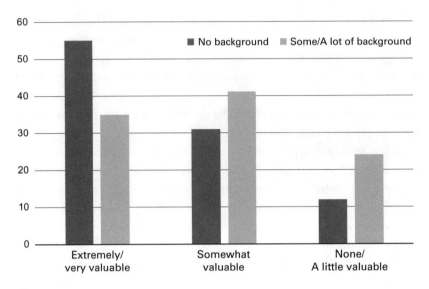

Figure 5.9
Educational value by prior healthcare experience

FUTURE DIRECTIONS

Since the conclusion of the spring 2016 iteration of the course, one pair of mentors has initiated discussions to commercially offer an advanced version of their app after clinical trials are successfully completed. Another pair of mentors is hoping to try their app in actual patient care. Some of the team members enhanced the obesity management app suite with a uniform user interface and tighter integration of its component apps. An effort is underway to deploy the tool in the community.

A full MOOC and course redesign was completed in time for the fall 2017 OMSCS course. It brings the didactic material up to date with the rapid movement of health informatics technologies to open APIs and tools. It also incorporates feedback from the survey to (among other things) introduce FHIR from the outset of the course.

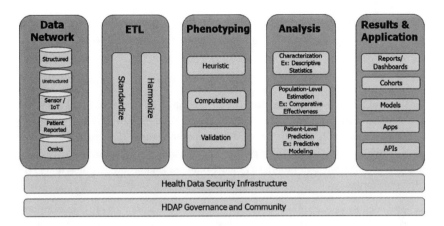

Figure 5.10
The Health Data Analytics Platform (HDAP) Architecture

In the spring of 2017, a team of former Introduction to Health Informatics students and TAs explored the development of a "platform" for the course as their project in David Joyner's CS 6460: Educational Technology course, which is also part of the OMSCS program. In summer 2017 they implemented that platform as a special project. As part of that project, they worked with Jon Duke's team at the Georgia Tech Research Institute (GTRI) to complete an initial version of a new FHIR/OMOP-based Health Data Analytics Platform (HDAP) that was used by students in the fall 2017 and Spring 2018 OMSCS courses. As you can see from figure 5.10, HDAP provides more facile loading of specialized project-specific datasets into OMOP and easier access to analytic and other tools. It stores code modules that can be reused in other projects and it hosts team projects and displays them in an integrated "app gallery." The goal is for student teams to benefit from seeing the work of others and to spend less time setting up project infrastructure and more time focused on the design and implementation of their solutions.

Finally, course participation now routinely exceeds 250 OMSCS students per semester necessitating a more automated and "open" approach to project recruitment and management. Software for that purpose is under development by a team of former OMSCS students/TAs over the summer of 2018.

Notes

1. A simplified health data model that is instantiated in JSON-formatted FHIR Resources (or, optionally, in XML) and a REST API to Create, Read, Update, and Delete (CRUD) those resources. EHRs and other clinical data repositories are FHIR-enabled by writing code (a FHIR adapter) that can respond to HTTP queries (such as Read) by retrieving the needed data from their proprietary model and repackaging and returning it in FHIR Resource format.

2. User identity is determined using OpenID Connect. Access rights to clinical records are determined using OAuth2. OAuth scopes are used to communicate (and negotiate) access requirements to Clinical, Contextual, and Identity data.

References

Bender, D., & Sartipi, K. (2013). HL7 FHIR: An agile and RESTful approach to health-care information exchange. In *Proceedings of the 26th IEEE International Symposium on Computer-Based Medical Systems*. Piscataway, NJ: IEEE.

Boston Children's Hospital SMART on FHIR Growth Chart App. (2017) Retrieved from https://gallery.smarthealthit.org/boston-childrens-hospital/growth-chart.

Cox, J. C., Sadiraj, V., Schnier, K., & Sweeney, J. F. (2016). Higher quality and lower cost from improving hospital discharge decision-making. *Journal of Economic Behavior & Organization, 131*, 1–16.

Ghassemi, M. M., Richter, S. E., Eche, I. M., Chen, T. W., Danziger, J., & Celi, L. A. (2014). A data-driven approach to optimized medication dosing: A focus on heparin. *Intensive Care Medicine, 40*(9), 1332–1339.

Hripcsak, G., et al. (2015). Observational health data sciences and informatics (OHDSI): Opportunities for observational researchers. *Stud Health Technol Inform, 216*, 574–578.

Hübler, M. J., & Buchman, T. G. (2007). Mathematical estimation of recovery after loss of activity: I. Renal failure. *Journal of Trauma and Acute Care Surgery, 63*(1), 232–238.

Johnson, A. E. W., Pollard, T. J., Shen, L., Lehman, L.-W. H., Feng, M., Ghassemi, M., et al. (2016). MIMIC-III, a freely accessible critical care database. *Scientific Data, 3*, 160035. https://doi.org/10.1038/sdata.2016.35.

Kassin, M. A., Owen, R. M., Perez, S. D., Leeds, I., Cox, J. C., Schnier, K., et al. (2012). Risk factors for 30-day hospital readmission among general surgery patients. *Journal of the American College of Surgeons, 215,* 322–330.

Leeds, I. L., Sadiraj, V., Cox, J. C., Gao, S. X., Pawlik, T. M., Schnier, K. E., et al. (in press). Discharge decision-making after complex surgery: Surgeon behaviors compared to predictive modeling to reduce surgical readmissions. *American Journal of Surgery.*

Leeds, I. L., Sadiraj, V., Cox, J. C., Schnier, K. E., & Sweeney, J. F. (2013). Assessing clinical discharge data preferences among practicing surgeons. *Journal of Surgical Research, 184,* 42–48.

Mandel, J. C., Kreda, D. A., Mandl, K. D., Kohane, I. S., & Ramoni, R. B. (2016). SMART on FHIR: A standards-based, interoperable apps platform for electronic health records. *Journal of the American Medical Informatics Association, 23*(5), 899–908.

Nielsen, M. A. (2015). *Neural networks and deep learning.* Determination Press.

Perez, G. (2017). Peer feedback tool. Retrieved from https://www.peerfeedback.io.

Richardson, et al. (2001). *Crossing the quality chasm: A new health system for the 21st century.* Washington, DC: Institute of Medicine.

Rowley, J., & Ghassemi, M. M. (2015). Heparin dosage estimation. https://hepstack-stage.herokuapp.com.

Smith, M., et al. (2012). *Best care at lower cost: The path to continuously learning health care in America.* Washington, DC: National Academies Press.

US Centers for Disease Control and Prevention (CDC). (2016, February 23). *Chronic disease overview.* http://www.cdc.gov/chronicdisease/overview/.

II

CONDUCTING RESEARCH IN BLENDED COURSES

6

RESEARCH METHODS IN BLENDED LEARNING

Robert S. Kadel and Lauren Margulieux

Educational research takes many forms, from quantitative studies that measure changes in learner outcomes to qualitative studies that attempt to describe why some students succeed when others do not. Both approaches are appropriate with respect to blended learning, but each produces its own kind of evidence. For example, a researcher might wonder how the use of video instruction affects students' comprehension of a particular topic. One researcher might use a qualitative design, such as a focus group, to show the video to a group of students and then ask them to describe what they understood from it. A second researcher might use a quantitative design, such as a concept inventory, asking students to answer specific quizlike questions about the content and calculating the average score on the concept inventory. Still a third researcher might use a hybrid design, both quantitative and qualitative, first interviewing students who have watched the video to determine what major themes emerge among the descriptions given by several students. These themes could then be used to construct survey questions ("Based on what you saw in this video, rate your understanding of each topic listed below ..."), which could be administered to a wider audience of students, thereby measuring average comprehension along a scale. Which design you should use depends on what question you are trying to answer.

The research studies included in this edited volume use variations and combinations of the techniques described in this chapter. We encourage the reader to refer back to this chapter when there are research details that are unclear. In this chapter, we consider a range of such research designs that can be used to understand blended learning in college and university settings, including the pros and cons of choosing different methods. Please note, though, that one chapter cannot comprehensively cover this area. We provide a list of resources, including Babbie (2012), Cohen (1988), Creswell (2013), Dziuban et al. (2016), and Tokunaga (2016), at the end of the chapter that the reader can use to explore topics further.

FUNDAMENTAL CONCEPTS THAT ARE OFTEN MISUNDERSTOOD

It is worth noting the value that different methodologies have in the scholarship of teaching and learning (SOTL). Scholars have been debating the value of SOTL for nearly three decades (Boyer, 1990), but it has become a burgeoning field mostly since the early 2000s. In this time, SOTL has become more robust and rigorous, and SOTL research is making a valuable contribution to the academy. One goal of this chapter is to demonstrate that the most valuable SOTL research is grounded in research methods that have a long history in psychology, sociology, learning science, and educational research.

If you are reading this book, you have likely done research and might be confused about why we are explaining types of research questions and data to an audience familiar with methods. Learning scientists and educational researchers often approach research questions with different parameters about context, experiments, and interpretation of results than traditional social and behavioral scientists. The learning sciences attempt to explain how learning happens and how instruction can be improved through innovative processes tied to how we process information (see, e.g., Schank, 2011). Blended learning is one such innovation, and this section describes how learning scientists think about research questions and data to help you understand the research methods and results described in the blended learning research and case studies included in this book.

Specifying Research Questions with Variables

Many educational research questions come from observing something unexpected in the classroom or reading about a new method of instruction. For example, you might find that a student tried a new way of studying that was effective and you want to know if it would be effective for other students. Or you might have read about classrooms using a "flipped blend" (Margulieux et al., 2016) and want to know if using that model would improve learning outcomes in your class. Your research methods will depend heavily on what type of research question you have.

The aspect of your course or instruction that you are changing will be one of the independent variables that you are exploring in your research. For example, if you are comparing one method of studying to another, then the variable you are examining is study method. Data that you collect about how those study methods affect students—for example, test scores—will be the dependent variable that you include in your research. Independent variables in educational research are usually related to a characteristic, such as gender, a behavior, such as time spent interacting with course materials, or an instructional method or material, such as blended learning. Dependent variables measure the effects of independent variables and include behaviors and performance, such as a grade on a test.

Independent and Dependent Variables

Independent variables are those variables that explain, describe, or categorize what you are studying, like gender or time spent in online discussion forums.

Dependent variables are those variables you are trying to impact, such as final grade in a course. They are so named because they *depend on* the values of the independent variables. Males may perform differently from females, and time spent in online discussion forums may have a differential impact on final grade. Final grade depends on the values of the independent variables.

There are two main types of research questions of interest to SOTL: relational and causal. A good educational research question identifies the group that you are studying, such as online students, and the variables that you intend to measure. Good research questions are also open-ended. They typically start with "how," "what," or "why," and cannot be answered with a simple yes or no. For example, the answer to "How do men and women act differently?" provides much more information than "Do men and women act differently?"

Relational Questions Relational questions (see table 6.1) ask about the relationships among variables, but they do not ask about the cause and effect between variables. Relational questions often ask if a change in one variable is related to a change in another variable. For example, a question might ask how the number of lectures missed is related to course grade. People often equate a relationship between variables with a causal relationship, which says that a change in one variable *causes* a change in the other. However, correlation is not causation for reasons that are detailed in chapter 8.

Causal Questions Causal questions (see Table 6.1) ask about the cause-and-effect relationship among variables. These types of questions are the most demanding because they require the researcher to manipulate the independent variable predicted to cause an effect. Sometimes researchers would like to find a causal relationship between variables but are unable to manipulate an independent variable for practical or ethical reasons. For example, you cannot assign students to a religion for practical reasons nor assign people to smoke cigarettes for ethical reasons; therefore, you cannot determine that religion or smoking causes something else.

Operationalizing Variables

In educational research, one of the dependent variables will almost always be some kind of learning. To measure learning, we have to define exactly what we mean. Learning could be measured by grades on assignments, such as exams or projects, performance on standardized tests, such as concept inventories, or self-report, such as feelings about learning. All of these options are possible,

Table 6.1
Understanding research questions

Type of question	Definition	Example	Explanation
Relational	Asks about relationship among variables.	How does behavior in discussion forums differ between men and women?	The answer to this question relates the gender of students to a forum behavior.
Causal	Asks about cause-and-effect relationship among variables.	How does number of forum posts by the instructor affect the average number of posts by students?	The answer to this question establishes cause and effect between instructor and student behavior.

though some are more defensible in scientific research (more on validity later). As a researcher, you need to operationalize, or clearly articulate in objective and measurable terms, what you mean when you say learning, or any of your other dependent variables. You might need to operationalize your independent variables too. For example, instead of saying you'll measure "peer-to-peer interaction," say "number of posts on a peer-to-peer forum and number of contributions during peer-to-peer discussions in class."

Types of Data

Once you have operationalized your variables, you will have a better sense of how to measure them. This section goes into more detail on measurement, and the sections that follow discuss data collection. Your measurements provide the data that you will analyze. There are two main types of data. Quantitative data represent the world with numbers that can be statistically analyzed. They are necessary for relational or causal research questions. For example, quantitative data could tell us the average number of forum posts per student or the number of times that students watched a video. Quantitative measures are appropriate when you want to test a hypothesis (e.g., that students in one group outperform those in another), but they tend to be close-ended, which does not allow for exploration.

Qualitative data are more open-ended than quantitative data and are often used for descriptive research questions. For example, qualitative data could tell us what a student posts on a forum or what notes a student took while watching a video. Qualitative measures are appropriate when you want to explore a phenomenon (e.g., how students use forums), but they are too detailed and time consuming to make it possible to amass a large amount of evidence to strongly support a hypothesis. Qualitative data can be quantified by using coding schemes that turn descriptions into numbers. For example, for coding a forum in a physics class, you could use a coding scheme that counted the number of times students mentioned each of Newton's laws of motion. Quantifying data allows qualitative data to be used in statistical analyses and for relational and causal questions. We provide additional details about coding qualitative data in chapter 8. The reader should also reference Picciano (2016).

Levels of Measurement

Levels of measurement (table 6.2) describe the type of quantitative data that you have by categorizing the relationships among values of a variable. Higher numbers do not always mean higher value in data. For example, if you're recording the race of the learners, you might code "Caucasian" to be 1, "Hispanic or Latino" to be 2, and so on for purposes of analysis. This coding does not mean that Hispanic or Latino is more valuable than Caucasian, but it is merely a way of distinguishing between the two. On the other hand, if you're measuring learners' test scores, then a score of 80 would have a higher value than a score of 70. Levels of measurement categorize these relationships to determine which statistical tests are appropriate to analyze your data. There are four levels of measurement.

Nominal—Lowest Level of Measurement For nominal data, you are basically replacing the name of a value with a number. As in the race example above, the number does not imply anything about the relationship between values. For another example, if you separated students into groups, the group number would not provide any information about the value of the group.

Table 6.2

Levels of measurement

Level of measurement	Definition	Example	Explanation
Nominal	Numbers are placeholders for categories.	0 = male 1 = female	Data don't provide information about relationship between values.
Ordinal	Numbers provide rank order but not exact difference between categories.	1 = low 2 = medium 3 = high	Data provide information about rank but not exact differences.
Interval	Numbers provide information about difference between categories, but there is no defined zero.	1 = strongly disagree 2 = disagree 3 = neutral 4 = agree 5 = strongly agree	The difference between 1 and 2 is equal to the difference between 2 and 3.
Ratio	Numbers provide information about difference between categories and zero means an absence.	0 = 0 forum posts 1 = 1 forum post 2 = 2 forum posts 3 = 3 forum posts 4 = 4 forum posts	The difference between 1 and 2 is equal to the difference between 2 and 3, and 0 means no posts were made.

Ordinal For ordinal data, you can rank-order the values, but the distance between values is not meaningful. For example, you could code prior education as high school degree = 1, some college = 2, college degree = 3, etc. You could rank these values from less education to more education, but the difference between 1 and 2 is not necessarily the same as the difference between 2 and 3.

Interval For interval data, the difference between values is meaningful. For example, if learners rate how much they liked an activity on a scale of "0—not at all" to "10—a great deal," then the difference between 4 and 5 is equal to the difference between 5 and 6. For interval data, zero is just another number on the scale; it does not indicate an absence of something. In this example, the scale could just as easily start at "1—not at all," and the meaning would be the same.

Because interval data lacks a true zero, it does not necessarily follow math principles. For example, on an interval scale like the one above, a student who answered 10 did not like the activity twice as much as a student who answered 5 because 5 represents a neutral point and 10 represents liking the activity a great deal.

Ratio—Highest Level of Measurement   For ratio data, the difference between values is meaningful and zero indicates an absolute zero, or a lack of something. For example, course grades or test scores are ratio because the difference between 70 and 80 is the same as the difference between 80 and 90, and a grade of 0 means that nothing about the topic was known (or demonstrated to be known). Because ratio data has a true zero, it follows math principles. For example, a grade of 100 should indicate that the student has mastered the content twice as well as a grade of 50.

Typically, you want the highest level of measurement that makes sense for the data. For example, you'd rather have numeric grade values, which are ratio, than letter grade values, which are interval or arguably ordinal. The higher your level of measurement is, the less restricted and more sensitive your statistical analyses can be. You must balance level of measurement, though, with meaningfulness. For example, it would not make sense to replace highest level of degree earned (high school, bachelor's, master's, etc.), which is ordinal, with number of years in school (13, 14, 15, 16, etc.), which is ratio, because that would not be meaningful.

Note: There are few differences between analyzing interval and ratio data, so if your data don't have an absolute zero point, that's not a problem.

TYPES OF DATA IN EDUCATIONAL RESEARCH

Demographic Data

Demographic data are used to describe relevant characteristics of the participants in your research. We collect demographic data to justify that our sample is representative of the population we are targeting. We might also run correlational analyses and crosstabulations (described in chapter 8) between dependent measures and demographic data to see if participant characteristics are affecting the results. Any distinguishing characteristics of or within the population should be measured in the demographics. These data typically are not used heavily in the analysis but are mainly used to describe the sample. Demographic variables might include gender, age, employment status, highest level of education completed, ethnicity, race, academic major, GPA, number of years in college, relevant prior experience, and primary language.

Survey Data

Surveys are prominent in educational research for measuring students' opinions. Data collected from survey research can be any level of measurement. For example, if you ask the question "Did you like this instructor?" you could collect ordinal data (e.g., "no," "some," or "yes") or interval data (e.g., "1—very little," "2," "3—some," "4," "5—a lot"). You must be careful when treating survey data as interval, though, because it can easily be misleading. For example, if half of the participants choose "1—very little" and the other half choose "5—a lot," then you don't want to report that your mean response was "3—some." Though statisticians will correctly point out that survey data is ordinal, it is a common practice to treat it as interval data as long as it makes sense.

Interval data is commonly collected with Likert-type scales (Likert, 1932). The classic Likert (pronounced "lick-ert") scale is a 5-point scale, as depicted in table 6.3.

Likert-type scales can range from 3 to 7 points, depending on how much sensitivity is desired. People tend to be less reliable when making more than 7 distinctions, so providing more choices can lead to troublesome data. If you want to force people to choose an option other than neutral, provide an even number of choices to avoid a neutral option. The anchors/endpoints for

Table 6.3
Example of a Likert scale

Strongly disagree	Disagree	Neutral	Agree	Strongly agree
1	2	3	4	5

Likert-type scales can be anything, but people are most familiar with "strongly disagree" to "strongly agree."

More information on constructing effective survey questions can be found in Fowler (2013) and Sapsford (2006). A thorough study of blended learning using a survey design can be found in Dringus and Seagull (2016). Chapter 11 in this volume by Margulieux discusses survey research and basic analysis of survey data. Chapter 4 in this volume by Joyner includes a more sophisticated description of data collection and analysis using surveys.

MAKING COMPARISONS: PRE- AND POSTTEST DESIGNS

Pre-Post Design

In educational research, we are often trying to measure what students learn. To do this, we need to measure the level at which students start, meaning their prior knowledge, and the level at which students finish after a course or intervention. The type of design that measures before (pretest) and after (posttest) a course or intervention is called a pre-post design (table 6.4). This design is good at measuring any sort of change from before the research started to after the research started, such as how students' knowledge differs from the beginning to the end of the course.

Example

Research question—How do physics students' learning outcomes differ when they complete homework problems in a group instead of by themselves?

Research design—Give students a test at the beginning of the semester, ask students whether they complete problems in a group or by themselves, give students the same test at the end of the semester, compare test performance between those that completed problems individually and those that worked in groups.

Researchers sometimes include multiple posttests in this type of design. For example, if you wanted to measure prior knowledge before a course, learning at the end of a course, and retention six months after the course, then you could administer the same test at those time intervals. Technically, that would be considered a pre-post-post design.

Post-Only Design

If you need to collect data only after the intervention, then you can use a post-only design. This design is good at measuring student attitudes or behaviors that develop over a course but are not present at the beginning. For example, the course evaluation surveys that students complete at the end of the semester are a post-only design. This design is appropriate because students likely don't have a strong opinion about the course at the beginning of the semester. Like the pre-post design, this type of design can include multiple posttests to create post-post designs.

Example

Research question—How do composition students' discussions differ when they use online forums instead of in-class discussion?

Research design—Assign students to use online forums or come to class discussions, measure their discussions (e.g., number of contributions per person) near the end of the course, compare performance between those that used online forums and those that discussed in class.

MAKING COMPARISONS: NONEXPERIMENTAL, EXPERIMENTAL, AND QUASI-EXPERIMENTAL DESIGNS

The type of research design that you need depends on the type of research question that you have. Descriptive and relational questions can be answered with nonexperimental designs, and causal questions must be answered by experimental designs. Note: These design categories are independent from pretest

Table 6.4

Pre- and posttest designs

	Definition	Example	Explanation
Pre-post design	Takes measurements before and during/after intervention to capture change.	Give the same test at the beginning (pretest) and end (posttest) of a course.	By comparing the pre- and posttests, the learning gains can be determined.
Posttest	Takes measurements during/after intervention to capture outcomes.	Give a survey (posttest) to measure students' opinions at the end of a course.	Survey responses show students' opinions at the end of the course.
Multiple posttests	Takes measurements at multiple points during/after intervention.	Give the same test at the beginning (pretest), middle (posttest), and end (posttest) of a course.	Multiple posttests allow researchers to track progress throughout the course.

and posttest designs, so you can have a pre-post nonexperimental design or a pre-post experimental design.

Nonexperimental Design (Descriptive and Relational Questions)

In nonexperimental designs, researchers are measuring phenomena as they exist in the world, and they are not systematically manipulating anything. Interactions between researchers and the participants in the study should be limited to what is necessary for collecting data. To collect data, researchers might ask participants to fill out surveys or use another type of measure. If direct interaction with participants is impossible or might invalidate the data by biasing participants, an observational approach might be appropriate. In observational research, researchers do not directly interact with participants, but they collect data by carefully observing participant behaviors. An example of observational research would be counting the number of contributions from each student in an in-class discussion.

Experimental Design (Causal Questions)

In experimental designs, researchers systematically control the environment and manipulate a variable to measure how its intervention affects another variable. In order to control for the effects of the environment in which the research takes place—for example, teacher quality, educational resources, and student background—researchers keep all of these constant and/or use randomization. Suppose a researcher wanted to test whether a blended course format is more effective than a traditional lecture-based format. She would begin by selecting a professor who was well versed in both pedagogical types and who would, by definition, have the same knowledge of the content of the course no matter how that content is delivered. The researcher would then set up two classes of students, where one would use a traditional lecture format and the other a blended design. Given a pool of, say, 100 students, 50 would be randomly assigned to the lecture class and 50 to the blended class. Randomization ensures that each class will very likely have the same differences in student characteristics, such as differences in race, gender, socioeconomic status, and prior knowledge of the subject matter. Both classes of students are essentially equal in terms of the teacher's ability, the content being delivered, and the students' background characteristics. The only thing that varies is the teaching method being used.

Quasi-Experimental Design (Causal Questions, with Caveats)

Quasi-experimental designs (QEDs) use the same logic as experimental designs, seeking to manipulate one or more independent variables between two similar groups and measuring the difference in some dependent variable measured for each group. However, in a QED, researchers accept that the effects of the environment cannot be controlled as easily. To draw on the example above, a researcher may seek to determine the differences between a lecture-format class and a blended class but does not have the ability to randomly assign students to either format.

In a QED, the goal of the researcher should be to establish how similar the two groups of students are. For example, if demographic and background information about the two groups of students shows that they are similar—that is, have generally the same proportions of males and females, the same proportion of freshmen, sophomores, etc., and about the same average GPA at the start of the semester—then it is possible to argue that the design still controls for these extraneous factors. If these facts cannot be established, it is still possible to statistically control for the differences between groups, but those statistical procedures go beyond the scope of this book. We recommend Holmes (2014) and Shadish, Cook, and Campbell (2001) for further information. For examples of quasi-experimental designs used to evaluate blended learning environments, we point the reader to Brooks and Sandfort (2016) and to chapter 9 in this volume by Webster, Kadel, and Madden.

VALIDITY AND RELIABILITY

Key to understanding relationships between different types of data are the concepts of reliability and validity. When we talk about validity in research measurement, we are talking about the extent to which the measurement we use actually measures what we think it measures. When we talk about reliability in research measurements, we are talking about the extent to which the same participant would give you the same score on a measurement that was administered more than once. In other words, validity and reliability question whether your measures will be legitimate and consistent, respectively.

A quick and easy way to think about validity and reliability is to consider throwing darts at a bull's-eye (see figure 6.1). The goal of the challenge is to hit the bull's-eye as many times as possible. If a dart thrower consistently throws a tight grouping, but they are not on the bull's-eye, we would say he is reliable but not valid. He keeps hitting the same spot, but it's not the spot he wants. If another dart thrower hits the target six inches to the left of the bull's-eye on one throw, six inches to the right on the next throw, six inches above on the third throw, and six inches below on the fourth throw, *on average*, she is valid but she is not reliable. The average of her throws converges on the bull's-eye, but any single throw is not accurate. If a third dart thrower's hits are all over the place and nowhere near the bull's-eye even on average, his throws are neither reliable nor valid. Finally, a dart thrower who throws a tight grouping right on the bull's-eye is both reliable and valid. If you have low validity or reliability, then you will have a lot of error in your data and be more likely to make errors in your conclusions.

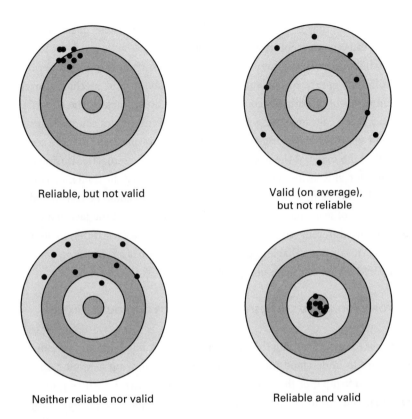

Reliable, but not valid

Valid (on average),
but not reliable

Neither reliable nor valid

Reliable and valid

Figure 6.1
Bull's-eye diagrams comparing reliability and validity

In educational research, we often think of validity in terms of how accurately we can measure student learning. For example, suppose a professor is teaching an engineering course on statics. He wants to start the term by measuring how much his students already know about the topic, so he asks them to fill out a concept inventory that essentially quizzes them on what they know. Unfortunately, the concept inventory he has chosen contains questions about both statics and dynamics. It would be considered an invalid measure of students' understanding because it is asking some questions about a topic that the students may or may not have already studied. Those questions are irrelevant, thus the concept inventory is not valid.

Meanwhile, suppose another engineering professor wants to measure how much different groups of students have learned about fluid mechanics over three semesters of offering the course. During the first semester, she administers a quiz that a colleague had written for his fluid mechanics course. During the second semester, she changes several of those quiz questions to more accurately reflect the material she has emphasized during the semester. During the third semester, she decides to use a quiz that accompanied the fluid mechanics textbook she was using. Each of these quizzes, by itself, could be considered a valid measure of learning, to a greater or lesser degree. But the fact that each quiz contains different questions and possibly emphasizes different topics means that it is not a reliable measure of student learning. Learning cannot be compared across the three groups of students.

POPULATIONS AND SAMPLES: HOW MUCH ERROR CAN YOU TOLERATE?

In addition to understanding the difference between reliability and validity, it is necessary to understand the difference between studying a whole population or just a sample of that population. A population is the whole group of people that you are interested in studying. For example, a population might be the students in a particular major, those at a particular university, or those in a particular country. In most cases, we are not able, nor is it necessary, to include everyone in a population in a study, so we rely on samples, or representative subsets, from those populations. For instance, if you were interested in a project about improving physics education (i.e., the population of physics students), you might use students in an intro physics class as your sample. Sampling introduces potential error into the research because samples can differ (e.g., students in one physics class are not the same as those in another), whereas a population is all inclusive. Additional information on drawing conclusions about a population from a sample is included in the inferential statistics section of chapter 8.

Error is anything that might influence the results of a study in a way that is inconsistent or that is not being measured. For example, personal issues may affect a student's performance in a course. Unless the study is about coping with personal issues, this is likely to be a source of error and impact the results of the research. People are incredibly complex, and human-subjects research inherently has error because people's performance in a study can be influenced by these complexities—time of day, day of week, events that happened yesterday, and even what the subjects think the research is about.

All measurements include some degree of error as well. For example, if you ask participants for their age, you can have two participants who are "25" with almost a year difference in age unless you measure with more specificity, which probably would not be worth your time. Other measurements used in educational research are no different. To manage this error, human-subjects research employs null hypothesis significance testing, where we use statistics to determine whether a phenomenon is likely due to error or not. We state our research questions as null hypotheses (usually, that what we are attempting to measure did not occur) and alternative hypotheses (that what we are attempting to measure did occur). In the positivist scientific tradition, we gather data to attempt to refute the null hypothesis, in effect saying, "I reject the conclusion that nothing happened; in other words, something happened!" Consider the example in table 6.5.

When analyzing quantitative data, we use statistical analyses to determine if a phenomenon is less than 5% likely to be due to error, reported as $p < 0.05$. Said another way, $p < 0.05$ means that we have 95% confidence that the result is due to differences in the independent variable (in the example in table 6.5,

Table 6.5
Example of a hypothesis to be tested

Null hypothesis (H_o)	There is no difference in quiz scores between those who used supplemental video instruction and those who did not.
Alternative hypothesis (H_a)	There is a statistically significant difference in quiz scores between those who used supplemental video instruction and those who did not.

use of supplemental video instruction), not just chance. We can reject the null hypothesis and be 95% confident in accepting the alternative hypothesis. Results that meet the $p < 0.05$ standard are considered evidence, but not proof, that a phenomenon exists. More sophisticated statistical analyses, called effect sizes, can tell you how strong or weak a phenomenon is, but they fall outside of the null hypothesis significance testing paradigm.

Differences that exceed the $p < 0.05$ standard are considered statistically significant. When describing results, it is correct to use the full phrase "statistically significant" instead of only "significant," because readers might infer the nontechnical meaning of significant. The opposite of statistical significance is "statistically nonsignificant." Never say "insignificant" unless you intend the nontechnical meaning. It is important that you do not confuse *statistical* significance with *meaningful* significance. Results can be statistically significant but not meaningful for a number of reasons. Sample size affects statistical significance, and even minor differences in very large samples can be found to be statistically significant. For example, if you are analyzing a massive open online course (MOOC) with 50,000 learners, then a 0.3% difference in quiz scores between groups could be statistically significant. But a 0.3% difference likely isn't meaningful in the big picture. Similarly, results can be statistically nonsignificant but meaningful. For example, if you expected online and in-class groups of students to perform differently and they did not, then nonsignificant results are meaningful. To use the vernacular, even a nonresult is a result.

METHODS FOR COLLECTING QUALITATIVE DATA

While the collection of quantitative data is often preferred in educational research, it is not always appropriate or the most effective means of testing a hypothesis. Qualitative research methods can be used to collect more detailed and descriptive information than a survey, quiz, or concept inventory can provide. Interviews with students and faculty, observation notes detailing in-class interactions, web-page text and images, news articles, even song lyrics—these are all sources of qualitative data. And the goal of gathering information from these kinds of sources is to determine patterns in the information *and* significant deviations from those patterns. Deciding which type of qualitative data collection method to use depends on your research question and the type of data you need. For example, if the information you seek to gather is of a personal nature, it is more appropriate to arrange one-on-one interviews than to conduct a focus group. The following section provides details on several common qualitative methods that are used in educational research.

In-Depth Interviews

A common approach to understanding an event, interaction, or phenomenon is to conduct in-depth interviews with those involved. For example, if a researcher wanted to understand students' impressions of learning in a blended class, he might draw a random sample of students from the class and ask them questions about their experiences. Key to this process is the use of an interview protocol (aka interview guide). The interview protocol is constructed based on the researcher's underlying hypotheses about what is happening in the class. For example, based on reviewing the research literature on blended classes, a researcher might hypothesize that students in a flipped class might be surprised at the use of video instruction outside of class and problem-solving opportunities in class. (After all, this is not a typical way of structuring a college course.) Based on this hypothesis, the researcher would include in his interview protocol questions such as

• Tell me about your first day of class. What were you thinking or feeling when the professor said you would be watching her lectures on your computer outside of class time?
• How would you describe the time you spent working with other students on problems during class time?
• [Probe on] Did you feel it was time well spent? Tell me more about that.

Notice the "Probe on" prompt. This is an important part of the interview protocol. There is a good chance that the respondent will tell the researcher whether or not time was well spent when answering the original prompt (How would you describe the time ...?). However, if the respondent does not happen to cover information about the quality of class time, the interviewer has a prompt to remind him to ask about it.

Each interview is usually audio-recorded and transcribed. By recording the interview, rather than trying to take notes, the researcher can focus attention on the person being interviewed and the flow of the conversation. Key to using interview protocols is to remember not to let them shackle you, the researcher. There is a reason we also refer to them as interview *guides*, because they are designed to guide the conversation but not to constrain it. If a respondent has relevant information, then the interviewer should allow the respondent to speak her mind, even if what she is describing is not covered by the interview protocol. However, if the respondent ends up on long tangents, then the protocol can be used to help the researcher guide her back to the topic at hand.

The transcripts of several interviews, then, are used to determine patterns among responses, to find quotations that are telling or typical, and to identify any outliers or deviations from the main themes. For examples of in-depth interviews used in studying blended learning, we point the reader to Skibba (2016) and to chapter 7 in this volume by Burnett, Menagarishvili, and Frazee.

Focus Groups

Focus groups have been widely used in marketing and advertising for several decades. Typically a focus group might be used to show a typical "audience" (representative of those advertisers are trying to reach) concepts for several new advertisements of a product. The group would debate the pros and cons of each and help researchers determine which ad would most likely persuade them to buy the product. In educational research, focus groups have taken on a different role, allowing learners, educators, parents, and so on the opportunity to share experiences and reflect on the experiences of others.

A focus group is a special kind of interview. The one-on-one interview process described above has great value, especially when the researcher does not want each respondent's answers to be influenced by others or when researching sensitive or possibly embarrassing topics. There are a number of ethical questions to consider when conducting interviews, especially on sensitive topics, and the reader is encouraged to consult Babbie (2012) and the resources listed in his chapter on qualitative field research.

On the other hand, there are times when a researcher may *want* to have respondents react to the responses of others. One student in a flipped class may describe an experience where his class partner did not show up for class regularly, and he expresses his frustration at this. Another respondent hears this and realizes that she felt the same way about her partner but handled it in a different way. The focus group is an ideal environment to allow respondents to have this back-and-forth conversation in real time. Picciano (2016) also discusses ways to apply this same logic to the analysis of asynchronous discussions, such as discussion forums (see pp. 85–88).

As with interviews, focus groups rely on a moderator's guide, which is akin to the interview protocol. The moderator's guide provides structure for the discussion and is usually grounded in one or more hypotheses that the researcher hopes to test. Again, though, the researcher should not feel completely bound to the questions in the moderator's guide and should allow respondents to add information that she feels is important even if it had not occurred to her or other members of the research team before.

Focus groups typically need to be video-recorded. As with interviews, the recording is transcribed for analysis; however, it is difficult to transcribe a focus group with multiple participants with only an audio recording because it is difficult to know who is speaking. It is helpful to color-code focus-group transcripts such that everything respondent 1 said is in red, everything respondent 2 said is in blue, and so on. See chapter 8 for more on coding qualitative data. For additional information on conducting focus groups, the reader should consult Krueger and Casey (2008). An example of focus groups used to evaluate blended learning can be found in DeCarrio Voegele (2016).

Observations

It is often the qualitative researcher's job to understand what is happening in a particular situation by watching individuals actively participate in that situation. For example, a researcher may want to understand how students interact during the active learning time in a blended class and to determine if there are any differences in interaction by gender, age, or ethnicity. To assist in this process the researcher will need to develop an *observation protocol*, which is somewhat similar to an interview protocol or focus-group moderator's guide. The observation protocol is again grounded in certain hypotheses that are usually formed ahead of time by examining the research literature. Observation protocol prompts can be written either as statements or questions (or both), such as "Watch each small group of students to determine if one or more participants is speaking more often than others" and "Does anyone in the group seem to be giving more instructions or directives than others?"

When developing the observation protocol, it is important that the researcher be aware of any biases that the protocol might bring into the collection of data. For example, if the research literature indicates that males will often monopolize conversations in blended engineering classes, the protocol should *not* state: "Do males in the class tend to take over conversations from females?" Instead, the protocol should be stated more objectively: "Observe one or more male-female pairs. Who appears to be speaking the most in each pair?"

The data generated from observations usually takes the form of field notes where the researcher writes down or types out what she saw as well as responses to the observation prompts. However, a researcher should be cautioned against trying to take note of *everything* such that she is missing key interactions because she is staring at her laptop. Instead, she should consider writing down field notes immediately after the class has concluded. The information is still fresh in her mind. It is important not to linger when taking field notes because important points can be forgotten quite easily even after only a few hours. If it is possible and not deemed too intrusive, the researcher may want to ask permission to video the class or portions of the class.

A common concern with observational research is the so-called *Hawthorne effect*. The Hawthorne effect states that by observing a phenomenon the observer causes an inherent change in the phenomenon. In other words, when students know they are being observed, they may change their typical behavior. One common method for mitigating the Hawthorne effect is to make multiple observations of the same subjects over time. That is, instead of observing just one class session, the observer should ask to observe several classes over a number of days. Once research subjects become comfortable with the presence of the researcher, they will often return to their typical patterns of behavior. How much observation is required is a matter of judgment and experience, but in our experience in education, a class should be observed a minimum of three times. The observer should sit in a quiet or unused area of the room where his presence will be the least intrusive, though being certain to choose a vantage point(s) where all students can be observed, even if that means moving from one location to another throughout the class.

Participant Observation

A special type of observational research has been established in sociology and cultural anthropology where the researcher actually participates in the environment she is observing. The goal of participant observation is to gather lots of information over long periods of time during which the researcher becomes familiar to and with the subjects being observed. This helps account for the Hawthorne effect over time. However, participant observation requires that the researcher be able to participate fully in each event—in other words, not holding a video camera or typing on a computer while the event is taking place. An observation protocol is still used, though it is typically more general and easier to memorize. The protocol should also be flexible enough that developments in the research can be taken into account as more is learned about the subjects and their experiences. Two classic participant observational studies worth attention are Ammerman (1992), *Bible Believers: Fundamentalists in the Modern World*, and Howell (1972), *Hard Living on Clay Street: Portraits of Blue Collar Families*.

Document/Artifact Analysis

Qualitative researchers will often examine information that has been recorded at a previous point in time, such as student research papers, web pages, books, research posters, and even diagrams and pictures. The goal of this type of analysis is similar to the above: to determine patterns among the documents or artifacts that are being analyzed. For example, Marino (2011) analyzed high school world history textbooks to determine how much coverage they gave to topics ranging from artistic representations of religion to economic and technological change.

A common tool in document and artifact analysis is content analysis wherein the researcher establishes algorithms for characterizing and categorizing texts. In the Marino example mentioned above, the author established measures of "coverage" by tabulating chapter titles, subheadings, and the total number of pages devoted to each topic. Content analysis will often drill down to the number of words devoted to a particular topic or the number of times a certain word (or its synonyms) appears in the text.

THE ROLE OF GROUNDED THEORY: DEDUCTIVE VERSUS INDUCTIVE

Each of the above types of data collection relies on the use of some sort of guide—an interview protocol, a focus-group moderator's guide, an observation protocol, and so on. Each of these would be driven by the hypothesis being tested. These approaches are all deductive in nature. There is an exception to this type of methodology, however, in *grounded theory*: "Grounded theory is an inductive methodology that attempts to derive a theory from an activity, process, or interaction and is *grounded* in the views of the participants" (Picciano, 2016, p. 91, emphasis in original). In short, studies that employ grounded theory are less concerned with trying to test a particular hypothesis and more concerned with constructing a theory of interaction based on the available data.

CONCLUSION

Paramount to conducting research in blended learning (or in any educational field) is writing specific research questions. Everything follows from the research question: the method of data collection, the hypotheses to be tested, and the interpretation of results. Other chapters in this part of the book explore these principles and analyses of data collected on blended college classes.

Chapter 8, in particular, builds on the research methods described here and discusses how best to analyze the data you have collected.

References

Ammerman, N. T. (1992). *Bible believers: Fundamentalists in the modern world*. New Brunswick, NJ: Rutgers University Press.

Babbie, E. (2012). *The practice of social research* (13th ed.). Belmont, CA: Wadsworth.

Boyer, E. L. (1990). *Scholarship reconsidered: Priorities of the professoriate*. New York: Carnegie Foundation for the Advancement of Teaching.

Brooks, D. C., & Sandfort, J. R. (2013). Trial and error: Iteratively improving research on blended learning. In A. G. Picciano, C. D. Dziuban, & C. R. Graham (Eds.), *Blended learning: Research perspectives* (Vol. 2, pp. 141–149). New York: Routledge.

Cohen, J. (1988). *Statistical power analysis for the behavioral sciences* (2nd ed.). Hillsdale, NJ: Erlbaum.

Creswell, J. W. (2013). *Research design: Quantitative, qualitative, and mixed methods approaches* (4th ed.). Thousand Oaks, CA: Sage.

DeCarrio Voegele, J. (2016). Student perspectives on blended learning through the lens of social, teaching, and cognitive presence. In A. G. Picciano, C. D. Dziuban, & C. R. Graham (Eds.), *Blended learning: Research perspectives* (Vol. 2, pp. 9–103). New York: Routledge.

Dringus, L. P., & Seagull, A. B. (2016). A five-year study of sustaining blended learning initiatives to enhance academic engagement in computer and information sciences campus courses. In A. G. Picciano, C. D. Dziuban, & C. R. Graham (Eds.), *Blended learning: Research perspectives* (Vol. 2, pp. 122–140). New York: Routledge.

Dziuban, C. D., Picciano, A. G., Graham, C. R., & Moskal, P. D. (2016). *Conducting research in online and blended learning environments: New pedagogical frontiers*. New York: Routledge/Taylor & Francis.

Fowler, F. J. (2013). *Survey research methods* (5th ed.). Thousand Oaks, CA: Sage.

Holmes, W. M. (2014). *Using propensity scores in quasi-experimental designs*. Thousand Oaks, CA: Sage.

Howell, J. T. (1972). *Hard living on Clay Street: Portraits of blue collar families.* Prospect Heights, IL: Waveland Press.

Krueger, R., & Casey, M. A. (2008). *Focus groups: A practical guide for applied research* (4th ed.). Thousand Oaks, CA: Sage.

Likert, R. (1932). A technique for the measurement of attitudes. *Archives de Psychologie,* *140,* 1–55.

Margulieux, L. E., McCracken, W. M., & Catrambone, R. (2016). A taxonomy to define courses that mix face-to-face and online learning. *Educational Research Review, 19,* 104–118.

Marino, M. P. (2011). High school world history textbooks: An analysis of content focus and chronological approaches. *History Teacher, 44*(3), 421–446.

Picciano, A. G. (2016). Qualitative research in online and blended learning. In C. D. Dziuban, A. G. Picciano, C. R. Graham, & P. D. Moskal (Eds.), *Conducting research in online and blended learning environments: New pedagogical frontiers* (pp. 84–96). New York: Routledge/Taylor & Francis.

Sapsford, R. (2006). *Survey research* (2nd ed.). Thousand Oaks, CA: Sage.

Schank, R. (2011). *Teaching minds: How cognitive science can save our schools.* New York: Teachers College Press.

Shadish, W. R., Cook, T. D., & Campbell, D. T. (2001). *Experimental and quasi-experimental designs for generalized causal inference* (2nd ed.). Independence, KY: Cengage.

Skibba, K. (2016). Choice does matter: Faculty lessons learned teaching adults in a blended program. In A. G. Picciano, C. D. Dziuban, & C. R. Graham (Eds.), *Blended learning: Research perspectives* (Vol. 2, pp. 203–212). New York: Routledge.

Tokunaga, H. T. (2016). *Fundamental statistics for the social and behavioral sciences.* Thousand Oaks, CA: Sage.

7

STUDENT ATTITUDES ABOUT TEAMWORK IN FACE-TO-FACE AND BLENDED TECHNICAL COMMUNICATION CLASSES

Rebecca E. Burnett, Olga Menagarishvili, and Andy Frazee

MIX Taxonomy Classification: The course is blended. The students in the blended course receive content through online videos and in-class lectures. They also receive feedback on their applications of content both via technology and in class. The FTF course includes many technology-supported aspects, but most of the instruction is delivered in class.

Research Method Classification: The research method is a quasi-experimental, pre-post-post test design. Students completed a survey with open-ended questions about their attitudes toward aspects of the class at the beginning, middle, and end of the semester. Student responses were coded qualitatively and reported both qualitatively (i.e., quotes from students) and quantitatively (i.e., counts of comments about a theme). In general, the researchers found little difference between the FTF and blended versions of the classroom.

Technical communication has a well-established, theoretically grounded history of teaching small, face-to-face classes, with an emphasis on active, experiential engagement. Typical technical communication activities include creating and interpreting written, oral, and visual artifacts such as specifications, documentation of computer code, proposals, reports, instructions, apps, and websites for a variety of workplace contexts, purposes, and audiences. The goal of technical communication teachers is to engage students in the collaborative work of writers and communicators—that is, to promote effective attitudes and engender productive practices in planning, drafting, writing, designing, revising, and presenting—rather than simply to tell or show them how others do it. Because of this emphasis on hands-on, experiential learning, technical communication teachers have long presumed that students' active engagement involves working face to face. We were curious about what happens, then, when technical communication is taught as a large, blended (online and face-to-face) class—effectively challenging decades of disciplinary assumptions about what appropriate technical communication pedagogy entails.

In this chapter, we address student attitudes in relation to face-to-face (FTF) and blended classes, student collaboration, and active learning. We focus on descriptions of in situ classes, offering observations that may provide suggestions for teachers and curriculum developers interested in blended learning. Our study is part of a larger IRB-approved, mixed-methods project investigating upper-level undergraduate students' attitudes, processes, and performances in a pair of linked courses: computer science (CS) and technical communication (TC).

Our research question asks what characterizes student attitudes about working with team members in FTF and blended TC classes. The focus on teamwork is relevant since most workplace documents have a collaborative component in their design and/or development (Lunsford and Ede, 1990). We begin by briefly explaining the context of the TC classes we examine. We follow with a discussion of our methodology, including a level of detail that is typical in our discipline, articulating rather than simply presuming concepts. Next, we present and discuss our quantitative data and offer observations using excerpts from our qualitative data. We conclude by considering implications for teachers, researchers, and developers, encouraging increased attention to active learning in designing courses.

The results of this study might be helpful for designing and teaching FTF, blended, and online TC courses, as well as for understanding the importance of active learning strategies in technical communication pedagogy. More generally, the results may be helpful in designing and managing team-oriented projects in blended learning contexts.

CONTEXT

In the first part of this section, we present details about the way TC was formerly offered to CS undergraduate students at Georgia Tech. We next describe this project's challenge to the status quo, which leads to our particular interest in three factors—blended learning, active learning, and student attitude—as the foci of our inquiry. The third part of this section of the chapter considers concepts that shape the teaching of TC: rhetoric, problem solving, situated cognition, knowledge transfer, and collaboration.

Background

Prior to 2013, Georgia Tech's CS students took a one-semester, 23-student, stand-alone TC course as part of their degree program. This TC course was similar to those in many universities, focusing student attention on workplace communication problems, processes, and deliverables. Student outcomes addressed five areas: rhetorical awareness, organization and support, design for medium, conventions, and process. In such TC courses, students typically complete both individual and team projects—often for actual clients—including, for example, instructions, user testing, proposals, reports, project/code documentation, specifications, brochures, infographics, presentations, and various kinds of social media. Students are especially encouraged to understand the importance of working collaboratively, responding to workplace contexts, designing ethical/legal documents, creating effective arguments, balancing visual and verbal elements, and designing usable deliverables for particular audiences.

The College of Computing agreed that attention to TC was important; however, they wanted the course to focus more on TC in the context of computer science so students would be better communicators in their future professional work. Furthermore, CS alumni indicated that they wanted even more attention devoted to TC in computer science. In response to this alumni feedback, the College of Computing invited the Writing and Communication Program to work with them to create another approach: a two-semester, team-taught course sequence that integrated CS and TC.

A committee consisting of faculty and administrators from CS and TC spent the academic year 2012–2013 redesigning two existing one-semester, three-credit courses—the 50-student junior capstone CS course and the 23-student stand-alone TC course—to create linked, two-semester, 50-student CS/TC courses, earning a combined six credits. The linked courses were FTF, team taught by one CS instructor and one TC instructor. The linked courses were initially offered in fall 2013.

The new linked courses continued CS/TC disciplinary preferences for project-based curriculum; thus, assignments necessarily consider detailed contexts, actual audiences, real arguments, effective designs, and expected language conventions, as well as feasibility, budget, schedule, and personnel. In these linked courses, students could find their own client, but more typically, the projects came from CS/TC instructors who had a list of client projects. These projects ranged from employers who often hire CS graduates to internal university departments with specific needs, so that a client might be a corporate or nonprofit professional or a university professor or staff member. Student teams request particular software development projects, which are typically apps, based on team interests and skill sets. Modeling workplace practice, communication is part of each stage of software development, as reflected in these assignments used in the linked courses:

(1) Statement of Work (proposal for the project)

(2) Feasibility Report (report arguing ways to create the project)

(3) Presentation (oral team presentation of work accomplished)

(4) Detailed Design Document (specifications, explanations, analysis, and visual representations about project's architecture)

(5) Progress Report (report about work planned, accomplished, and yet to be done)

(6) Project Postmortem (analysis of project process and product)

(7) Final Presentation (oral team presentation of work accomplished and product demo)

By summer 2015, we also developed a blended, largely online section of the courses in response to student and faculty interest. During our study, students met with instructors for a percentage of the primary instructional time (i.e., time the instructors met with the class group for teaching purposes, such as lecturing or facilitating active learning).

• *Face-to-face classes.* In the FTF section of the course, students saw each other regularly in a classroom throughout the semester. For the primary instructional time, the FTF section met face to face 100% of the time. Even though they met face to face, students used a range of digital tools, both in and out of class. For example, they accessed the learning management system (T-Square, Georgia Tech's version of Sakai) to receive the course schedule, read assignment sheets, and submit assignments; they used Google Drive, Piazza, and WordPress (or blog alternative) for tasks including peer review and work on assignments and projects.

• *Blended classes.* In the blended section, students met face to face for approximately one-third of the primary course instruction time, whereas they met online (both synchronously and asynchronously) for approximately two-thirds of the time—for example, via T-Square, Google Drive, Piazza, and blogs, the same technology used in the FTF section. Some weeks, students met face to face once or twice; other weeks, students completed all of their work online. In addition, students in the blended section viewed some video lectures.

Each FTF section worked in five ways: *whole class* (50 students), *class discussion/working groups* (25-student subsections of the whole class), *teams* (5- to 6-member teams, both self-selected and teacher assigned), *peer review groups* (two teams, both self-selected and teacher assigned), and *individuals*. Each *blended section* worked in four ways: *whole class, teams, peer review groups,* and *individuals.* Depending on the nature of the class activities for a particular day, students met with the whole class, their working section, their team, or by themselves. This meant students needed to track when they were required to attend class and what was expected on a particular day.[1]

Focus of Inquiry

A second part of the context defines three factors—blended learning, active learning, and student attitude—that influence our teaching and shape our research question. We begin by discussing the ways blended learning challenges technical communication disciplinary conventions that courses should be taught in FTF sections—even as many institutions are moving to online teaching for courses in STEM disciplines. Next, we discuss active learning, which we saw as a purposeful way of promoting student engagement and potentially engendering effective attitudes. Finally, we discuss student attitudes, which affect performance and behavior, which, in turn, influence learning.

Blended Learning   In this study, we use the term *blended learning* to mean a course that blends some percent of FTF learning (usually in teacher-determined times and places) and some percent of online learning (usually in student-determined times and places).[2] Blended learning has benefits that are unlikely with FTF education because of its online components. For example, online learning is one possible solution to challenges of enrollment, making classes available to student populations that normally do not have access to them. Online learning also appeals to many students and responds to their desire for scheduling flexibility. Despite the benefits of online learning, a recent study about teaching TC reported that "statistically, it took [instructors] significantly more time and effort per student—approximately 20%—to teach an online technical communication course than it took to teach the same course FTF" (Whorley and Tesdell, 2009, p. 149), with the increased time being used for "reading and responding to discussion boards/forums/blogs ... [and] record keeping" (p. 144). Nonetheless, online learning blended with FTF learning is more effective than either alone. Nearly 20 years ago, Chadwick (1999) conducted a study demonstrating that blended learning (what he called "multi-modal instruction," a blend of FTF and online instruction) "appears more effective than single-mode instruction."

We are particularly interested in recent research that supports Chadwick's findings, confirming blended learning as having "a consistent positive effect in comparison with no intervention, and to be more effective than or at least as effective as non-blended instruction for knowledge acquisition" (Liu et al., 2016). We are curious about whether we'll find, like Liu and colleagues who explored blended learning in the health professions, that blended learning enables "students to review electronic materials [as well as other materials] as often as necessary and at their own pace, which likely enhances learning performance" (Liu et al., 2016).[3]

Because blended learning may productively influence student attitudes, it has the potential to increase student learning. We are interested in whether we'll find that CS/TC students prefer to "do written activities online but engage in discussion in person" (Kemp and Grieve, 2014). Our study population informally voiced a preference for interacting via technology—even when FTF interaction was the norm for the course.

Active Learning We are interested in active learning strategies that are effective in both FTF and blended TC classes. Active learning is "the process of having students engage in some activity that forces them to reflect upon ideas and how they are using those ideas" (Prince, 2004, p. 160). Students need to be active participants, not passive recipients.[4]

The umbrella of active learning (Linton et al., 2014) includes a range of strategies used by our students in completing their work in our courses, including designing/responding, listening/responding, reading/responding, and viewing/responding to artifacts (e.g., texts, podcasts, images, films, and videos). The strategies are not mutually exclusive. So, for example, cooperative learning could be used to analyze a case study; similarly, peer discussion is typically part of problem-based learning. Overall, active learning strategies lead to multimodal, client-based projects (Cooper et al., 2016). The active learning strategies we introduced in our classes reinforced a range of conceptually oriented tasks (Ruiz-Primo et al., 2011); emphasized collaboration, including collaborative planning, collaborative learning, and cooperative learning (Burnett, 1991; Bruffee, 1995; Johnson, Johnson, and Smith, 1998); and encouraged problem solving, including problem-based learning (Dochy et al., 2003). These strategies were used in all sections of the CS/TC courses, but the strategies were sometimes developed and implemented differently in the FTF sections and blended sections.[5]

Our approach is supported by a number of studies arguing that "collaboration improved learner performance regarding higher-order thinking activities when learners discussed the problem and suggested potential solutions to the problem" (Ku, Tseng, and Akarasriworn, 2013, p. 922; Johnson and Chung, 1999; Mergendoller, Bellisimo, and Maxwell, 2000). These studies supporting the merits of active learning are reinforced by a meta-analysis examining 225 studies and reporting that "active learning increases scores on concept inventories more than on course examinations, and ... active learning appears effective across all class sizes—although the greatest effects are in relatively small ($n \leq 50$) classes" (Freeman et al., 2014, p. 8410). In summary, we concur with Ku and colleagues (2013, p. 922) that "active and constructive learning, deep processing of information, critical thinking, and goal-based learning ... [are] valid in online collaborative learning environments."

Student Attitude We focus on three factors in our study that appear to affect student attitude: students' preferences, pedagogical attention to students, and students' active engagement. We agree with Kemp and Grieve (2014) when they argue that students' preferences need to be addressed in research; specifically, they encourage researchers to consider students' "perceptions and experiences" that have been largely ignored. For us, this meant, for example, considering the ways student perceptions about attendance affect their attitudes. While many faculty in the College of Computing do not take attendance, in our classes, attendance is required. Once CS students became aware of this requirement, they informally expressed resistance to attending FTF sections and expressed a preference for the blended sections. Similarly, students' preferences about technology influence their attitudes. For example, many students prefer "working collaboratively in an online environment" (Ku et al., 2013, p. 928). Our anecdotal observations support this, since the second time the linked courses were offered, the online section filled more quickly.

For some students, simply knowing they merit special pedagogical attention appears to improve their attitude. For example, students in an introductory physics course demonstrated improved attitude when they were in sections using an alternative pedagogy such as peer discussion (rather than in a traditional lecture), showing "positive attitudinal gains related to alternative curricula" (Zhang, Ding, and Mazur, 2017, p. 010104–1). In our study, a similar kind of attention came by integrating active learning strategies into both the FTF and the blended sections. Students in our linked classes knew that our use of blended learning was for pedagogical purposes rather than to overcome "barriers of distance and time, economies of scale, and [to introduce] novel instructional methods" (Cook, 2007, p. 37), a position sometimes promoted by Georgia Tech in providing a rationale for the institute's online courses.

Finally, we are concerned with the ways student attitude is affected by active engagement. Vygotsky believes engagement facilitates individual cognitive growth and knowledge acquisition, and that peer collaboration can help learners in problem solving. He argues that learners better understand new ideas or concepts with help or feedback from a teacher or peer (Vygotsky, 1978), thus extending the "zone of proximal development." In this study, engagement through peer interaction is an active learning strategy, one that our student teams used in several ways, including peer review, collaboration, small-group problem solving, responding to each other's blogs, and whole-class discussion.

Concepts That Shape the Teaching of Technical Communication

Both the FTF and blended sections of our courses were explicitly situated within a theoretical frame based on rhetorical awareness, problem solving, situated cognition, knowledge transfer, and collaboration. These factors are conventional and widespread in technical communication courses, frame our discussion, and influence our interpretation of our results.

Rhetorical Awareness Rhetoric is the core of effective communication (including technical communication); Aristotle called it "the best available means of persuasion" (Aristotle, n.d., book 1).

Rhetoric is the overarching theory framing our courses. *Rhetorical awareness* includes students' attention to, among other things, overlapping purposes (e.g., informing, instructing, persuading, balancing textual and visual information, urging safety compliance, and urging legal compliance), multiple audiences (e.g., internal and external, expert and nonexpert), complex contexts, appropriate processes, affordances of a range of modes and media, and design. Rhetoric is a critical concern in technical communications both as a discipline and a profession. Furthermore, effective communication is identified as a competency required by the Accreditation Board for Engineering and Technology (ABET), which accredits college and university programs in computing and other disciplines (Accreditation Board for Engineering and Technology, n.d.; Passow, 2012).

All our students deal with these rhetorical concerns in designing and developing their CS/TC projects, though they give some concerns more attention than others, depending on the project. Sometimes the primary focus might be on audience and context. For example, one of our student teams created an app for a user audience of patients to find and schedule a doctor's appointment quickly and remotely (requiring awareness of context, including time and physical location). Another student team developed Roadtrippr, an app to help the audience of hungry users pinpoint preferred restaurants during particular dining times along a travel route (requiring awareness of time and physical location).

Problem Solving Because technical communication often focuses on fuzzy, ill-structured problems, *problem solving* is necessarily a second theoretical frame of our courses (as well as an ABET competency; Passow, 2012). While the criticality of both individual and team problem solving has long been established (Johnson 1988), problem solving is acknowledged as increasingly important in the workplace, as recent engineering graduates attest (Passow, 2012).

In our courses, developing expertlike processes for problem solving is addressed by CS/TC faculty who recognize, as research has long indicated, that a team's problem-solving competence is highly dependent on the problem-solving competence of the individuals on that team (Bransford et al., 1986; Chi, Glaser, and Farr, 1988). The processes that our teams use to solve problems are also highly dependent on the ways they engage in collaborative processes and manage various kinds of conflicts (Burnett, 1996). Engaging in successful individual and collaborative problem solving has benefited teams in this study. For example, one team addressed a problem some users had in matching their current skill sets with available workplace positions. The student team created an app for a social network, providing resources to help students track their current qualifications and also to plan and obtain skills to become qualified for the positions they wanted.

Situated Cognition A third overarching theoretical frame for technical communication, *situated cognition*, argues the importance of what Brown, Collins, and Duguid (1989, p. 33) call "authentic activity," noting that such activities are framed by culture and are socially constructed. Brown and his colleagues have long argued the value of activities in which students use knowledge in context, what they (and others, e.g., Collins, 1989) call cognitive apprenticeships and what we call problem-based client projects that "connect context with domain-specific knowledge" (Johnson and Chung, 1999). As Marra and others (2014, p. 226) explain, "Meaning is derived by learners from the contexts in which they are working or learning. ... Knowledge that is anchored, or 'situated,' in specific contexts is more meaningful, more integrated, better retained, and more transferable."

The importance of situated cognition is particularly relevant to our students' team projects—for example, creating an app to automatically generate schedules for individual students based on specific academic/professional requirements. In general, our students' client-based projects are designed to use workplace processes and intended for workplace applications (e.g., developing an app tracking transportation routes, creating a program for monitoring temperature in CDC labs). In these situations, student teams need to recognize and understand the context of the problem they're addressing in order to create a functional solution.

Knowledge Transfer To be successful in technical communication, students must be able to engage in a fourth overarching theoretical frame that encourages the process of *knowledge transfer*, which affects individual, team, and organizational success (Argote and Ingram, 2000). For example, students need to transfer knowledge from previous courses and workplace experiences to solve the client problems in our courses, to transfer knowledge (e.g., processes, best practices, client information) from one individual on their team to other members of the team, and to recognize the value of generalizing the processes they learn in our courses to future academic and workplace situations. Moreland and Myaskosky (2000, p. 117) make the case that groups who are trained together and/or receive "information about one another's skills" have improved performance. Such processes include understanding and articulating the value of sharing (rather than hoarding) information on a team, selecting technologies for sharing, planning processes and schedules for sharing information, and then confirming and monitoring that information has been received, understood, and used.

Knowledge transfer has a strong history: Ensign (2008, p. 4) argues that "new knowledge form[s] the basis for a firm's [or a team's] competitive advantage." Johnson and Chung (1999) support such transfer of competencies as important in dealing with "problems in a wide variety of knowledge domains." While virtually all projects developed by our students in the CS/TC courses involve knowledge transfer, some demonstrate it effectively. For example, one of our student teams created an educational tool to help young users see what happens inside a computer processor and created a computer game that allows users to check in as often as they like to perform time-limited actions. Knowledge transfer enables students to generalize the processes and strategies they learn in the linked courses to other courses, to internship and co-op experiences, and eventually to the workplace.

Collaboration Teamwork is ubiquitous in the workplace (as well as an ABET competency; Passow, 2012); thus, *collaboration* is a fifth overarching theoretical frame of TC courses. Collaborative interaction can be described in a number of ways (Burnett, Cooper, and Welhausen, 2013)—from diagrams (Six Sigma, 2012) to models (Parraguez, Eppinger, and Maier, 2015) to theory (Spinuzzi, 2012). Collaboration in the digital age is part of a distributed network that, as Spinuzzi (2007, p. 268) argues, "is deeply interpenetrated, with multiple, multidirectional information flows ... performed by [shifting] assemblages of workers and technologies." Spinuzzi (2007, p. 268) has argued that "under these circumstances, singularity (monocontextuality) is impossible to sustain at any significant scale; multiplicity (polycontextuality) is inevitable."

In our courses, learning how to best collaborate is addressed primarily by the TC faculty, though certainly acknowledged by the CS faculty; all of them help students collaborate on four- to five-member teams and with their clients. While students learn the basics of collaboration, such as reasoning and problem solving (Johnson and Chung, 1999), they also need to manage relationships and deal with cultural factors (St. Amant, 2015) because collaboration now often means polycontextuality, not only in the process of creating artifacts, but also in their use. For example, our students' team projects have included creating and implementing a facial recognition tool for fleet vehicle companies to make sure the correct driver is in the correct truck while taking care of a shipment.

With the frames of rhetorical awareness, problem solving, situated cognition, knowledge transfer, and collaboration in place, we now begin to explore issues raised by our research question; thus, we consider blended learning, class scale, active learning, and student attitude. In discussing the study itself, we present our methodology for collecting and analyzing in situ data from the linked CS/TC courses. Following a discussion of the rationale for our methodology, we present and analyze data, focusing on student attitudes about teamwork that characterize their experience in FTF or blended sections.

METHODOLOGY

Because this is a classroom study, we have an obligation to balance our research needs with our classroom responsibilities. In this study, all collected data fulfill some aspect of the course outcomes and have a pedagogical benefit to students. In this section of the chapter, we describe our study, introduce student participants, explain what we told students about the study, describe the survey instrument used for data collection, summarize our coding, and explain our approach to interrater reliability.

Our Study

Developing blended versions of our TC courses presented us with an opportunity to look more closely at students' attitudes and engagement, believing that habits of mind (including attitude) affect engagement and performance (e.g., Lovelace and Brickman, 2013). In our overall study, we collected data from students in the FTF and blended sections about three factors: *process* (including managing time, drafting, collaborating, providing feedback, and process tracing), *attitudes and behaviors* (toward team members, toward culture, and toward communication), and *performance* (assessed quantitatively and qualitatively). However, in this chapter, we only consider students' attitudes toward team members in their responses to one survey question.

Study Participants

In fall 2015, our study focused on two sections of an upper-level TC course (linked with CS). All 98 students enrolled in these particular sections were invited to participate in this study; 72 (73.5%) agreed to participate. One section was FTF; the other was blended. Of the 72 participants, 38 (52.8%) were in the FTF section and 34 (47.2%) were in the blended section. These students were CS majors who were at least juniors and taking the linked course as their junior design requirement. The combined FTF and blended sections enrolled 72.4% males and 27.6% females. All students were comfortable using English in the classroom, although for many, English was not their first language.[6]

Students who participated in the study had the opportunity to erase a class absence and to skip two of 20 assigned blog posts without penalty. While some students may have participated in the study due to intellectual interest, most students likely participated because of these potential benefits.

All data collected for the study were part of students' regular, required coursework. Students were explicitly told that their participation in the study was voluntary and had no influence on their course grade; their course instructor had no access to the list of study participants during the course, which is ethically important to ensure that students do not feel coerced to participate. A very small number of students were excluded from analysis because they didn't submit all the required coursework.

Informed Consent

At the beginning of the study, the researcher visited the classes, spoke with the students, and provided each student with an IRB-approved Fact Sheet and Informed Consent Form for the study. Students were told about the study: "The purpose of the study is to contribute to the international conversation about what constitutes effective ways to learn to be better writers and communicators and to learn about similarities and differences in students' attitudes, processes, and performances in two types of blended classes in technical communication—one that is largely *face-to-face* and the other that is largely *online*." The researcher also explained what this study does *not* do:

• We do not analyze individual language correctness.
• We do not show individual or team grades for assignments.
• We do not show individual videos without asking for additional permission.
• We are not doing a case study that looks at individual participants or specific teams.
• We are not interested in individuals but in collective, aggregated data. The power of aggregated data comes from having a large number of individuals who fall into categories.

Students understood that their participation was voluntary and that they would do "exactly the same work for the study as they're doing for the class. Participating in the study requires NO additional or extra work." The categories of classwork and categories of study data were identical.

Surveys

In our overall study, we investigated student attitudes with brief online surveys, each asking open-ended questions, administered three times each semester.[7] Here, we use the responses to one survey question to consider whether an FTF or blended approach appears to influence students' attitudes toward teamwork.

Using SurveyMonkey, we constructed very brief online surveys. Our research question in this chapter focuses on students' attitudes and behaviors toward team members, drawing on responses to the survey question about problems with teamwork because of its criticality in the academy and workplace. Such problems (e.g., dealing with various kinds of conflict) are a common complaint, both in technical communication classes and in the workplace.

The survey question we discuss here was asked three times during the semester, with the question slightly modified according to the time in the semester (beginning, middle, end):

• Beginning of semester (August 26, 2015): "What problems do you anticipate working with your team members? List as many as you want."

• Middle (October 1, 2015) and end of semester (November 5, 2015): "What problems do you have working with your team members? List as many as you want."

Repeating the question about team attitudes and behaviors enabled us to track students' evolving perceptions as they became more knowledgeable about the ways technical communication is practiced in computer science. As part of their coursework, students completed their required surveys outside of class; they were expected to aggregate and use their survey data as evidence in their end-of-course reflective memo about their professional development. For the study, the data from the surveys were preliminarily aggregated in SurveyMonkey and then transferred to and analyzed in NVivo.

Coding

Coding is the process of characterizing data—for us, the survey responses—to determine patterns. In this process, we quantify the qualitative survey responses by reading (and rereading) them, identifying categories of repeated terms and concepts—in this case, those about teams. Based on our categories, we were able to determine patterns of responses. We formed our categories from the data itself (rather than beginning with preconceived categories we imposed on the data) and worked to keep the students' "words intact in the process of analysis ... to maintain [their] presence" (Mills, Bonner, and Francis, 2006, p. 7), so these intact responses could help illustrate the categories. This grounded approach enabled us to establish "links between the ideas being conceptualized from the data" (p. 5). Our development of the coding categories was recursive, with multiple iterations to refine the definition of each category.

Like other researchers who use grounded theory, we appreciate that the approach "is about concepts that emerge from data" (Holton, 2010, 22). Using all the data from the broader study, we developed these coding categories that are equally relevant to this particular study.

- **Rhetorical awareness.** The focus is on *rhetorical elements*, coding these concepts in student responses: Considering audience. Determining context. Focusing on purpose. Articulating argument. Respecting ethics. Selecting register, style, diction. Increasing comprehensibility.
- **Development.** The focus is on *content*, coding these concepts in student responses: Determining scope. Elaborating ideas. Selecting and analyzing evidence or support. Determining completeness (e.g., sufficiency, relevance, necessary information, expansion). Deleting unnecessary information.
- **Organization.** The focus is on *order/sequence*, coding these concepts in student responses: Structuring elements (e.g., introductions, body, and conclusions). Determining content for each section (e.g., classification). Sequencing (e.g., of ideas, information, or sections). Establishing coherence (e.g., connections among ideas or ideas and evidence).
- **Conventions.** The focus is on *professional standards, skills, and tools regarding language, presentation, and design*, coding these concepts in student responses: Conforming to professional expectations of grammar and mechanics. Complying with specifications. Satisfying requirements, rules, details (e.g., length, labeling). Attending to form/format referring to the superstructure. Referring to sample documents. Referring to prerequisite skills, tools, and competencies.
- **Design.** The focus is on *visual elements*, coding these concepts in student responses: Using design principles for print and digital artifacts. Using images (e.g., tables, graphs, charts). Making artifacts visually accessible. Considering aesthetics.
- **Process.** The focus is on *individual action or activity*, coding these concepts in student responses: Composing (e.g., putting ideas into words, initiating

projects). Managing process (e.g., moving past writer's block; moving from one step, phase, or stage to another; managing a project, managing time/ schedule; understanding continuum of the work). Practicing recursive processes (e.g., brainstorming, researching, outlining, writing, revising, editing, proofreading).

• *Genre.* The focus is on *material deliverables,* coding these concepts in student responses: Naming an artifact (e.g., letter, report, presentation, memo, blog post).

• *Fairness.* The focus is on *logos,* coding these concepts in student responses: Creating transparency and accuracy. Avoiding distortion of information. Considering logic.

• *Community.* The focus is on *the class or team, on the presence of another person,* or *on interaction with other(s),* coding these concepts in student responses: Interacting with others (e.g., team members, clients, superiors, instructors). Initiating/engaging in conversation. Dealing with individual/team balance, roles, collaboration, or working environment. Managing anxiety related to teamwork. Having difficulty interacting/engaging with others. Dealing with stress, nervousness, interpersonal scariness—all related to interaction.

• *Nonresponse.* The focus is on *no response,* coding off-task comments or expressions of disinterest.

Six of the coding categories (rhetorical awareness, development, organization, conventions, design, and process) that we identified from the data also appear in the Georgia Tech Writing and Communication Program's assessment rubric. That these categories are what students talk about is programmatically affirming, but it is not surprising. One of the goals of our Writing and Communication courses is to give students the vocabulary and tools to analyze, talk about, and strengthen their writing, speaking, designing, and collaboration. The visible presence of rhetorical concepts in students' work and their ability to talk about these concepts are likely because they're emphasized on assignment sheets, in analysis of professional documents, in class discussions, in self- and peer review sessions, and in grading criteria.

Interrater Reliability

A coding scheme needs to be consistent—to work for a range of raters and produce the same results over time. Attention to interrater reliability is a common practice among qualitative and mixed-methodology researchers who are concerned with the degree of consensus among raters.

We determined the interrater reliability for our broad study from which the question about teamwork has been taken for this chapter. After reading 100% of the dataset multiple times, the primary coder (Coder #1) developed a coding scheme. Our interrater reliability quantifies the degree of agreement between Coder #1 and Coder #2. While Coder #1 independently coded 100 percent of the student responses, Coder #2 independently coded approximately 20% of the student responses. We have no way to assess a "true score" (Hallgren); instead, we are concerned that the coders interpret the coding categories in similar ways.

After each calibration round of independent coding for the broad study, the two coders reviewed their agreement and refined the coding scheme. The question addressed in this chapter was included in the overall interrater reliability. The two coders noted that disagreements were due to inadequacies (e.g., omitted characteristics, overly broad categories, imprecise boundaries) in coding definitions.

The coders spaced their calibration sessions at least 24 hours apart. With each succeeding round of coding, they refined the category definitions, leading to generally improved agreement. In the initial calibration round, the coders had 67% agreement; in round 2, they had 77% agreement; in round 3, they had 83% agreement. In the remaining five calibration rounds, they had between 84% and 92% agreement.

For each calibration round, the coders refined the definitions. For example, after calibration round 1, the two coders agreed that "clarity" and "clear" would be coded as part of rhetoric, with the idea that communication needs to be clear for an audience and situation. After calibration round 2, the two coders agreed, for example, that references to "following the rules" would be coded as part of conventions. After calibration round 3, the two coders agreed, for instance, that references to an "individual" would be coded as process, while references to "others" would be coded as community. After the final rounds of calibration, Coder #1 recoded 100% of the data, using the revised coding scheme. Those recoded data are reflected in the presentation of data and the analysis that follows.

DATA AND ANALYSIS

One of the most interesting findings in our data is that students expressed more than minimal concern about only four areas related to teamwork.[8] As table 7.1 shows, responses in both the FTF and blended sections indicated awareness of teamwork. Students in both sections expressed some concern about process, community, and rhetorical awareness, while students in the blended section expressed some concern about development in working with team members. Students appeared to trust that the team members would want to contribute to the mechanical and creative tasks fairly, but they had concerns about how to actually make that happen.

Interestingly, almost no students in either the FTF or blended sections expressed concern about team problems in managing genre, organization, conventions, design, or fairness (see the discussion above about ways student responses to the survey question were coded). Table 7.1 shows low percentages of students concerned with these areas; 0% is the most typical response, with an occasional response of 3% and 4%.

All the coding categories intersect with the three factors we've introduced in this chapter (blended learning, active learning, and student attitude). The three factors are useful to curriculum designers and developers interested in ferreting out distinctions between FTF and blended classes, between passive and active learning, and among negative, neutral, and positive attitudes. As a result, in the following subsections, we indicate some of the places where our data most clearly signal a connection to these broader factors.

Process
The largest percentage of students' survey responses expressed some concern about *process* in relation to team members—focusing on individual actions or

Table 7.1

Student responses to question about attitudes/behaviors toward communication—What problems do you anticipate/have working with your team members?

| | Early question (late August) | | | | Developing question (late September) | | | | End-of-semester question (early November) | | | |
| | FTF | | Blended | | FTF | | Blended | | FTF | | Blended | |
	Individual responses/total # of Aug FTF surveys	Percentage	Individual responses/total # of Aug Blended surveys	Percentage	# of Sept FTF surveys Individual responses/total	Percentage	# of Sept FTF surveys Individual responses/total	Percentage	# of Nov FTF surveys Individual responses/total	Percentage	# of Nov Blended surveys Individual responses/total	Percentage
Rhetorical awareness	2/44	5%	6/34	18%	0/31	0%	0/27	0%	1/35	3%	2/31	7%
Genre	0/44	0%	1/34	3%	0/31	0%	0/27	0%	0/35	0%	0/31	0%
Development	1/44	2%	0/34	0%	0/31	0%	6/27	22%	0/35	0%	0/31	0%
Organization	0/44	0%	0/34	0%	0/31	0%	0/27	0%	0/35	0%	0/31	0%
Conventions	0/44	0%	0/34	0%	0/31	0%	1/27	4%	0/35	0%	1/31	3%
Design	0/44	0%	0/34	0%	0/31	0%	0/27	0%	0/35	0%	0/31	0%
Process	30/44	68%	16/34	47%	13/31	42%	2/27	7%	21/35	60%	13/31	42%
Fairness	0/44	0%	0/34	0%	0/31	0%	0/27	0%	0/35	0%	0/31	0%
Community	27/44	61%	27/34	79%	13/31	42%	14/27	52%	16/35	46%	18/31	58%
Nonresponse	5/44	11%	3/34	9%	12/31	39%	12/27	44%	10/35	29%	9/31	29%

activities, such as composing, managing processes, and practicing recursive processes. While the differences between the FTF and blended sections are not large, table 7.1 shows that at the beginning of the semester, 68% of the students in the FTF section anticipated problems related to process in working with team members, contrasted with 47% of the students in the blended section who expressed concern. This percentage of students expressing concern is indicative of their attitude.

By the end of the course, the anxieties anticipated by students about process were slightly lower than at the beginning of the course, but higher than in the middle. Our data suggest that at the end of the semester, 60% of the students in the FTF section were worried about process in working with team members, while 42% in the blended section were worried about such problems. The difference might be due to end-of-semester stress—that is, the blended section afforded more flexibility in terms of meetings and completing tasks.

The following typical student responses about process (see the methodology discussion) signal attention to individual actions and/or activities. These examples show the focus of students' anxieties about management of the process—specifically attending to issues of time, efficiency, and schedule—was similar in both FTF and blended sections:

- "I feel like the hardest problem will be finding a time when we are all free to work on the project."—*CS/TC Student, FTF Section, Developing Survey*
- "Rarely being able to instantly communicate [is a problem]."—*CS/TC Student, FTF Section, End-of-Semester Survey*
- "Coordinating meeting times will likely also be a challenge, especially if our respective schedules aren't amenable to it, and with all of the other obligations we will have for other classes."—*CS/TC Student, Blended Section, Early Survey*

Learning in our classes—whether in an FTF or blended classroom—is necessarily a process. This process is active in two ways: first, in the use of specific pedagogical methods, and second, in the engagement of students, engagement that demonstrates positive student attitudes. Throughout the semester, students explicitly articulated their concern about process, but the students in the blended sections were consistently somewhat less concerned. We speculate that physical distance, which required students to use already-familiar digital tools, was easier and less stressful for these students than FTF interaction. In addition, many CS students informally conveyed to their TC teacher a preference for working online rather than FTF—for example, students in the fall 2015 FTF section occasionally asked their TC instructor if some of the FTF activities could be online and if future sections of the course could be online.

Community

A considerable percentage of students expressed concern about *community*, which we defined as the presence of another person or interaction with other(s)—initiating and engaging in conversation; dealing with individual/ team balance, roles, collaboration, and the working environment; managing anxiety or difficulties related to teamwork; and dealing with the stress of inter-action. As table 7.1 shows, at the beginning of the semester, 61% of the students in the FTF section anticipated problems related to community in working with team members, contrasted with 79% in the blended section.

By the end of the semester, anxieties anticipated by all students about com-munity in relation to their team had been reduced; 46% of the students in the FTF section worried about community in working with team members while 58% in the blended section worried about community problems. Information about ways to address potential problems with their teams was disseminated during the semester; we speculate that this information led to some of the reduction in concerns.

Student responses indicated that they were concerned about interacting with others. These representative student responses demonstrate awareness of relationships, commitments, and division of labor necessary for a team to function well:

• "I anticipate problems dividing the workload evenly."—*CS/TC Student, FTF Section, Early Survey*
• "I tend to take on more responsibilities instead of confronting problems with team members—if someone isn't doing their share, I simply do the work

instead of encouraging full participation."—*CS/TC Student, FTF Section, Early Survey*

• "The only issue is making sure everyone participates equally."—*CS/TC Student, Blended Section, End-of-Semester Survey*

Our use of active learning contributed to the creation of multiple and overlapping communities in the FTF and blended sections: whole class, class discussion/working groups, teams, and peer review groups. We speculate that belonging to communities increases students' confidence. Nonetheless, we speculate that students' level of concern about relationships, commitments, and division of labor is a holdover from other classes in which these problems interfered with their work. We also speculate that the blended section expressed higher percentages of concern because students perceived that relationships, commitments, and division of labor may be more difficult to negotiate at a distance, despite their familiarity with tools for interacting at a distance.

Rhetorical Awareness

A third area in which some students expressed concern about working with their team was *rhetorical awareness*, which we defined as attention to rhetorical elements, such as audience, context, purpose, argument, ethics, and a range of language issues affecting style and comprehensibility. Table 7.1 shows that only 5% of the students in the FTF section anticipated problems related to rhetorical awareness in working with team members, whereas 18% of the students in the blended section initially anticipated such problems. However, as table 7.1 also shows, by the end of the course the anxieties anticipated by all students were both minimal and similar.

These representative student responses indicate that students were attuned to rhetorical elements, in these cases concerns with audience—that is, with users as well as with personal attitudes and behaviors in relation to interactions with team members:

• "Not wanting to have a user-driven approach. Assuming we know what users want always."—*CS/TC Student, FTF Section, Early Survey*

• "I don't see many problems working with my teammates. The biggest one that I could foresee is that I am not a very assertive person, and if one team member doesn't pull their own weight, I'll be disadvantaged trying to convince them otherwise."—*CS/TC Student, Blended Section, Early Survey*

CS students at Georgia Tech do a lot of teamwork in virtually every class, and they sometimes experience problems, so their anticipation of that pattern repeating itself is not surprising. We speculate that the lower percentage in the FTF section may be due to students thinking that meeting face to face could potentially result in fewer interpersonal problems. Because of the course content, which early on included explicit information about ways to work in teams, by midsemester, the anxieties of students about rhetoric and teams appear to have been quelled. We suspect that being involved in active learning helps the students be rhetorically engaged in classroom activities; however, when this active learning takes place in a blended classroom, the learning environment may appear more explicitly complex to students. We speculate that while this complexity may make teamwork more complicated, the affordances of media required for blended learning may also push students toward a nuanced sense of rhetorical categories and strategies.

Development

A fourth area in which some students expressed concern about working with their team was *development*, which we define as focusing on content—for example, determining scope, elaborating ideas, selecting and analyzing evidence or support, determining completeness, and deleting unnecessary information. The students' response is surprising because only those in the blended section responded—and only then in the middle of the semester. The rest of the students did not identify development related to their team as a concern at any time.

Students who responded focused on several aspects of content: scope, elaboration, evidence, and completeness or sufficiency, including these representative examples:

- "We don't meet [face to face] very often so each of our meetings have a relatively short time period to be productive."—CS/TC *Student, Blended Section, Middle Survey*
- "Some problems that we have are being off topic. ..."—CS/TC *Student, Blended Section, Middle Survey*

We speculate that in the middle of the semester, the task of preparing a client project seemed especially challenging to students in the blended section; even though they were comfortable with the online tools, they didn't have much face-to-face contact (and thus a sense of control) with team members. By the end of the semester, the collaborative strategies they'd been taught in the course had actually worked, and their anxieties diminished. Active learning helped students develop content; by working in communities, students had more sources/resources for developing content.

IMPLICATIONS

Early in this chapter, we argued that blended learning, active learning, and student attitude are important in our exploration of this research question. The instructors expected that the students' distance from the instructors as well as from their classmates would affect their attitudes. It didn't much. While we found some differences in student attitudes in the two sections of the class, the responses about attitudes toward teamwork were more often similar than different. The FTF and blended sections we have described were much the same in many ways: same outcomes, same instructors, and the same client-based, problem-solving approach. One explanation for the similarities (both in what mattered and what didn't matter) might be that many of the CS students saw working online as equally or more comfortable than working face to face.

Blended Learning

Because Georgia Tech has a strong technological infrastructure, we weren't concerned with often-cited disadvantages of blended learning that include "up-front costs and technical problems" (Cook, 2007, p. 37). We also didn't investigate the ways blended learning functions broadly in technical communication. However, we did consider the ways it affected student attitudes about teamwork in our linked courses. The results of our study suggest that the blended environment does not reduce students' positive engagement in teamwork and thus works as an approach to teaching technical communication when teams are central in the pedagogy.

Our belief that blended learning is a workable pedagogical approach is supported by studies about blended learning (e.g., Harris et al., 2016). Like us, Harris and his colleagues (2016, p. 591) affirm the value of blended learning; they assume that the value of and attitudes toward the "delivery of online oral communication learning" support desirable outcomes such as students' "intrinsic interest, behavioral intentions, and perceived usefulness of the technology." Results such as theirs reinforce our belief that blended learning is viable as an approach for the CS/TC students in our classes.

Active Learning

We believe that another likely explanation for the similarity of students' responses in the FTF and blended sections is that both sections used well-defined active learning strategies. While FTF interaction does change things (e.g., responsiveness to subtle and nuanced facial expression and body language, increased awareness of paralinguistic cues, sense of bonding with people in physical proximity), we speculate that the similarities in attitudes are because the instructors used the same active learning strategies in both the FTF and blended sections. Specifically, active learning requires intense and regular engagement and writing, regardless of the distance from the instructors or other students. Active learning exemplifies student centeredness, so students connect and interact with the content, regardless of whether the section is FTF or blended.

Given our belief that active learning equalized the interaction in the two FTF and blended technical communication sections, we argue that active learning strategies should be widely used in technical communication pedagogy, whether FTF or blended, whether in small or larger classes. The CS students in our study strongly believed computer coding, not communication, was the center of their universe. Active learning helped them counter this misperception by providing strategies to focus their attention on communication and help them understand its relevance to their client-based projects as well as their careers. Not only does the following list define active learning strategies (*italicized*) used by students in this study, but the strategies can also be used in other technical communication courses to encourage individual engagement and team interaction.

- **Moving from theory to practice** included active learning strategies such as these: *Blogging* about ways principles of technical communication apply to computer science discourse as well as to client projects. Engaging in *active reading* (e.g., annotating, locating examples, analyzing artifacts). Participating in *peer discussions*, both in class and online.
- **Interacting with class materials** included active learning strategies such as these: *Reading* textbook and supplementary class materials, including sample workplace artifacts. *Viewing* and *listening* to peer presentations, TED Talks, and instructor videos. *Blogging* about ways instructor videos influence project practices.
- **Responding to processes and drafts** included active learning strategies such as these: Participating in *peer critique/review* of drafts for written, oral, and visual work products created by team members and classmates. Providing *self-interviews* about individual processes and performances.
- **Planning, drafting, reviewing, and revising artifacts** included active learning strategies such as these: Completing *conceptually oriented tasks*. Creating *written artifacts* (e.g., proposals, feasibility reports, analytical reports, specifications). Creating *oral artifacts* (e.g., Prezi, PowerPoint). Creating *visual artifacts* (e.g., tables, graphs, diagrams, maps, photos, and data visualizations).
- **Engaging in professional development** included active learning strategies such as these: Completing *surveys* about individual processes and performances. Engaging in *self-assessment* about one's own processes and drafts. *Reflecting* on team engagement and artifact quality.

All of the active learning strategies we note can be done in dyads, triads, small groups, teams, and whole classes. The most important thing to note is that active learning was much the same for the FTF and blended classes; the instructor tried to make content, activities, and assignments as similar as reasonably possible.

Student Attitude

Teamwork is a critical professional competence. Information about its importance and guidelines about ways to engage in it are readily available from both academic centers for teaching excellence (e.g., the University of Waterloo) and for-profit training programs (e.g., Happy Manager). Ironically, even though teamwork is ubiquitous, students often receive little formal or informal instruction about it and little guidance about developing positive, productive attitudes toward it. As noted earlier in this chapter, collaboration—foundational for building and maintaining teams—is an ABET competency (Passow, 2012). Given the importance of successful teamwork, students in both the FTF section and the blended section demonstrated surprisingly little concern about it.

In both sections, the most frequent response by students was that they had few concerns (or even no concerns) related to genre, development, organization, conventions, design, or fairness. Students' attitude can be explained by their having considerable classroom experience but little professional experience with teamwork; despite instructor advice to the contrary, many students still operated in the divide-and-conquer model, which works with relatively simple projects that could have been completed just as well individually were it not for time constraints. Typical responses in both the FTF and blended sections indicated some awareness of what might be required to make a team successful, which begins to explain that students in both sections expressed concern about process, community, rhetorical awareness, and development in working with team members.

We are confident that in this study students in the FTF and blended sections were not disadvantaged by the blended learning pedagogy or the increased class size—because of the intense attention to active learning in both sections. Schaubroeck and Yu (2017) have argued that equal attention should be given to developing strategies and technologies for FTF and virtual/online teams in the workplace. We recommend a similar balance in the classroom, with the technical communication curriculum including explicit instruction for both FTF and virtual/online teams, with active learning as a substantive component of instruction, and with the encouragement to recognize and use the factors contributing to productive teamwork.

LOOKING FORWARD

We end by suggesting four takeaways to be considered by teachers as well as course designers who are interested in ways to strengthen student teamwork in FTF and blended classes.

• **Use active learning as a core pedagogy for both FTF and blended classes.** We are pleased about the ease of embedding active learning in blended classes. For us, using active learning to teach teamwork seems like a natural fit, since it fosters motivation and engagement, and students thus have increased comprehension of ideas and practices. We believe that the use of active learning in both FTF and blended sections is the primary factor that reduced differences between the sections in this study. We are especially interested that student responses related to teamwork in our FTF and blended sections were often so similar, countering the belief that students prefer and perform better in FTF sections.

• **Use the affordances of technology to support teamwork and interaction for both FTF and blended classes.** In our study, the use of technology was pedagogically appropriate. It supported course outcomes, it was available and well supported by the institute's infrastructure, and our students were already comfortable with many technologies and receptive to new ones. Technology can effectively facilitate teamwork; we believe that virtually all FTF and blended classes should use technology for a range of competencies, including discussions, individual and collaborative composing and reviewing, design, dissemination to various audiences, and individual as well as collaborative archiving.

• **Increase explicit attention to rhetorical factors to help students become more skillful with teamwork, regardless of whether the class is FTF or blended.** Depending on their prior experience, students will have varying levels of familiarity and competence in using rhetorical factors. We can help them assess their own knowledge and give them tools and experience to become better team members. While students in this study exhibited considerable comfort with factors such as *genre, organization, conventions, design,* and *fairness* in their teamwork, they expressed discomfort in dealing with *process, community, rhetorical awareness,* and *development* in working with team members and needed help in developing these competencies.

• **Recognize and help students learn to manage the complexities of teamwork in both FTF and blended classes.** Students arrive in our classes with experience in teamwork and collaboration; however, their experience has not necessarily been positive or productive, and it almost never has been supported by explicit guidance or instruction. We need to teach students explicit strategies and tools related to teamwork and collaboration, regardless of whether they are in an FTF or blended class. We cannot presume they are successful or skillful collaborators just because they've been on teams before. For example, the students in this study learned to analyze and assess their own teamwork, they learned that teamwork occurs in different settings and for various purposes, they learned to manage conflict, and they developed some strategies for giving and responding to feedback. Similar explicit guidance needs to be given to all students.

Given our findings that students' responses about teamwork are remarkably similar in both FTF and blended classes, we encourage further research to investigate the weight of various influence(s): disciplinary focus, pedagogy using active learning, embedded technology, attention to rhetorical factors, and strategies for teamwork.

Notes

1. Class observations of the FTF section showed a high level of engagement and interaction. Two class observations showed participation by 100% of the students in the

class, offering accurate and substantive responses to class activities. Review of the materials for the blended section showed a similarly high level of student engagement and interaction.

2. Technical communication teachers seldom lecture, choosing instead from a range of active learning strategies that promote engagement and enthusiasm (Bonwell, 1991). Further, many of us purposely avoid the term *flipped classroom*, largely used by those in disciplines for whom using in-class time for active learning is a new development in their pedagogy. In writing studies (e.g., introductory and advanced composition; writing/communication across the curriculum/disciplines; business, technical, and science communication), the classroom has *always* been "flipped" because active learning has been both common and best practice for many decades—small-group and whole-class discussions as well as individual, small-group, and whole-class activities and projects (Brame, 2013).

3. Research disagrees about the role of blended learning in causing feelings of isolation. For example, Liu et al. (2016) say that in a blended learning environment, students "are less likely to experience feelings of isolation or reduced interest in the subject matter," whereas Cook (2007) indicates that a disadvantage of blended learning is its social isolation.

4. Teachers need to counter students' mistaken notions that active learning means that students do all the work and teachers do nothing. We advocate making clear that the teacher creates and monitors the class infrastructure, that the teacher facilitates activities, and that the teacher provides substantive feedback on both processes and in-process artifacts. Teachers also need to provide information and justification about the pedagogical value of peer editing, reviewing, and feedback, since most students come with a "blind leading the blind" view of peer activities that teachers explicitly need to change, so students learn the value of these activities for both their academic and professional work.

5. The current iteration of the course eliminates the individual CS and TC assignments identified in this chapter; instead, all assignments fulfill requirements for both CS and TC.

6. At Georgia Tech, TOEFL scores (and similar tests) are encouraged but optional for nonnative undergraduate admissions; therefore, a few entering students find English conversation challenging. By the time they have reached their junior year, most students are comfortable using English in the classroom. In addition, because of cultural differences, some students prefer not to speak in class, so assessing their oral competence in a large class is difficult.

7. Sarah Heywood (Daniel Guggenheim School of Aerospace Engineering, Georgia Institute of Technology, Class of 2018) was an invaluable member of our research team by helping to sort and analyze the survey data.

8. All student responses are direct quotations, without correction for mechanical, grammatical, or stylistic infelicities. Inattention to conventions shows the speed and lack of proofreading of the survey responses. Also, students knew their course grades for the surveys were based on completion and content, not on mechanical, grammatical, or stylistic conventions.

References

Accreditation Board for Engineering and Technology (ABET). (n.d.). About ABET. http://www.abet.org/about-abet/.

Argote, L., & Ingram, P. (2000). Knowledge transfer: A basis for competitive advantage in firms. *Organizational Behavior and Human Decision Processes, 82*(1), 150–169.

Aristotle. (n.d.). *Rhetoric,* book 1, chap. 2. https://rhetoric.eserver.org/aristotle/rheti-2 .html.

Bonwell, C. C. (1991). *Active learning: Creating excitement in the classroom* (ASHE-ERIC Higher Education Report, Vol. 1). Washington, DC: School of Education and Human Development, George Washington University. https://www.ydae.purdue.edu/lct/HBCU/ documents/Active_Learning_Creating_Excitement_in_the_Classroom.pdf.

Brame, C. (2013). *Flipping the classroom.* Vanderbilt University Center for Teaching. https://cft.vanderbilt.edu/guides-sub-pages/flipping-the-classroom/.

Bransford, J., Sherwood, R., Vye, N., & Rieser, J. (1986). Teaching thinking and problem solving. *American Psychologist, 41*(10), 1078–1089.

Brown, J. S., Collins, A., & Duguid, P. (1989). Situated cognition and the culture of learning. *Educational Researcher, 18*(1), 32–42.

Bruffee, K. (1995). Sharing our toys: Cooperative learning versus collaborative learning. *Change: The Magazine of Higher Learning, 27*(1), 12–18.

Burnett, R. E. (1991). Cooperative, substantive conflict in collaboration: A way to improve the planning of workplace documents. *Technical Communication (Washington, DC), 38*(2), 532–539.

Burnett, R. E. (1996). Some people weren't able to contribute anything but their technical knowledge: The anatomy of a dysfunctional team. In A. H. Duin & C. Hansen (Eds.), *Nonacademic writing: Social theory and technology* (pp. 123–156). Hillsdale, NJ: Erlbaum.

Burnett, R. E., Cooper, L. A., & Welhausen, C. A. (2013). How can technical communicators develop strategies for effective collaboration? In J. Johnson-Eilola & S. A. Selber (Eds.), *Solving problems in technical communication* (pp. 454–478). Chicago: University of Chicago Press.

Chadwick, S. (1999). Teaching virtually via the web: Comparing student performance and attitudes about communication in lecture, virtual web-based, and web-supplemented courses. *Electronic Journal of Communication, 9*(1). http://www.cios.org/EJCPUBLIC/009/1/00915.HTML.

Chi, M. T. H., Glaser, R., & Farr, M. J. (1988). *The nature of expertise.* Hillsdale, NJ: Erlbaum.

Collins, A. (1989). *Cognitive apprenticeship and instructional technology* (Technical Report No. 474). Urbana-Champaign: Center for the Study of Reading, University of Illinois.

Cook, D. A. (2007). Web-based learning: Pros, cons and controversies. *Clinical Medicine, 7*(1), 37–42.

Cooper, I. M., Williams, C. G., Ivins, W. K., Jones, C. M., & Turner, M. S. (2016). Developing work-ready software engineers using real-world team-based projects as a catalyst for learning. *Journal of Computing, 5*(2), 24–33.

Dochy, F., Segers, M., Van den Bossche, P., & Gijbels, D. (2003). Effects of problem-based learning: A meta-analysis. *Learning and Instruction, 13,* 533–568.

Ensign, P. C. (2008). *Knowledge sharing among scientists: Why reputation matters for R&D in multinational firms.* London: Palgrave Macmillan.

Freeman, S., Eddy, S. L., McDonough, M., Smith, M. K., Okoroafor, N., Jordt, H., et al. (2014). Active learning increases student performance in science, engineering, and mathematics. *Proceedings of the National Academy of Sciences of the United States of America, 111*(23), 8410–8415.

Hallgren, K. A. (2012). Computing inter-rater reliability for observational data: An overview and tutorial. *Tutorials in Quantitative Methods for Psychology, 8*(1), 23.

Harris, K. M., Phelan, L., McBain, B., Archer, J., Drew, A. J., & James, C. (2016). Attitudes toward learning oral communication skills online: The importance of intrinsic interest and student-instructor differences. *Educational Technology Research and Development, 64*(4), 591–609.

Holton, J. A. (2010). The coding process and its challenges. *Grounded Theory Review, 09*, 265–289. http://groundedtheoryreview.com/wp-content/uploads/2012/06/GT-Review -vol-9-no-11.pdf#page=34.

Johnson, D., Johnson, R., & Smith, K. (1998). *Active learning: Cooperation in the college classroom*. Edina, MN: Interaction Book Co.

Johnson, S. D. (1988). Cognitive analysis of expert and novice troubleshooting performance. *Performance Improvement Quarterly, 1*(3), 38–54.Johnson, S. D., & Chung, S. P. (1999). The effect of thinking aloud pair problem solving (TAPPS) on the troubleshooting ability of aviation technician students. *Journal of Industrial Teacher Education, 37*(1), 7–25. http://scholar.lib.vt.edu/ejournals/JITE/v37n1/john.html#feltovich.

Kemp, N., & Grieve, R. (2014). Face-to-face or face-to-screen? Undergraduates' opinions and test performance in classroom vs. online learning. *Frontiers in Psychology, 5*, 1–11.

Ku, H.-Y., Tseng, H. W., & Akarasriworn, C. (2013). Collaboration factors, teamwork satisfaction, and student attitudes toward online collaborative learning. *Computers in Human Behavior, 29*, 922–929.

Linton, D. L., Pangle, W. M., Wyatt, K. H., Powell, K. N., & Sherwood, R. E. (2014). Identifying key features of effective active learning: The effects of writing and peer discussion. *Life Sciences Education, 13*(3), 469–477.

Liu, Q., Peng, W., Zhang, F., Hu, R., Li, Y., & Yan, W. (2016). The effectiveness of blended learning in health professions: Systematic review and meta-analysis. *Journal of Medical Internet Research, 18*(1).

Lovelace, M., & Brickman, P. (2013). Best practices for measuring students' attitudes toward learning science. *CBE Life Sciences Education, 12*(4), 606–617. http://www.jmir .org/2016/1/e2/.

Lunsford, A., & Ede, L. (1990). *Singular texts/plural authors: Perspectives on collaborative writing*. Carbondale, IL: SIUP.

Marra, R., Jonassen, D. H., Palmer, B., & Luft, S. (2014). Why problem-based learning works: Theoretical foundations. *Journal on Excellence in College Teaching* , 25(3–4), 221–238.

Mergendoller, J. R., Bellisimo, Y., & Maxwell, N. L. (2000). Comparing problem-based learning and traditional instruction in high school economics. *Journal of Educational Research, 93*(6), 374–383.

Mills, J., Bonner, A., & Francis, K. (2006). The development of constructivist grounded theory. *International Journal of Qualitative Methods, 5*(1), 25–35.

Moreland, R. L., & Myaskosky, L. (2000). Exploring the performance benefits of group training: Transactive memory or improved communication? *Organizational Behavior and Human Decision Processes, 82*(1), 117–133.

Parraguez, P., Eppinger, S. D., & Maier, A. M. (2015). Information flow through stages of complex engineering design projects: A dynamic network analysis approach. *IEEE Transactions on Engineering Management, 62*(4), 604–617.

Passow, H. J. (2012). Which ABET competencies do engineering graduates find most important in their work? *Journal of Engineering Education, 101*(1), 95–118.

Prince, M. (2004). Does active learning work? A review of the research. *Journal of Engineering Education, 93,* 223–231.

Ruiz-Primo, M. A., Briggs, D., Iverson, H., Talbot, R., & Shepard, L. A. (2011). Impact of undergraduate science course innovations on learning. *Science, 331*(6022), 1269–1270.

Schaubroeck, J. M., & Yu, A. (2017). When does virtuality help or hinder teams? Core team characteristics as contingency factors. *Human Resource Management Review, 27*(4), 635–647.

Six Sigma. (2012). The activity network diagram. Six Sigma Daily. http://www.sixsigmadaily.com/the-activity-network-diagram.

Spinuzzi, C. (2007). Technical communication in the age of distributed work. *Technical Communication Quarterly, 16*(3), 265–277.

Spinuzzi, C. (2012). Working alone, together: Co-working as emergent collaborative activity. *Journal of Business and Technical Communication, 26*(4), 399–441.

St. Amant, K. (2015). Culture and the context of communication design. *Communication Design Quarterly Review, 4*(1), 6–22.

Vygotsky, L. (1978). *Mind in society: The development of higher psychological process.* Cambridge, MA: Harvard University Press.

Whorley, W. L., & Tesdell, L. S. (2009). Instructor time and effort in online and face-to-face teaching: Lessons learned. *IEEE Transactions on Professional Communication, 52*(2), 138–151.

Zhang, P., Ding, L., & Mazur, E. (2017). Peer instruction in introductory physics: A method to bring about positive changes in students' attitudes and belief. *Physical Review Physics Education Research, 13,* 010104. https://doi.org/10.1103/PhysRevPhysEducRes.13 .010104.

ANALYZING QUANTITATIVE AND QUALITATIVE DATA FOR
BLENDED LEARNING

Lauren Margulieux and Robert S. Kadel

The previous research method chapter (chapter 6) focused on how to collect data, different considerations in ensuring that the data you collect are accurate measures of what you are studying, and why it is important to be specific about who you are collecting data from. This chapter takes that data and puts it through useful analyses that help you draw conclusions.

How you analyze your data will depend on your data's level of measurement and what your question is. This chapter starts with some of the fundamental concepts of understanding quantitative data and analyses. Then it describes the statistics appropriate for various types of data and research questions. We conclude this chapter with a description of how to analyze qualitative data.

DISTRIBUTION OF SCORES

Suppose you would like to learn more about the quiz scores of students in a large lecture course to understand how much your students have learned.

Note: Letters that denote statistical terms should always be italicized. For example, when N represents sample, it should be italicized: N = sample.

You have 1,055 students across all sections of this course. Because *N* denotes sample size, you would say you have an "*N* of 1,055" or "*N* = 1,055." A lowercase *n* indicates a subsample. If 500 of your students were in morning classes and you only wanted to talk about that group, you'd say you have "*n* = 500." You could create a chart that shows bars for each score and the number of students who earned each score. The number of students is plotted on the *y*-axis and the scores are plotted along the *x*-axis. It might look something like figure 8.1.

DESCRIPTIVE STATISTICS

Descriptive statistics provide summaries of your data. They are intended to describe the data in your sample rather than drawing conclusions beyond your sample of participants. For example, if you had two groups with average test scores of 85 and 88, you could use descriptive statistics to say that one group

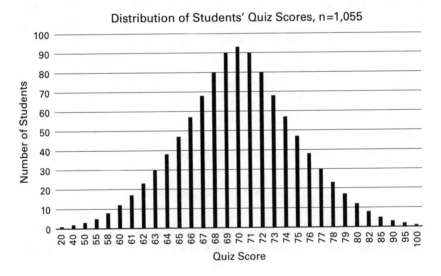

Figure 8.1
Example of normal distribution using student quiz scores

scored higher than the other. This difference does not necessarily mean that there is a statistically significant difference between the two groups (i.e., that the difference is likely not due to chance), and you could not claim that you would expect to see the same difference in other classes. You would need inferential statistics to determine if the difference is statistically significant and could be expected in other classes.

Measures of Central Tendency: Mean, Median, and Mode

In educational research, we are typically comparing groups of students to other students, especially for quantitative measurements. In this type of paradigm, the measurement of interest is a group's score rather than an individual's score. The mean (M), or average score, is typically the most appropriate descriptive statistic to represent a group with a normal distribution. If you have skewed data, then you might consider using the median, or middle score, instead.

Returning to our earlier chart of normally distributed data, you can see that the most frequently observed score is a 70. This is also called the mode—the value of any variable that is observed the most. If you were to sum up all the scores and divide by 1,055, you would find that the mean (or arithmetic average) score is also 70. Lastly, if you were to sort the 1,055 in a list from lowest score to highest score and split that list right down the middle, the value at the middle is the median and would also be 70 in this case. Given the distribution of scores in the above chart and that the mean, median, and mode all equal 70, you have a normal distribution of data. When you chart a line that connects the tops of all the bars in the chart, you will have a bell-shaped curve, thus the familiar bell curve, also called the normal curve, as shown in figure 8.2.

Parametric statistical tests (i.e., the tests that are typically used) are designed for data that are normally distributed. Distributions can deviate from the normal distribution in kurtosis or skewness. Kurtosis, meaning how flat or tall the distribution is, largely does not matter for parametic statistical tests as long as the distribution is symmetrical. If your data are skewed in one direction or the other (see figure 8.3), then you likely cannot use parametric tests. Data can also be multimodal, meaning that it has more than one peak.

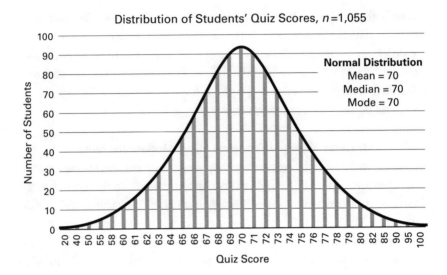

Figure 8.2
Creating the normal curve from an example of student quiz scores

Skewed and multimodal distributions are analyzed with nonparametric tests. This chapter only has space to discuss parametric tests, so for more on topics such as kurtosis, skew, and nonnormally distributed data, see Hanushek and Jackson (1977).

A Measure of Dispersion: Standard Deviation

Besides the mean, we typically also want to know how homogeneous a group's scores are. For example, a group that has an average test score of 85 with all individual scores in the 80s is more homogeneous than a group that has an average test score of 85 with individual scores between 70 and 100. Standard deviation (*SD*) is a unit that allows you to describe how dispersed scores in a group are. In the test-score example, the first group's scores are closer together, so the standard deviation would be lower than in the second group. You can more easily visualize differences in standard deviation in figure 8.4.

If data follow a normal distribution, about 68% of scores will fall within one standard deviation of the mean, 95% of scores within two standard deviations,

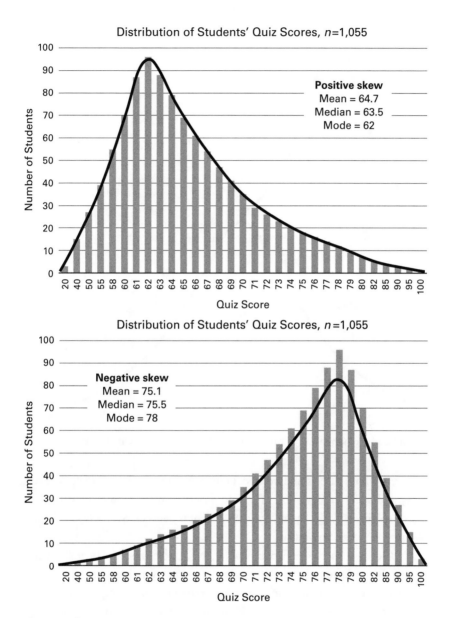

Figure 8.3a–b
Examples of positively and negatively skewed distributions using student quiz scores

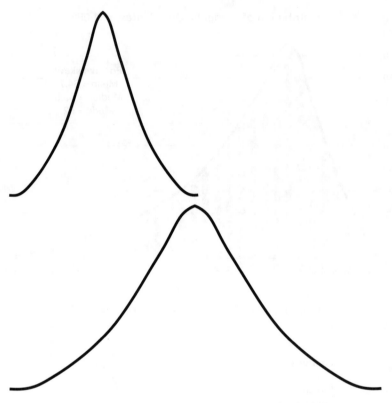

Figure 8.4a–b
Examples of the normal curve with a small (left) and a large (right) standard deviation

and 99% within three standard deviations. For example, if a group has a mean of 85 and standard deviation of 2 (and a normal distribution), then 68% of scores will be between 83 and 87, 95% of scores between 81 and 89, and 99% of scores between 79 and 91.

As discussed in the previous chapter, error accounts for inconsistencies in data due to factors that are beyond your control, variables that you are not measuring, or inaccuracies in your measurements. For example, you cannot control or measure whether some students' performance on a test suffered because they were up late the previous night. The more error that you have in your data, the higher your standard deviation will be. The higher your standard deviation is, the harder it will be to determine whether your intervention has a statistically significant effect. Inferential statistics, which are used to test for statistical significance, compare the amount of error to the size of the effect. Therefore, if you have high error, you will need a large effect for it to be statistically significant. To continue the example above, if the purpose of the test was to measure whether supplemental video instruction helped students to learn the material, but you have a subset of students whose test performance is off because they are tired, the effect of the supplemental video instruction would have to be large to offset the effect of being tired on test performance.

INFERENTIAL STATISTICS

The purpose of inferential statistical analysis is to determine if the differences between groups are greater than what would be expected due to chance. Inferential statistics allow you to make some generalizations about your findings beyond your sample. If you tested the effect of supplemental video instruction and found that students who viewed the videos scored 5 points higher on a test than students who did not, it would matter if the standard deviation were 2 points or 10 points. If the standard deviation were 2 points, then the mean of the intervention group is 2.5 standard deviations higher than of the other group, and the videos would have a statistically significant effect. If the standard deviation were 10 points, then the difference in means between the groups is not greater than what would be expected due to chance.

Correlational Analyses (Relational Questions)

For relational questions, you are trying to determine the type of relationship between two variables. A positive relationship suggests that as the value of a variable increases or decreases, the value of the other variable also increases or decreases, respectively. For example, as attendance in class increases, scores on a test increase. A negative relationship is the opposite and suggests that as the value of a variable increases or decreases, the value of the other variable decreases or increases, respectively. For example, as absences from class increase, scores on a test decrease.

These are both types of linear relationships; the relationship is constant across different levels of the variables. There are also curvilinear relationships in which the relationship changes across different levels of the variables. For example, as students' level of stress about an exam increases, their scores might increase up to a point, but at that point, excess stress might negatively relate to test scores. These types of curvilinear relationships cannot be analyzed with correlations. A scatterplot of the variables will show you the type of relationship you have. Scatterplots are charts that plot the values of two variables—for example, students' reported stress level going up the y-axis and student test scores going across the x-axis. Each student's pair of stress level and score is represented by a dot on the chart, and the collection of dots for all students creates a scatterplot allowing you to spot patterns in the relationship between the two variables.

Correlation versus Causation

In areas of the United States where there are more storks, more babies are born. This does not, however, mean that storks are bringing these babies. The two are correlated but not causally related.

For correlational analyses, a relationship should not be misinterpreted as causation for two reasons: the third-variable problem and the directionality problem. The third-variable problem states that a third variable, separate from those in the correlation, might be mediating the relationship. Storks tend to live in rural areas of the country, and according to the US Census Bureau, families from rural areas tend to have more children than families from urban areas. In this case, a third variable, the degree of land development, influences both. In the stress and test-score example from earlier, it is unlikely that stress primarily causes better test scores. More likely, stress causes more or better studying, which causes better test scores. The directionality problem states that it is unclear from a correlational analysis which variable is causing which. In the stress and test-score example, it is unclear whether high stress hurts test scores or poor test preparation causes high stress.

The type of correlational analysis you use will depend on the levels of measurement of the two variables you are studying. Two interval- or ratio-level (i.e., continuous data) variables can be analyzed using Pearson's r, also called the correlation coefficient. The correlation coefficient will be an r-value between -1 and +1. Negative numbers indicate a negative relationship, and positive numbers indicate a positive relationship. The closer the number is to +/-1, the stronger the relationship between variables. The closer the number is to 0, the weaker the relationship between variables. The strength of the relationship indicates how accurately you can predict one variable if you have a value for the other variable. In strong relationships, having values for both variables is somewhat redundant. In weak relationships, the value of one variable provides little information about the other. Many people misinterpret the strength of the relationship as the slope of the relationship, but a correlation coefficient of 1 does not mean that the variables have a 1-to-1 relationship.

Table 8.1 lists the heuristic cutoffs (Cohen, 1988) to describe strengths of relationships, but the meaningfulness of the strength of relationship depends largely on the variables that you are correlating. In educational research especially, correlation coefficients tend to be low because of the large variability in learners' prior knowledge, level of motivation, and so on.

The relationship between two ordinal or nominal variables can be analyzed by crosstabulating the data, in other words, calculating the number of observations that match across two variables. Consider an example where we crosstabulate the differences in 50 students' course grades by gender—that is,

Table 8.1
Heuristic guidelines for effect size of correlations.

Value of correlation coefficient	Strength of relationship
$r > .5$ or $> -.5$	Strong
$r = .5$ to $.3$ or $-.5$ to $-.3$	Moderate
$r = .3$ to $.1$ or $-.3$ to $-.1$	Weak
$r < .1$ or $< -.1$	No relationship

how many males earned As, Bs, Cs, etc., and how many females earned those same grades (table 8.2).

Reading across each row in the table, we can see that female students have the majority of As and Bs while male students have the majority of Cs, Ds, and Fs. (This is fabricated data; such differences are rarely this clearcut.) Furthermore, we can determine the statistical significance of the relationship between these two variables using such statistics as the χ^2 (chi-square) and Kendall's tau-b. These statistics generally calculate the difference between the observed values in the table and the "expected" values that one would see if there were no relationship, in other words, if males and females were evenly split in the numbers of As, Bs, Cs, and so on that they earned.

Finally, if you are analyzing a combination of interval variables with nominal or ordinal variables you would use statistical tests such as biserial correlations, point biserial correlations, or Spearman's rho. Standard statistical software such as R and SPSS can make these calculations, but it is important to consult

Table 8.2

Course grade * gender crosstabulation

			Male	Female	Total
			\multicolumn{2}{c}{Gender}	
Course grade	A	Count	2	10	12
		% within course grade	16.7%	83.3%	100.0%
	B	Count	3	8	11
		% within course grade	27.3%	72.7%	100.0%
	C	Count	7	3	10
		% within course grade	70.0%	30.0%	100.0%
	D	Count	9	2	11
		% within course grade	81.8%	18.2%	100.0%
	F	Count	5	1	6
		% within course grade	83.3%	16.7%	100.0%
Total		Count	26	24	50
		% within course grade	52.0%	48.0%	100.0%

a statistics guide to make sure you choose the statistic that is most appropriate for the data you are analyzing.

T-Test (for Interval or Ratio Data)

The statistics described above show us how two groups can be compared across one or more dependent variables. However, if you want to determine whether or not the difference between those two groups is statistically significant, you will want to use a t-test.

There are a few different types of t-tests based on how you collected data:

• For comparing between-subjects groups (the participants in the groups are mutually exclusive), use an independent-samples t-test. For example, if you taught one group of students with lectures and a different group of students with active learning, then you could compare their test performance using an independent-samples t-test.

• For comparing groups that are within-subjects (participants are the same in both groups), use a paired-samples t-test. For example, if you taught one topic via lectures and another topic with active learning, and the same students learned both topics, you could compare their performance on questions about each topic using a paired-samples t-test.

• For comparing a group to the mean from literature or another study, use a one-sample t-test (this is not common). For example, if you were comparing scores on a concept inventory from your class to the mean score from the literature, then you could use a one-sample t-test.

T-tests will give you a t-value, which is basically the ratio of the difference between groups to the error within groups. The larger t is, the bigger the difference between groups compared to the error within each group. For example, if the difference between group means was 10, the t-value will be larger if the standard deviation were 5 than if it were 15. The t-value can be positive or negative depending on whether you have a positive or negative relationship between groups. You can determine if that value is statistically significant based on the p-value (i.e., $p < 0.05$ is statistically significant), or you can determine how large the difference between groups is using Cohen's d, an effect-size statistic.

Effect Size

One type of effect size is essentially the difference between two group's means divided by the standard deviation (Coe, 2002). For example, if a group of students in a lecture-based course had an average final exam score of 83 and a group of students in a blended course had an average score on the same final exam of 87, there is a 4-point difference between them. But we divide this difference by the pooled standard deviation of both groups so that it is "standardized" (i.e., on the same scale and easy to compare). This is particularly useful in conducting meta-analyses where multiple effect sizes from multiple, replicated studies can be combined to determine an overall effect of a particular intervention. For more information, we point the reader to Glass et al. (1981). Table 8.3 lists the heuristic cutoffs (Cohen, 1988) to describe the size of effects based on Cohen's d, but the meaningfulness of the strength of relationship depends largely on the variables you are correlating.

ANOVA (for Interval or Ratio Data)

If you are comparing more than two discrete groups, then you will want to use analysis of variance, ANOVA. For example, suppose you have quiz scores for three groups of students who were taught with three different instructional methods, and you want to determine whether the instructional method had a significant effect on these quiz scores. ANOVA will do that for you. This is comparing three groups within one independent variable; however, ANOVA can also be used to compare multiple groups within multiple independent variables. For example, you simultaneously test the effect of three different

Table 8.3
Heuristic guidelines for effect size of Cohen's d.

Value of d	Size of effect
$d > .8$	Large effect
$d = .8$ to $.5$	Medium effect
$d = .5$ to $.2$	Small effect
$d < .2$	No effect

instructional methods and the effect of two types of feedback (i.e., a 3×2 design), which would mean that you have six groups. For each of your three instructional methods, half of the students would receive one type of feedback, and the other half would receive the other type of feedback. Testing multiple interventions simultaneously like this allows you to explore how interventions interact with each other (e.g., if one type of instruction is particularly strong with one type of feedback but not with the other).

ANOVA can tell you if there is a main effect of a variable (a difference between groups within an independent variable) and if there is an interaction between independent variables (a difference in an independent variable's effect based on the value of another independent variable). For example, if you had two interventions that you were testing, it could be the case that getting one or the other intervention would not improve test scores (dependent variable). In this scenario, there would be no main effect of either independent variable, meaning that by themselves neither variable improved scores. If students who received both interventions performed better on the test, then that would be an example of an interaction. The effect of each intervention relies on the other intervention being given.

The type of ANOVA you use will depend on whether you have a between- or within-subjects design and the relationships among dependent variables. A standard ANOVA assumes a between-subjects design and affords one dependent variable to be analyzed at a time. If you have a within-subjects or mixed design or you expect dependent variables to be related, then you'll need to use another type of ANOVA (you will find more information in Keppel and Wickens, 2004).

ANOVA will give you an F-value, which is basically the ratio of the differences among groups to the error within groups. It is the same framework as t-tests. The larger F is, the bigger the difference among groups compared to the error within groups. For example, if the group means were 4, 6, 8, and 10, the F-value will be larger if the standard deviation were 1 than if it were 3. The F-value can only be positive. You can determine if that value is statistically significant based on the p-value (i.e., $p < 0.05$ is statistically significant), or you can determine how large the effect is using the effect-size statistic f. Table 8.4

Table 8.4

Heuristic guidelines for effect size of Cohen's f.

Value of f	Size of effect
$f > .4$	Large effect
$f = .4$ to $.25$	Medium effect
$f = .25$ to $.1$	Small effect
$f < .1$	No effect

provides the heuristic cutoffs (Cohen, 1988) to describe the size of effects based on Cohen's f, but the meaningfulness of the strength of relationship depends largely on the variables you are correlating.

Post Hoc Analyses

An ANOVA will tell you whether there is a difference among your groups, but because you are comparing more than two groups, it will not tell you between which groups the difference occurs. For example, if you were comparing three groups and found a statistically significant F-value, it could be the case that groups 1 and 2 are equal but group 3 is different, or it could be the case that groups 2 and 3 are equal and 1 is different. To determine the specific pattern of results within an ANOVA, you'll need to conduct post hoc tests. More information about post hoc tests can be found in Keppel and Wickens (2004).

Linear Regression

Regression is an analysis technique for determining how much of the performance on a dependent variable can be predicted by the independent variables, demographic characteristics, and/or performance on other dependent variables. If you're thinking that it sounds a lot like ANOVA, then you are right. ANOVA, however, requires that the levels of your independent variable are discrete, and it is typically used for analyses with few predictors. Regression can use continuous independent variables and typically attempt to account for as much of the variance in the dependent variable as possible; therefore, they are typically used for analyses with several predictors. Regression also focuses on how well each predictor explains the dependent variable. A regression coefficient, or β, refers to the slope of the relationship between the independent/predictor and dependent variables (unlike correlation). For example, $\beta = 2$ means that for each unit increase in the predictor variable, the dependent variable increases by 2 units. Meanwhile, the R^2 statistic is used to tell you how much of the variance in the dependent variable is accounted for by all of the predictor variables taken together. A summary of all of the analyses that we have discussed can be found in table 8.5.

Demographic Analyses

One of the reasons to collect data about demographic information is to determine if characteristics of the participants affect performance on the dependent variables. It is good practice to run correlations between demographic data and dependent variable data to see if there is in fact a relationship between the two. Be careful, though, because much demographic data cannot be tested

Table 8.5
Summary of statistical analyses and their appropriate use.

Statistic	Type of question	When to use
Mean	Descriptive	Find the average score of a group
Standard deviation	Descriptive	Find the average error of a group
Correlation coefficient	Relational	Determine the strength of the relationship between two variables
T-test	Causal	Determine if difference between groups on dependent variable is caused by independent variable with two levels
ANOVA	Causal	Determine if difference among groups on dependent variable(s) is caused by independent variable(s) with two or more levels
Regression	Causal	Determine how much of the variance in a dependent variable is attributable to other variables (e.g., demographics, independent variables)

with the standard Pearson's *r*. If you do find that one of your demographics is correlated with a dependent variable, then you will want to ensure that there are no meaningful differences among groups on that demographic character-istic. Otherwise it will be difficult to argue that the differences on the depen-dent variable are due to the independent variable instead of the demographic difference. For example, in analyzing differences in test scores among high schoolers, some who have been taught in a blended class and others in a traditional lecture class, you will want to control for socioeconomic status. Several decades of research have demonstrated that academic performance is affected by the socioeconomic status of the students—those from lower-income backgrounds tend to perform less well than students from higher-income backgrounds. You can determine whether SES affects performance by gathering data about SES and testing for correlation between SES and performance.

WORKING WITH QUALITATIVE DATA

The previous section of this chapter dealt with analyses of quantitative data. Quantitative data analyses are highly valuable for describing a broad range of responses. However, if you want to get more depth of information, you will probably at some point end up working with qualitative data. Several methods are used in educational research to gather information about the *quality* of an event—what was said or observed, by whom, to whom, for what reasons, and so on.

This section provides a brief overview of methods for working with such information. For more detailed descriptions, we point the reader to Friese (2014), Gibson and Brown (2009), Miles, Huberman, and Saldana (2014), and finally Creswell and Plano Clark (2011), which is particularly useful for mixed-method research where qualitative analyses are combined with quantitative.

Analyzing Qualitative Data

While content analysis is one commonly used method of analyzing qualita-tive data, it is more *quantitative* than the analyses used by most qualitative researchers. In other words, while it might be tempting to try to reduce words to numbers, that is not the general goal of qualitative research. Qualitative researchers are less interested in the "what" questions than they are in the "how" and "why" questions. Content analysis gives us the what but leaves out the how and why.

Recall that the goals of qualitative research are to determine patterns in the data, to identify examples or quotations that demonstrate those patterns, and to identify outliers or deviations from those patterns. To make such classifications, qualitative data must be *coded*, in other words, analyzed for major themes. Suppose that a researcher has transcripts of interviews with three students who each participated in a blended learning environment. He would begin with the first interview, reading the transcript through thoroughly, and then going back and highlighting important sentences that exemplify the thoughts, feelings, and opinions of the respondent. He would then repeat that process with the second interview transcript and then the third.

Coding the data is a process of making general notes or descriptions about each of these quotations. For example, interview 1 might include the statement, "When I saw the professor's first video and how she drew equations on the screen, it made a lot more sense." Interview 3 might include the statement, "It was helpful to see the equations written out in the videos." The researcher would highlight each of these sentences and would label them each with the word *equations*, denoting that each describes opinions about the professor's equations. The researcher would repeat this process, understanding that not every statement made by one respondent will match statements made by all other respondents, but still looking for those overall patterns. Codes are often gathered into *clusters*, and these clusters can be somewhat fluid. The more data one analyzes, the more apparent some themes will become. Meanwhile, some codes that seemed quite important in the first interview might seem less so when looking at interviews 2 and 3. This will change the way the codes are clustered.

It is also good practice when analyzing qualitative data to have more than one researcher code the data. This helps ensure that the codes and clusters are viewed consistently by multiple reviewers and that the conclusions to be drawn from the data are as accurate as possible. In doing so, the researcher should be concerned with interrater reliability (IRR), the extent to which consistency can be established among multiple reviewers. Chapter 7 in this volume provides an example of IRR applied to open-ended survey questions used in a blended course. For more information on IRR, the reader should consult Gwet (2012).

Another key to qualitative data analysis is that it sometimes involves a combination of deductive and inductive reasoning. A researcher may have certain hypotheses about the how respondents will react to different topics. (Remember, those hypotheses might have been used to guide the interview protocol.) Testing those hypotheses by analyzing the statements respondents make is a form of deductive reasoning. However, it is also possible that in reading interview transcripts and the like, the researcher will discover themes that she had not previously thought of. The more prevalent these themes become, the more likely the researcher is to have to adapt her hypotheses and conclusions to account for new data. This is inductive reasoning. Taking this to its limit, *grounded theory* is an approach that specifies no a priori theories and asks the researcher to create theories based entirely on patterns in the qualitative data.

Before computers were introduced into qualitative data analysis, a common approach to coding data and establishing themes was to write or type identified quotations on index cards. The cards could be moved around and sorted into different piles. They might even be color-coded to provide a second level of information. Following from our previous example, all yellow cards could refer to student activities that took place in the classroom while all pink cards could refer to student activities that took place outside the class. But within each color, there would be different themes in the quotations, which could be organized to establish themes.

More recently, programs such as NVivo and ATLAS.ti have come to replace much of the manual work of coding data with what is known as CAQDAS (pronounced "CACK-dahs"; short for Computer Assisted Qualitative Data Analysis Software). These programs do *not* do the analyses for the researcher. The human element is still essential to analyzing data. But they do allow the researcher to highlight quotations, code and color-code information, cluster codes, create network diagrams showing the relationships between themes, help with content analysis by counting occurrences of words, and work handily with video and images. Such tools can be extremely valuable in creating reports based on qualitative data.

YOUR END GOAL: TELL THE STORY

A good qualitative analysis should allow the researcher to generate a narrative about what was observed. There is a reason that many ethnographic or qualitative reports are published as books (as opposed to journal articles). It often takes a full monograph to report on all the work that went into the study and all the information that came out of it. Nevertheless, smaller qualitative studies, such as those included in this volume, can be presented as case studies or snapshots of how a particular strategy or tool was used in the classroom.

Moreover, reliability is considered less important in qualitative research than validity. Qualitative studies can become so large, time consuming, and expensive that it is often impractical to try to replicate them to establish consistency of findings. Instead, the researcher should be absolutely concerned with making sure that the results are valid—that they will stand up to scrutiny in terms of both theory and methods.

The depth of information produced by qualitative studies rivals the breadth of information produced by quantitative studies. Neither approach should be considered better or worse than the other; they simply have their appropriate places in the spectrum of educational and social research. With this in mind, and with the information contained in this chapter, the reader should better understand why certain methods were chosen to demonstrate blended learning, its challenges, and its successes.

References

Coe, R. (2002). *It's the effect size, stupid: What effect size is and why it is important.* Paper presented at the British Educational Research Association Annual Conference, Exeter, UK.

Cohen, J. (1988). *Statistical power analysis for the behavioral sciences* (2nd ed.). Hillsdale, NJ: Erlbaum.

Creswell, J. W., & Plano Clark, V. L. (2011). *Designing and conducting mixed methods research.* Thousand Oaks, CA: Sage.

Friese, S. (2014). *Qualitative data analysis with ATLAS.ti.* Thousand Oaks, CA: Sage.

Gibson, W., & Brown, A. (2009). *Working with qualitative data.* Thousand Oaks, CA: Sage.

Glass, G., McGaw, B., & Smith, M. L. (1981). *Meta-analysis in social research.* London: Sage.

Gwet, K. L. (2012). *Handbook of inter-rater reliability: The definitive guide to measuring the extent of agreement among raters.* Gaithersburg, MD: Advanced Analytics.

Hanushek, E. A., & Jackson, J. E. (1977). *Statistical methods for social scientists.* New York: Academic Press.

Keppel, G., & Wickens, T. D. (2004). *Design and analysis: A researcher's handbook* (4th ed.). Upper Saddle River, NJ: Pearson Prentice Hall.

Miles, M. B., Huberman, A. M., & Saldana, J. (2014). *Qualitative data analysis: A methods sourcebook.* Thousand Oaks, CA: Sage.

9

BLENDED DYNAMICS—DOES SIZE MATTER?

Donald R. Webster, Robert S. Kadel, and Amanda G. Madden

MIX Taxonomy Classification: This course is blended. It closely resembles a flipped course as students receive content online before class and receive feedback while applying content in class. In addition, the students receive feedback while applying content after class through an online quizzing system that gives them multiple chances to attempt problems, making the assessment more formative than summative.

Research Method Classification: The research method the instructor selected is a quasi-experimental design. The two experimental groups, one that had a medium class size and one that had a large class size, were separated by semester and had the same instructor. Student performance was measured through a concept inventory and course exams. Student perceptions were measured through an in-class survey, the institutional end-of-course survey, and an engagement survey.

INTRODUCTION

Blended learning has shown some preliminary success in STEM courses. Analyses of the pedagogy's effectiveness include studies on introductory chemistry and calculus courses (Eichler and Peeples, 2016; Scott et al., 2016).

Successful trials in engineering courses include Velegol et al. (2015), who, in an introductory course, found that students like the flexibility of the course format and enjoy the interaction with the instructor and other students during class time. In a blended introductory Dynamics course, Swithenbank and DeNucci (2014) found higher scores on a common final examination relative to that of a traditional course. Similarly, Webster et al. (2016) demonstrated gains in problem-solving skills and conceptual understanding via a blended classroom approach in an introductory Fluid Mechanics course. Experiments in blended learning with a Computational Fluid Dynamics course show that the collaborative learning environment successfully increased student satisfaction (Sauret and Hargreaves, 2015). While these and other examples suggest advantages of the blended classroom approach, there are outstanding questions to be addressed about effectively implementing the pedagogy in STEM courses, including the issue of the impact of class size on the intervention.

This study examines the influence of class size on blended classroom pedagogy in an engineering mechanics course. In this chapter, the term *blended* will be used to describe the course format (following the taxonomy described in Margulieux et al., 2016) and encompasses the approach that has also been described as a *flipped classroom*. In the blended classroom approach, the often passive activity of listening to and watching a lecture is replaced with technologically mediated material outside of the class meeting. In-class activities are designed to engage students and encourage active learning. As detailed below, the study finds that this format is highly effective as class size expands due to the pedagogy's emphasis on maintaining a student-centric approach that provides flexibility, learning support, and active engagement.

The benefits of a blended classroom include (1) more one-on-one time with students, (2) improved student attendance at lectures, (3) self-paced learning, (4) "just-in-time" instruction, (5) opportunities for active and collaborative learning, and (6) increased engagement. The latter two benefits may be the most important. When conceptually challenging material is being introduced, increasing student engagement can improve student learning (Smith et al., 2005). Stickel and Liu (2015) also noted that increased student engagement is a key component in the success of the blended engineering classroom.

Barriers to increasing engagement may be overcome by shifting to a student-centric approach (Catalano and Catalano, 1999). Further, active learning and in-class collaboration approaches generally foster student engagement and enhance student performance (Prince, 2004; Felder and Brent, 2004; Albers and Bottomley, 2011; Freeman et al., 2014). In particular, Velegol et al. (2015) noted that the blended classroom format allowed students to become active learners. Gains in performance were directly related to increased student engagement, knowledge retention, and skill development (Velegol et al., 2015).

Studies that quantitatively measure the effectiveness of a blended classroom intervention are sparse, however, because collaboration and engagement can be hard to measure. On this note, Hotle and Garrow (2016) reported that while the literature suggests the blended learning format increases student engagement and satisfaction, very few studies have been able to isolate the effect of the intervention and measure a significant increase in assessment metrics relative to a traditional lecture-based approach.

Class size is an important consideration in any format, but it is particularly of interest for blended classrooms due to the personalized aspects of the approach. It has been suggested that there are potential economic benefits to the blended classroom approach because more students may be added to the classroom while still effectively maintaining student flexibility and personalized contact with the instructor (Hotle and Garrow, 2016). The converse (i.e., increased cost) has also been suggested due to the increased workload and time commitment necessary to effectively deliver a student-centric pedagogy (Catalano and Catalano, 1999). Roach (2014) noted that higher student-instructor ratios may be tolerated if blended classroom approaches allow for more personalized instruction. The potential downside is that the benefits of the individualized interaction with the instructor may necessarily decrease simply due to the demands of a larger population of students.

Measuring the impact of engagement and collaboration, especially for larger classes, is an important direction for research on the effectiveness of blended learning. Inherent challenges of large-scale classes include spatial constraints in the typical lecture hall, high student-instructor ratios, and technological barriers, among other factors. It is generally unknown whether the benefits of blended learning, as well as the personalized instruction of the blended classroom pedagogy, scale to larger class sizes. In fact, Hotle and Garrow (2016) report that they are unaware of any previous study that examines the influence of class size on the effectiveness of the blended classroom approach. There is, however, evidence that the benefits of active learning can scale up to large classes (up to 100) in an introductory physics course (Beichner et al., 2007).

To examine the scalability of this instructional approach, the authors designed a study to quantitatively and qualitatively assess the impact of class size on student performance and attitudes in a second-year (i.e., sophomore) engineering Dynamics course. The study examined two classes where the substantial difference between the classes is the size of the student groups: 37 in one course and 82 in the other. This chapter compares these two classes, which were offered in different semesters by the same instructor who employed a nearly identical blended classroom approach.

DESCRIPTION OF THE PEDAGOGY

Dynamics is a required course in the civil engineering and environmental engineering degree programs at the Georgia Institute of Technology (Georgia Tech). The course is part of an engineering mechanics sequence in both degree programs and the prerequisite is engineering Statics. Specific topics covered in the course include kinematics, kinetics, work-energy methods, and impulse momentum methods for both particle and rigid body applications. This particular course is limited to two-dimensional rigid body analysis. In Georgia Tech's curriculum, the semester-long, two-credit-hour course is intended for the second semester of the second year in both the civil engineering and environmental engineering degree programs. Typical enrollees include a mix of second-year and third-year students plus a small number of fourth-year students. The course meets for 50 minutes of class time two days each week on a Monday-Wednesday schedule. The primary course learning outcome is that students demonstrate an ability to appropriately apply fundamental analysis techniques to engineering dynamics applications.

In the instructor's opinion, the traditional lecture-based course format was deficient in its ability to provide an environment in which students could consistently obtain a depth of understanding of the material and thereby gain confidence in a range of problem-solving exercises. In his observation of the traditional lecture-based approach, students passively listened even with significant effort on the instructor's part to encourage participation and discussion. Class attendance was mixed; some students consistently attended and others attended infrequently. Note that attendance in the traditional format was not formally recorded and did not directly enter into the grading scheme. The instructor suspected that a significant fraction of the students were parroting homework assignment solutions from internet sources or unauthorized archives maintained by student groups. Students received personalized support only if they self-identified a deficiency and visited the instructor's office for help. The net effect was ultimately weak collective performance on the examinations and a lack of evidence that students had mastered the material. While student feedback on the traditional lecture-based class format was generally positive about the course effectiveness, student feedback also indicated a less-than-effective learning environment with few opportunities to engage:

- "It seemed like class was spent furiously writing down notes, and then trying to make sense of it later when it came time to do homework."
- "Homework was often frustrating and very time-consuming, but amount of effort expected was appropriate."
- "In spite of lecture attendance I still often had a really hard time with the homework (but lecture was always fast and the time was spent effectively, so I'm not sure what else could be done)."
- "The exams were a lot harder than any of the notes or homework examples. And I could work through the notes and homeworks with ease but struggle on the test."

With these observations as a backdrop, the instructor transformed the course into a blended format with the goal of engaging students with the subject and enhancing problem-solving skills through active participation.

Blended Course Design

The blended classroom approach for the Dynamics course is described in the flowchart in figure 9.1. Students watched online lecture recordings before the class session. The lectures were recorded by the instructor via the Tegrity recording software (McGraw-Hill Higher Education, Burr Ridge, IL). The Professional Education Division at Georgia Tech provided technical support for the lecture recording process, including managing software and licenses, maintaining the servers, and answering questions and problem reports. Lectures were recorded in the instructor's campus office without an audience present. A tablet PC and webcam were used as the recording hardware. The Open-Sankoré software (http://etmantra.com/open-sankore-a-free-software -for-smart-board-or-interactive-board) was employed on the tablet PC to create

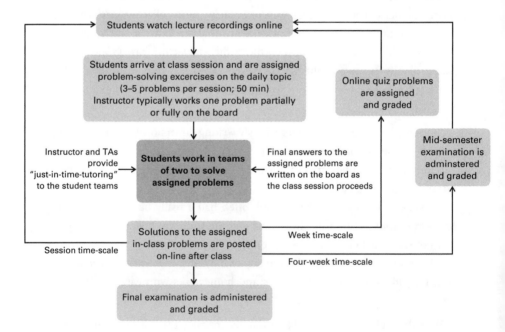

Figure 9.1

Description and sequence of the blended classroom format for the engineering Dynamics course

an electronic whiteboard. The instructor predominantly handwrote the lecture content on the electronic whiteboard using a stylus. The audio content and the instructor's face and upper torso were recorded using the webcam. Students had significant control during playback. Figure 9.2 shows a screenshot of an example lecture recording during playback. The main window displayed the electronic-whiteboard lecture content. Synchronously, the webcam recording was displayed in a smaller window. Students could expand the main window (i.e., the electronic whiteboard) to full screen, if desired. They also had the ability to make bookmarks and notes at key junctures as well as to pause, rewind, and fast-forward the recording. The playback speed could be set at normal and at up to two times faster.

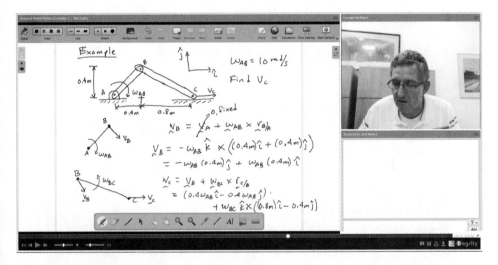

Figure 9.2
Screenshot of a lecture recording during playback. The largest window shows the electronic whiteboard created with the Open-Sankoré software. The lecture content was predominately handwritten with a stylus, as shown in this example. The synchronized webcam recording of the instructor is shown in a smaller window. Students may use the icons at the bottom left to control the playback, and they may make notes and bookmarks in the window at the bottom right.

Fifty-five to sixty-two short lecture recordings were created (table 9.1). The content followed that developed in previous live lectures during traditional lecture-based class offerings, with the significant difference that the content was presented in short and highly focused segments. The average lecture recording duration was slightly longer than 8 minutes (table 9.1). The content included both a theoretical introduction of the topics and examples of step-by-step problem solving. The pace of the lectures was brisk, but the progressively handwritten format facilitated students being able to follow along with note taking. In fact, students often took handwritten notes based on the lecture recordings just as they would in a live lecture. The seven recordings added for the spring 2015 semester were all sample problem-solving exercises, thereby increasing the number of example problems presented from 34 to 41 (table 9.1). Between zero and six lecture recordings were assigned prior to each class session, and the assignment was clearly documented in the class schedule (included in the syllabus) and on the class website. The class schedule in the

Table 9.1

Lecture recording and assignment information for each semester

	Fall 2013	Spring 2015
Number of lecture recordings	55	62
Number of example problems presented in lecture recordings	34	41
Average duration of the lecture recordings	8.3 minutes	8.2 minutes
Number of in-class problems assigned	76	82
Number of TAs	2 (one undergraduate and one graduate student)	3 (all graduate students)
Student-teacher ratio	12.3: 1	20.5: 1
Number of online quiz assignments	12	11
Aggregate number of online quiz problems	48	44

syllabus also stated the relevant section(s) of the course textbook (Meriam and Kraige, 2012) for the particular daily topic.

The primary focus of the in-class activities was to develop problem-solving skills and proficiency, which was addressed via assignments that required active participation. During the class sessions (two 50-minute sessions each week), students worked in teams of two to solve assigned problems addressing the session topic. The team size of two was selected to avoid situations where a student was left out of the conversation by being the third (or worse) wheel. Students selected their partner during the first week of the semester and the teams remained together for the full semester. The teaming process was constrained by forming four groups of students and instructing the students to select a partner from within the same subpopulation. The groups were created by ranking the students' incoming GPA (without informing them of the criterion) with the objective of forming teams consisting of students with comparable previous academic performance. The purpose was to prevent a more accomplished student from dominating the interaction with a less accomplished student. Concerns about partnering two weaker-performing students were alleviated by providing in-class support to the teams, as described below.

Up to five problem-solving exercises were assigned during each class session. The number of problems depended on the scope and complexity of the problems, which also were typically sequenced in terms of difficulty. The assigned problems consisted of homework-style problems from textbooks, examination problems from previous semesters, and problems written by the instructor. To create a collaborative space for students to interact, personalized whiteboards (81 cm × 53 cm) were provided to each team along with markers and erasers. The teams were not required to use the collaborative boards and their use diminished as the semester proceeded because the students often preferred to write on their individual assignment sheets. The total number of in-class problems assigned over the course of the semester was between 76 and 82 (table 9.1), and the added problems in the second semester were for sessions in which the majority of student teams finished early or to fill a noted topical gap. The subject of the problems for each session was directly linked to the session topic and the assigned lecture recordings. The instructor typically started the class session by working one of the problems on the board (either partially or fully) to refresh the topic of the lecture recordings, to allow the students to ask questions, and to get the students quickly engaged in problem-solving.

As a session proceeded, student teams worked on the remaining problems at their respective stations. The instructor and teaching assistants (TAs) roamed the room to answer student questions, pose questions to students, and discuss issues such as application relevance. The interaction could be described as "just-in-time tutoring" since questions typically came at the point in the problem-solving analysis at which the student teams were stuck or confused. As most instructors can appreciate, the student teams were highly receptive to the explanations of the instructor and TAs at that moment since they had reached a barrier to progressing with the analysis and realized that they needed help. It is important to note that this interaction was more "messy" than a traditional lecture in which the instructor is controlling the content and pace of the session; students were making mistakes, getting confused, asking questions, and working past challenges. In the blended classroom, the teams were working at their unique pace and controlling the sequence of exercises on which they worked. In the instructor's opinion, it is important to allow this flexibility, variation, and messiness to flourish because it ultimately provides a unique and tailored learning experience for each student.

The student teams demonstrated a broad range of performance. Teams that entered with a strong understanding of the material could complete the entire set of problems rapidly and thereby gain fluency by repetitive problem solving. Alternatively, teams that struggled with the material would typically ask numerous questions and might only finish one problem during the session. The benefit to those students was gaining basic skills and knowledge of the topic. In this way, the course format met students at their level of understanding and provided a framework for every student to learn and progress. The benefit to the instructor was to gain an understanding of where individual students were struggling and where they were excelling in order to guide future presentations and discussions.

The final answers to the problems were written on the board as the session continued to enable students to check their results. After the class session, the instructor's handwritten solutions to the problems were posted on the class website. Student teams that did not complete the full set of problems were given the opportunity to finish the problems and compare their work to the instructor's solutions. No credit was given for performance on the in-class problems. Instead, attendance was recorded and students who missed two or fewer sessions during the semester were rewarded with an additional 10% toward their final grade. This policy contrasted with that for the traditional lecture-based format, described above, in which attendance was not recorded and did not factor directly into the students' final grade. In practice, this policy had the effect of strongly encouraging attendance and participation in the class sessions, with only a small number of students failing to earn the attendance credit. In the instructor's opinion, the lack of graded credit for the in-class problems was a key factor in the success of the course. Students were free to work at their own pace rather than rush and stress out about getting all the problems completed. The approach created an environment in which they could make mistakes and ask questions without penalty.

To assess comprehension, online quizzes were assigned each week, with quiz problems selected to be topically consistent with the problems previously worked in class. The WileyPlus online system was used in connection with the textbook employed (Meriam and Kraige, 2012). Once the problem was assigned, each student received a unique set of input parameters. Hence, the system required them to perform the analysis and calculations for their unique set of numbers. Students were allowed to make three attempts at the solution with immediate feedback on the correctness of their submission. In the event that they did not correctly answer the problem by the third attempt, they gained access to the published solution to the problem in PDF file format (with a standard set of parameter values). Scores on the online quizzes were recorded and incorporated into the students' final grade in the course. The number of quizzes was 11 or 12, and the total number of quiz problems was between 44 and 48 (table 9.1).

Another key aspect of the course success was that it possessed an organized structure such that students could easily find the needed links and materials at the correct moment in the semester. The motivation was to create a simple and intuitive organization that would eliminate frustrating student searches for material and instead allow them to focus on learning the course subject. The class website, together with the schedule published in the syllabus, facilitated the organizational structure. Folders on the website were created for each class session and named by the respective date of the session. All links and materials for the session were included there, including links to all assigned lecture recordings, the assigned in-class problems for the session, and (after class) the solutions to the in-class problems. Links to the online quiz assignments were also created in the folders corresponding to the due date. By following the website folder structure, students could chronologically complete the assignments without ambiguity.

Three midsemester examinations (roughly four weeks apart) and a final examination provided the primary assessments of student achievement. The examinations consisted of problem-solving exercises that were manually graded by the instructor. Examinations were graded based on the students' demonstrated ability to (1) identify an effective approach to the problem-solving exercises, (2) set up the problem-solving technique including a sketch, if needed, (3) correctly apply the principle(s) for the analysis, and (4) perform the calculations to produce the solution.

STUDY DESIGN AND ASSESSMENT

Comparing the two blended classroom implementations of the Dynamics course, the substantial difference is that in the fall 2013 class the student count was 37, whereas in the spring 2015 class it was 82. The instructor was consistent across the classes, and the approach was nearly identical. Two TAs were employed in the classroom of the smaller class, leading to a student-teacher ratio of 12.3 to 1 (table 9.1). A higher student-teacher ratio (20.5 to 1) was present in the classroom of the larger class, which had three TAs (table 9.1). Note that the two individuals employed as TAs in fall 2013 were also employed in spring 2015. A few additional minor differences are noted above and summarized in table 9.1. The number of lecture recordings increased from 55 to 62 in the second offering of the course, due to the instructor's desire to increase the number of example problems presented. The number of in-class problems increased slightly from 76 to 82, largely due to the need to add problems to sessions in which the majority of students completed the assignment early. Due to slight differences in the calendar for the fall and spring semesters, 12 quizzes were assigned in fall 2013 for a total of 48 quiz problems, and 11 quizzes were assigned in spring 2015 for a total of 44 quiz problems (table 9.1).

It also should be noted that the classroom environments were substantially different (figure 9.3). The smaller fall 2013 class was in a general-purpose classroom that seats up to 66. The chairs rolled easily on casters over the carpet. The tables were designed for two students to sit comfortably and they could be moved if necessary (although not on casters). The instructor and TAs could easily move between the table rows in the classroom. In contrast, the larger spring 2015 class was in a tiered lecture hall since it was the only room with sufficient size for the class (with a capacity of 95 students). The chairs were again on casters, but the tables extended the full length of the rows and were fixed to the floor. The spacing between neighboring tables was limited, which hindered the instructor's and TAs' movement to the center of the rows. The restricted movement had the potential to limit the just-in-time tutoring interactions. The instructor attempted to limit these adverse effects by purposely walking through the rows periodically to interact with student groups along the entire row. This typically required maneuvering awkwardly around the furniture and stepping over backpacks and other items on the floor. Student groups often asked questions as the instructor passed close by, which suggested the proximity of the instructor encouraged their willingness to ask for help. Hence, the purposeful effort to walk between the rows was beneficial despite the awkwardness. The whiteboard and audiovisual equipment had been recently installed in both rooms and were equivalent (and modern).

The Dynamics Concept Inventory (DCI) Assessment Test was administered twice during the class to assess conceptual gains from the intervention. This

Figures 9.3a–b
Images of the classrooms. The first image shows the general-purpose classroom used for the fall 2013 class, and the second image shows the gently tiered lecture hall used for the spring 2015 class.

is a validated instrument designed to evaluate student learning and curricular innovations (Gray et al., 2005). It consists of 29 questions with multiple-choice answers that require minimal computation. The DCI was selected for this study due to the fact that its conceptual nature allows administration pre- and postsemester for subsequent comparison of student gains. It was administered during the first week of the semester and again during the last session of the semester. The DCI was not announced in advance on either occasion in either class and was administered by a neutral third party. It is important to note that the instructor did not review the content of the assessment test in advance.

Figures 9.3a–b (continued).

The instructor employed an identical final examination in each class. It consisted of five problem-solving exercises that comprehensively covered the full semester of course material. The examinations were hand-graded by the instructor using the same rubric (i.e., scoring guide to evaluate the quality of students' constructed responses).

To assess engagement and student response to the format, during the 11th week of the semester, students in both classes were asked to anonymously complete a survey (handwritten; administered in class) to provide feedback on their perceptions of the course format. The survey included the following questions:

• What aspects of the blended classroom format do you prefer over a traditional-style course?

- What aspects of a traditional-style course do you prefer over the blended classroom format?
- Do you find the lecture recordings to be helpful? More or less so than a traditional classroom lecture?
- At what moment in the class did you feel most engaged with what was happening?
- At what moment in the class did you feel most distanced from what was happening?
- Would you recommend this course format to a friend?

Students were asked to complete an engagement survey, using questions from the National Survey of Student Engagement (Center for Postsecondary Research, 2012). The survey covered 14 questions about student collaboration, skill development, and the use of higher-order thinking skills. Students were asked how often they performed certain tasks, such as how often they worked with other students on projects during class time, and responses were given using the following scale: never, occasionally, often, or very often.

During the final three weeks of the semester (including final examination week), students submitted the online Course-Instructor-Opinion-Survey (institute-administered) on a voluntary and anonymous basis.

RESULTS

Data were available for 37 students who completed the fall 2013 course and 82 students who completed the spring 2015 course. Crosstabulating students' major, gender, and year in school by the semester during which they took the course (fall 2013 or spring 2015) yielded fairly consistent results between the two classes (table 9.2). The fall 2013 class was 68% male, whereas the spring 2015 class was 55% male, but this difference is not statistically significant. In fall 2013, 68% of the students were civil engineering majors and 30% were environmental engineering majors. In spring 2015, 78% of the students were civil engineering majors and 22% were environmental engineering majors. These differences, too, were not statistically significant. However, the two groups did

Table 9.2
Student demographic information by semester taken

| | | | Semester | | Total |
			Fall 2013	Spring 2015	
Gender	Female	N	12	37	49
		% w/in semester	32.4%	45.1%	41.2%
	Male	N	25	45	70
		% w/in semester	67.6%	54.9%	58.8%
Major	Civil engineering	N	25	64	89
		% w/in semester	67.6%	78.1%	74.8%
	Environmental engineering	N	11	18	29
		% w/in semester	29.7%	22.0%	24.4%
	Architecture	N	1	0	1
		% w/in semester	2.7%	0%	0.8%
Year	2nd year	N	19	22	41
		% w/in semester	51.4%	26.8%	34.5%
	3rd year	N	13	52	65
		% w/in semester	35.1%	63.4%	54.6%
	4th year	N	5	8	14
		% w/in semester	13.5%	9.8%	11.8%
Total		N	37	82	119

differ on one factor: the year in school (second, third, or fourth year). Table 9.2 shows that the majority of the fall 2013 students (51%) were second-year students compared with the spring 2015 students, where the majority (62%) were third-year students. However, this difference was not enough to warrant tests for nonnormally distributed data in the analyses that follow.

Table 9.3 shows that there were no statistically significant differences in the students' previous academic preparation and performance. Incoming GPA differed by only 0.04 points (table 9.3). The average total number of semester credit hours that students had completed prior to taking the course differed

Table 9.3

Prior academic performance for two student groups

	Semester	N	Mean	Standard deviation	Standard error mean	t (p-value)
Incoming GPA	Fall 2013	37	3.02	0.63	0.10	0.253
	Spring 2015	81	2.98	0.70	0.08	(0.80)
Total number of credit hours completed prior to course	Fall 2013	37	67.7	17.6	2.9	-0.644
	Spring 2015	81	69.8	15.6	1.7	(0.52)
Number of credit hours completed at Georgia Tech prior to course	Fall 2013	37	42.2	21.2	3.5	-0.490
	Spring 2015	81	44.2	21.2	2.4	(0.62)

by only 2.1 hours, and the average total number of semester credit hours that students had completed specifically at Georgia Tech prior to taking the course differed by only 2 hours (table 9.3).

Student Performance

Table 9.4 shows consistent average results on the presemester DCI (a mean of 8.8 points in fall 2013 compared with a mean of 9.0 points in spring 2015) and on the postsemester DCI (a mean of 10.6 points in fall 2013 compared with 10.5 points in spring 2015). T-tests of the differences between means yielded no significant differences between the two classes, lending support to the suggestion that the blended classroom model employed in both classes was equally effective regardless of class size. Furthermore, the effect size of the difference in presemester DCI mean scores, measured by the Cohen effect-size parameter, d, was 0.06. According to Cohen (1988), effect sizes can be classified as small where $d = 0.2$, medium where $d = 0.5$, and large where $d = 0.8$. Therefore, an effect-size parameter seen here of 0.06 indicates a practically nonexistent difference between the two groups of students. The effect size (d) of the difference in postsemester DCI mean scores was 0.03 (table 9.4). Again, this shows practically no difference between the two classes.

Table 9.4

Comparison of presemester and postsemester Dynamics Concept Inventory (DCI) Assessment Test scores and final examination scores

	Semester	N	Mean	Standard deviation	Standard error mean	Cohen effect-size parameter, d
Presemester DCI score	Fall 2013	37	8.8	3.2	0.52	0.06
	Spring 2015	82	9.0	3.9	0.43	
Postsemester DCI score	Fall 2013	36	10.6	3.9	0.65	0.03
	Spring 2015	65	10.5	4.9	0.61	
Final exam score	Fall 2013	36	76.9	14.9	2.5	0.25
	Spring 2015	82	80.2	13.0	1.4	

The scores on the DCI (both pre- and postsemester) were considered by the instructor to be fairly low, however. Note that the largest mean score reported of 10.6 (table 9.4) corresponds to 36.6% of the 29 problems answered correctly. A subsequent examination of the topics covered on the DCI revealed that 4 of the 11 topics included on the assessment test were not covered in this two-credit-hour course, and at least one additional topic was addressed in a limited manner (recall that the instructor did not review the DCI in advance to prevent "teaching to the test"). Since the DCI covered topics that the designers selected due to common misperceptions among students and since the course content didn't address a significant fraction of the exam content, it is not surprising in hindsight to have relatively low average scores on the assessment test (for both semesters and for both pre- and postsemester).

The pre/post differences on the DCI administered within each class were significant, however (see figure 9.4). The gain in students' conceptual understanding between the pre- and postsemester DCIs is consistent with the results of Webster et al. (2016) in a blended classroom format for a Fluid Mechanics course. Thirty-five students completed both the pre- and postsemester DCI in fall 2013, showing means of 8.9 and 10.7, pre- to postsemester, respectively, a difference of 1.8 points. A paired-samples t-test yielded a t-value of 3.60,

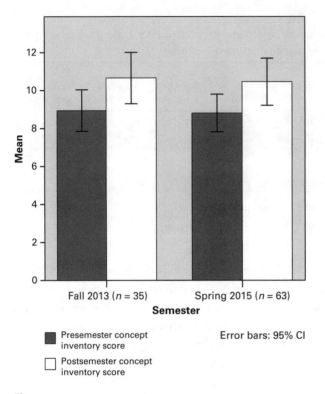

Figure 9.4

Comparison of presemester and postsemester Dynamics Concept Inventory (DCI) Assessment Test scores. The bars report mean values and the error bars report 95% confidence intervals.

significant at $p = 0.001$, and the Cohen effect-size parameter, d, was 0.53, measuring a medium effect of the course from the beginning to the end. In spring 2015, 63 students completed both the pre- and postsemester DCI, showing means of 8.8 and 10.5, pre- to postsemester, respectively, a difference of 1.7 points. A paired-samples t-test yielded a t-value of 3.83, significant at $p < 0.001$, and the Cohen effect-size parameter, d, was 0.35, a small-to-medium effect of the course from the beginning to the end.

One notable difference between classes is the average final examination score: 76.9 in fall 2013 and 80.2 in spring 2015 (table 9.4). This 3.3-point difference is not statistically significant, but it does show a small Cohen effect-size parameter of $d = 0.25$. The fact that students in the larger class (spring 2015) scored higher on the final examination than students in the smaller class does not indicate that the blended class model is less effective in larger classes. In this case, the opposite is true—students in a larger blended class slightly outperformed students in a smaller blended class.

In sum, within-class gains in conceptual ability across the semester were statistically significant and had small-to-medium effect sizes. But between-class differences were not significant, supporting our hypothesis that the blended classroom model was equally effective in both classes regardless of the size of the class. Students also demonstrated good problem-solving ability on the final examination, and the average score on the common examination was actually higher in the larger class.

Student Feedback

Fourteen questions from the National Survey of Student Engagement were used to establish collaboration, skill development, and the use of higher-order thinking skills. Survey responses were crosstabulated between the fall 2013 and spring 2015 classes, and chi-square tests established whether differences between the two classes were statistically significant. Responses to 12 of these questions indicated no significant difference between the classes, including:

During your class, about how often have you done each of the following?
- Worked with other students on projects during class time
- Tutored or taught the class materials to other students in the class

To what extent has this course emphasized the mental activities listed below?
- Memorizing facts, ideas, or methods from your course and readings so you can repeat them in almost the same form
- Analyzing the basic elements of an idea, experience, or theory such as examining a specific case or situation in depth and considering its components

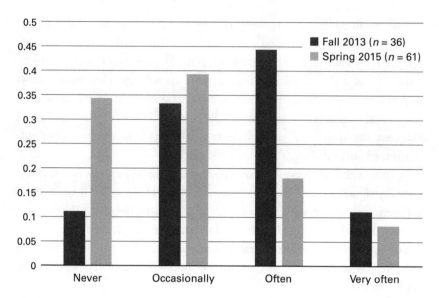

Figure 9.5

Histogram of student responses to the question "About how often have you asked questions during class or contributed to class discussion?" Data reported as fraction of students for the respective semester. Chi-square test results: $\chi^2 = 10.88$, $p < 0.012$, which reveals the distributions are not statistically similar.

• Synthesizing and organizing ideas, information, or experiences into new, more complicated interpretations and relationships

• Evaluating the value of information, arguments, or methods, such as examining how others gathered and interpreted data and assessing the accuracy of their conclusions

• Applying theories and/or concepts to practical problems or in new situations

To what extent has this course contributed to your knowledge, skills, and personal development in the following ways?

• Acquiring job- or career-related knowledge and skills

• Writing clearly, accurately, and effectively

• Thinking critically and/or analytically

- Learning effectively on your own, so you can identify, research, and complete a given task
- Working effectively with other individuals

Figures 9.5 and 9.6 show the results for the responses to the two questions that revealed a significant difference between the two classes:

During your class, about how often have you done each of the following?
- Asked questions during class or contributed to class discussion (figure 9.5)
- Worked with classmates outside of class to complete class assignments (figure 9.6)

It is proposed that the differences between classes with respect to students' likelihood to ask questions during class may have been due to class size

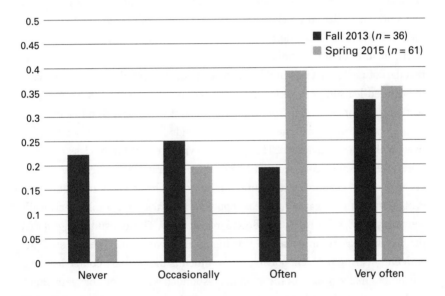

Figure 9.6
Histogram of student responses to the question "About how often have you worked with classmates outside of class to complete class assignments?" Data reported as fraction of students for the respective semester. Chi-square test results: $\chi^2 = 9.13$, $p < 0.028$, which reveals the distributions are not statistically similar.

and interpretation of the question. In both classes, students regularly asked questions of the instructor and TAs when working in pairs or small groups. However, if one perceives the question to refer to "asking a question while the whole class is listening," then figure 9.5 would indicate that students in the larger class may be less likely to ask a question while the instructor is at the front of the classroom interacting with the entire class. Since the class format, assignments, and process for selecting teams were the same in the classes, explanations for the differences in figure 9.6 are less clear. It is possible that more experience or maturity or previously developed friendships led to increased collaboration outside of class, since the demographics of the larger spring 2015 class included more third-year students and fewer second-year students (table 9.2). Based on the 12 similar responses and the potential explanations for the two queries yielding different responses, it is concluded that students in the larger class are reporting a level of engagement similar to the level experienced by their counterparts in the smaller class.

The results of the National Survey of Student Engagement also indicate that the course format was highly effective in engaging students and producing the desired learning outcomes. For instance, 90.5% of students (across both sections) responded "often" or "very often" about working with other students on projects during class time and 81.4% responded similarly for working effectively with other individuals. This provides evidence that the in-class activities were effective at encouraging students to collaborate. Similarly, the "often" or "very often" responses regarding analyzing the basic elements of an idea, synthesizing and organizing ideas, applying theories, and thinking critically were 84.5%, 78.4%, 88.7%, and 89.5%, respectively. These results suggest that the blended classroom pedagogy was highly effective at empowering students with engineering problem-solving skills, which is the primary course learning outcome. Finally, 79.4% of the students responded with "often" or "very often" to the question about learning effectively on their own, which suggests they gained confidence about continuing on their engineering educational pathway. These results support recent research that contends that active learning in a blended classroom can contribute to the development of cognitive skills such as critical thinking and problem solving (Yildiz et al., 2014; Cash, 2017).

In the institute-administered Course-Instructor-Opinion-Survey, student comments in the larger class (spring 2015) were equally, if not more, complimentary of the blended classroom format compared to the smaller class (fall 2013). Several students made extremely positive comments regarding the format, while expressing initial skepticism. For instance, one student wrote, "I loved the flipped classroom style of teaching. I was a little skeptical at first, but it ended up really working out." Another student commented on how the format allowed for a deeper understanding of the material: "[The] flipped classroom was really useful for getting a lot of practice doing problems. We used class time as more of an interactive assignment time which was much more helpful than just spending class time for lectures." This theme was echoed several times: "I love the reverse classroom system implemented in this class. Having lectures available for whenever I need to review anything and then having the TAs and the professor there to help was amazing. My favorite teaching format of any class I've ever had." Given that students continued to respond positively as the class size increased, their positive response in the surveys is another indicator of success with the format in terms of engagement.

The anonymous handwritten surveys revealed similar comments, but the responses to the question "Would you recommend this course format to a friend?" were more negative in the larger class. In the smaller fall 2013 class, the student responses to this question were: 27 "yes," 1 "no," and 5 "maybe." In the larger spring 2015 class, the student responses were: 40 "yes," 11 "no," and 4 "maybe." While both sets of responses were predominantly positive, the larger class had more "no" responses. Among the "maybe" responses, one student wrote, "Generally, I dislike flipped classes, but this one is structured well. It is not my preference, but I wouldn't turn people away from the class." This comment and the ones above suggest that the blended pedagogy needs to be well organized in order to encourage students to commit to the format. The survey responses for those students responding "no" indicate that they prefer to "be taught" the material and that they prefer to be able to "ask questions during lecture." While it may be their preference, "being taught" the subject matter is not the most effective means of learning, as reported in the literature on active learning and based on the instructor's observations. A few of the negative responses complained that the class format forced them to be engaged—which suggests a lack of self-awareness about how engagement helps them learn. The latter reason is not supported by the students' actual behavior. Both in previous traditional lectures and in the introductory period of the blended classroom sessions, few students have tended to ask questions. In fact, the data in figure 9.5 indicates that the number of students asking questions diminishes with class size, whereas engagement and performance are maintained as described above.

Table 9.5 shows mean values of the students' responses from the Course-Instructor-Opinion-Survey. The first five queries relate to the effectiveness of the instruction, which is influenced by the students' perceptions of the course format and the instructor. The results of the all-encompassing query "Considering everything, the instructor was an effective teacher" are 4.6 and 4.7 for the two classes, indicating a similar level of overall student satisfaction with the instruction despite the class-size difference. Independent-samples t-tests of the mean differences indicate no statistically significant differences between responses of the two groups of students on these five questions. The second five queries shown in table 9.5 relate most directly to the course itself. The mean values of the responses are again similar between classes, with four of the five results showing no statistically significant differences. The mean responses to one question, "Rate how prepared you were to take this subject," were statistically different (3.5 for fall 2013 and 4.0 for spring 2015). This is consistent with the above finding that the majority of the fall 2013 students were second-year students, while the majority of spring 2015 students were third-year. Overall, these quantitative results support the positive anecdotal comments presented above.

Figure 9.7 shows student-reported data (from the Course-Instructor-Opinion-Survey) for the number of hours spent per week on the course. More students reported spending 3–6 hours per week in the smaller fall 2013 class than in the larger spring 2015 class. Correspondingly, more students reported spending 9–12 hours in the larger spring 2015 class. The greater amount of

Table 9.5

Summary of results for the Course-Instructor-Opinion-Survey. Mean scores are for a 1-to-5 scale, as defined for each question. * indicates a significant difference

	Fall 2013	Spring 2015	t (p-value)
Number of responses	22	50	
Instructor's clarity in discussing or presenting course material. 5: exceptional; 1: very poor	4.4	4.5	-0.837 (0.406)
Instructor's level of enthusiasm about teaching the course. 5: extremely enthusiastic; 1: detached	4.2	4.5	-1.580 (0.119)
Instructor's ability to stimulate my interest in the subject matter. 5: made me eager to learn more; 1: ruined my interest	3.7	4.0	-1.444 (0.153)
Helpfulness of feedback on assignments. 5: extremely helpful; 1: not helpful	4.2	4.5	-1.801 (0.076)
Considering everything, the instructor was an effective teacher. 5: strongly agree; 1: strongly disagree	4.7	4.6	0.503 (.616)
Rate how prepared you were to take this subject. 5: extremely well prepared; 1: completely unprepared	3.5	4.0	-2.123 (0.037)*
How much would you say you learned in this course? 5: an exceptional amount; 1: almost nothing	4.3	4.4	-0.787 (.434)
Degree to which activities and assignments facilitated learning. 5: exceptional; 1: very poor	4.3	4.2	-0.112 (0.911)
Degree to which exams, quizzes, homework (or other evaluated assignments) measured your knowledge and understanding. 5: exceptional; 1: very poor	4.2	4.3	-0.948 (0.346)
Considering everything, this was an effective course. 5: strongly agree; 1: strongly disagree	4.4	4.4	-0.729 (0.469)

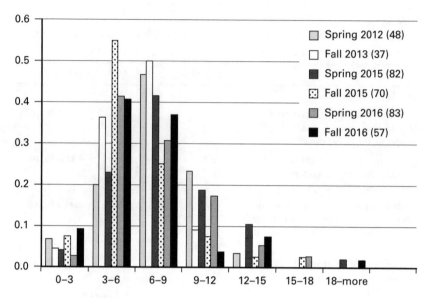

Figure 9.7
Student-reported hours per week spent on the course. Data are from the Course-Instructor-Opinion-Survey and are presented as the fraction of students in the class reporting for each range. The number of students in each class is shown in parentheses in the legend. Five classes were in the blended classroom format, and the spring 2012 class was in a traditional lecture-based format.

time spent on the course by these students may, in part, explain the higher average score on the final examination for the spring 2015 class (table 9.4). The spring 2015 distribution also shows approximately 10% of the students reported spending 12–15 hours per week. Comparison with data from three subsequent semesters of the course reveals that this is an atypical result with fewer responses in this range in other semesters (fall 2015, spring 2016, and fall 2016). Further, comparison to data from a previous traditional lecture-based class offered by the same instructor reveals a distribution that is very similar to the spring 2015 distribution, which suggests the blended classroom format is not overly demanding on student effort outside of the classroom sessions (consistent with conclusions in Webster et al., 2016). In fact, the percentage of students reporting spending between 3 and 9 hours per week was always the majority and was consistently in the range of 65% to 86% across all classes reported.

DESCRIPTION OF INSTITUTIONAL SUPPORT

During development and delivery of the blended classroom pedagogy, the instructor received institutional support through several mechanisms. First, he received advice about implementing the blended pedagogy from the director of the Center of Teaching and Learning, the assistant dean (of the College of Engineering) for Educational Research and Innovation, and a small number of faculty colleagues (mostly notably in biomedical engineering and physics). Second, he received a small discretionary account from the College of Engineering to be used toward acquiring the needed technology, specifically the tablet PC and webcam used for the lecture recordings. Georgia Tech's Professional Education Division provided support for the lecture recordings by managing software and licenses, maintaining the servers, and responding to questions and problem reports. During the semester, the instructor used the institute's course management system to host the class website. The teaching assistants were supported by the School of Civil and Environmental Engineering through normal mechanisms provided to courses in the school. This typically consists of financial support for several hours per week of "grading" by an assistant, and the funds were used here instead to support the in-class assistants.

During the research phase of the project, the instructor received support from Georgia Tech's Center for 21st Century Universities, an organization that, among other tasks, assists faculty with research on alternative pedagogies. The researchers conducted a review of existing literature on this topic, administered the DCI and in-class surveys, and organized and analyzed data, which included statistical hypothesis testing. The institute also provided support by administering and managing the online Course-Instructor-Opinion-Survey.

CONCLUSIONS

The blended classroom approach described in this chapter for an undergraduate engineering Dynamics course required a substantial shift from a traditional teacher-centric approach to a student-centric format in which the instructor acts as a guide through the material and provides "just-in-time" tutoring. In addition to describing the pedagogy, the main purpose of this chapter has been to examine the effectiveness of scaling the approach to larger classes.

The conclusion is that the course format scales very effectively to larger classes based on the instructor's perceptions, assessment of student performance, assessment of student engagement, and review of student feedback. Students in the larger class showed similar gains on the DCI and they produced a higher mean score on a common final examination. Further, student-reported opinions of the class and its effectiveness were similarly positive in the larger class and in many cases exceeded the perceptions in the smaller class. In particular, students reported a similar level of engagement, despite the substantial difference in class size.

Moving forward as departments and institutes struggle with the value proposition in delivering engineering education, blended classroom approaches such as the one described here may provide a means of delivering a high-quality educational experience to larger classes. In fact, the motivation to offer the larger class was driven by department budget constraints, making it desirable to combine two moderate-sized classes offered in parallel during a given semester into a single larger class. While the generally accepted opinion is that larger class size leads to poorer student engagement, satisfaction, and performance, the results of this study suggest that the individualized benefits of the blended classroom approach scale to a larger class with little to no loss in effectiveness. It is important to reiterate that the course described here is not an online course. Rather, the course accurately fits the "blended" description in the taxonomy presented by Margulieux et al. (2016) by balancing delivery via instructor with delivery via technology and balancing information transmission with praxis. In the course design, the main objective was to use online and electronic technologies to enhance the in-class experience and effectiveness. Whereas technology drives the out-of-class aspects of the course, the in-class experience is characterized by personalized tutoring interactions between students and instructors that lack advanced technology. In the instructor's observations and in student feedback, it is clear that student engagement and the in-class active learning are key to the success of the instructional approach. Hence, as instructors consider adopting similar approaches, it is recommended that besides taking technology considerations into account, they focus on designing the in-class activities and engagement aspects.

ACKNOWLEDGMENTS

Financial support from the Georgia Tech College of Engineering Dean's Office and the Speedwell Foundation are gratefully acknowledged. The research was conducted under IRB Protocol #H13458. Thanks to David Young, Anna Skipper, and Seongyu (John) Jung for their assistance in the classroom and to David Majerich for collecting data for the fall 2013 course. Thanks also to George Wright and the technical support staff at Georgia Tech's Professional Education Division.

References

Albers, L., & Bottomley, L. (2011). *The impact of activity based learning, a new instructional method, in an existing mechanical engineering curriculum for fluid mechanics.* Paper presented at the 118th ASEE Annual Conference & Exposition, Vancouver, BC.

Beichner, R. J., Saul, J. M., Allain, R. J., Deardorff, D. L., & Abbott, D. S. (2000). *Introduction to SCALE-UP: Student-centered activities for large enrollment university physics.* Paper presented at the ASEE Annual Conference & Exposition, Washington, DC.

Cash, R. M. (2017). *Advancing differentiation: Thinking and learning for the 21st century.* Minneapolis: Free Spirit.

Catalano, G. D., & Catalano, K. (1999). Transformation: From teacher-centered to student-centered engineering education. *Journal of Engineering Education, 88*(1), 59–64.

Center for Postsecondary Research. (2012). *National Survey of Student Engagement.* Bloomington: Indiana University School of Education.

Cohen, J. (1988). *Statistical power analysis for the behavioral sciences* (2nd ed.). Hillsdale, NJ: Erlbaum.

Eichler, J. F., & Peeples, J. (2016). Flipped classroom modules for large enrollment general chemistry courses: A low barrier approach to increase active learning and improve student grades. *Chemistry Education Research and Practice, 17*, 197–208.

Felder, R. M., & Brent, R. (2004). The intellectual development of science and engineering students. Part 2: Teaching to promote growth. *Journal of Engineering Education, 93*, 279–291.

Freeman, S., Eddy, S. L., McDonough, M., Smith, M. K., Okoroafor, N., Jordt, H., et al. (2014). Active learning increases student performance in science, engineering, and mathematics. *Proceedings of the National Academy of Sciences of the United States of America, 111*(23), 8410–8415.

Gray, G. L., Costanzo, F., Evans, D., Cornwell, P., Self, B., & Lane, J. L. (2005). *The Dynamics Concept Inventory Assessment Test: A progress report and some results.* Paper presented at the ASEE Annual Conference & Exposition, Portland, OR.

Hotle, S. L., & Garrow, L. A. (2016). Effects of the traditional and flipped classrooms on undergraduate student opinions and success. *Journal of Professional Issues in Engineering Education and Practice, 142*, 05015005– 105015005-11.

Margulieux, L. E., McCracken, W. M., & Catrambone, R. (2016). Mixing face-to-face and online learning: Instructional methods that affect learning. *Educational Research Review, 19*, 104–118.

Meriam, J. L., & Kraige, L. G. (2012). *Engineering mechanics: Dynamics* (7th ed.). Hoboken, NJ: Wiley.

Prince, M. (2004). Does active learning work? A review of the research. *Journal of Engineering Education, 93*, 223–231.

Roach, T. (2014). Student perceptions toward flipped learning: New methods to increase interaction and active learning in economics. *International Review of Economics Education, 17*, 74–84.

Sauret, E., & Hargreaves, D. (2015). *Collaborative learning approach to introduce computational fluid dynamics. Paper presented at the 2015 Australasian Association for Engineering Education (AAEE) Conference*, Geelong, Victoria, Australia.

Scott, C. E., Green, L. E., & Etheridge, D. L. (2016). A comparison between flipped and lecture-based instruction in the calculus classroom. *Journal of Applied Research in Higher Education, 8*, 252–264.

Smith, K. A., Sheppard, S. D., Johnson, D. W., & Johnson, R. T. (2005). Pedagogies of engagement: Classroom-based practices. *Journal of Engineering Education, 94,* 87–101.

Stickel, M., & Liu, Q. (2015). *Engagement with the inverted classroom approach: Student characteristics and impact on learning outcomes.* Paper presented at the 2015 Canadian Engineering Education Association Conference, Hamilton, Ontario.

Swithenbank, S. B., & DeNucci, T. W. (2014). *Using a "flipped classroom" model in undergraduate Newtonian dynamics.* Paper presented at the 121st ASEE Annual Conference & Exposition, Indianapolis.

Velegol, S. B., Zappe, S. E., & Mahoney, E. (2015). The evolution of a flipped classroom: Evidence-based recommendations. *Advances in Engineering Education, 4*(3), 1–37.

Webster, D. R., Majerich, D. M., & Madden, A. G. (2016). Flippin' fluid mechanics—Comparison using two groups. *Advances in Engineering Education, 5*(3), 1–20.

Yildiz, M. N., Petela, A., & Mahoney, B. (2014). Global kitchen project: Promoting healthy eating habits and developing 21st century skills among children through a flipped classroom model. In J. Keengwe, G. Onchwari, & J. N. Oigara (Eds.), *Promoting active learning through the flipped classroom model.* Hershey, PA: IGI Global.

III

COURSE DESIGN CASE STUDIES: SOLVING COMMON TEACHING ISSUES

10

BLENDING A FIRST-YEAR COMPOSITION COURSE USING
ASSASSIN'S CREED II

Amanda G. Madden

> **MIX Taxonomy Classification:** The course is blended. Students receive content both through the game and in class. Students also completed activities both in and out of class and received feedback on those activities from the instructor. The author provides recommendations for blending based on this novel way of teaching composition, including how to guide students to learn seriously from a popular videogame that they might play for entertainment.

In 2009, the *New York Times* published a review of Ubisoft's blockbuster videogame, *Assassin's Creed II*, quipping:

Over the next few semesters some teachers of Italian history will be surprised—not altogether pleasantly, I'm sure—as some of their new students confess that they have already explored 15th-century Florence and Venice in a video game. (The progressive professors will then find a way to incorporate the game into their lectures). (Schiesel, 2009)

Not being a serious gamer (rather an instructor of first-year composition and disciplinary expert in the Italian Renaissance), I found this statement both provocative and intriguing. It can be difficult to engage students in studying places and eras that are wholly unfamiliar to them, or more generally, to get them to invest in more than their grades in an introductory-level course most often taken to fulfill a requirement. So when presented with the opportunity to design a blended first-year composition course incorporating the game—I seized it. My research question was the following: Would using this immersive, adaptive text in lieu of lectures on the historical period result in increased student engagement and promote better learning outcomes?

First, this chapter provides context and gives a brief overview of the relevant literature on blended learning as it relates to composition—as noted, blending a composition course, particularly using a videogame is not typical, so the literature is sparse in both regards.

Second, the chapter discusses course design. When designing this course, I hypothesized that by using *Assassin's Creed II* as a textbook, students would become more engaged with the course material as measured by engagement metrics. These metrics include voluntary participation in class discussion and on Piazza (a platform for discussion forums), as well as traditional content assessment—a series of assignments designed to test students' historical knowledge as acquired by playing the game in conjunction with secondary readings. In essence, the videogame would become a sort of lab for the subject material.

Third, the chapter explores the impact of this design on student engagement and outcomes. As measured by student feedback, blending the classroom with a videogame did result in increased student engagement as compared to courses previously taught in first-year composition and European history. As one student noted on the course's Piazza discussion board, "Being able to visualize the Renaissance era, even graphically, was enough to push me to start learning," and many students echoed similar unprompted sentiments in course reflections and assignments.

Finally, I point the way to promising future research directions and applications. In particular, I propose that blending a writing-intensive intro-level humanities course using technology allows students not only to reflect on their learning but also on the use of technology—a necessary skill for the 21st-century workforce. Videogames are only one way of promoting active, technology-based learning. With the advent of virtual and augmented realities, students will most likely be learning more frequently in this manner and humanities and writing instructors have an unprecedented chance, if not the responsibility, to explore this type of learning.

First, some context and a brief word on the genesis of this course as it is relevant to understanding the course design and my goals in blending the course. I had been teaching writing-intensive introductory courses for several years before I had ever heard of "flipped" or "blended" classrooms. During the spring of 2012 in a postdoctoral research seminar on digital pedagogy, I first became aware of the concept and began to ponder the possibilities of blending a freshman composition course using technology—reading- and writing-intensive courses like composition traditionally rely on high levels of face-to-face, instructor-student contact. Discussing the potentials for asynchronous learning and writing-classroom redesign, my colleagues and I explored different types of technologies that could break us out of these traditional education formats embedded in the brick-and-mortar classroom. These included learning management systems (LMSs), discussion tools, video-production platforms, and videogames. After discussing videogames, I wondered how these games could stand in as immersive, interactive lectures for content delivery and whether this delivery mechanism would result in increased content mastery, engagement, and overall improved course outcomes.

While student engagement is often correlated with better performance in a course, engagement is negatively correlated with required courses that do not correspond to a student's chosen major. In this particular context, the course in question was part of a sequence of writing and composition courses required of all Georgia Tech students, like most undergraduate students regardless of major, in order to graduate. While programmatic expectations are consistent across the 20+ sections offered every semester, namely that the students learn to communicate multimodally and turn in a final portfolio of their best work, the sections themselves are content agnostic and the assignments are customized to individual instructors' preferences (Burnett et al., 2014). Many students tend to treat the courses as something to endure rather than enjoy, as is often reflected on the Course Instructor Opinion Survey (CIOS) scores and student feedback. In essence, engagement in these courses is often low regardless of the section's content, the instructor, or the learning gains.

Different pedagogical tactics have been adopted by writing instructors and composition programs to address the challenge of engaging students and to improve learning outcomes. These tactics include the incorporation of technology into writing instruction, the cognizance of 21st-century literacies and writing, broader definitions of media, and the reframing of composition as "multimodal," to name a few productive pedagogical directions. Blended pedagogy, however, has yet to be widely adopted in composition classes.

There are a multitude of reasons—more philosophical than practical—that blended learning is not typical of composition pedagogy. While this approach has been correlated with increased student engagement in STEM disciplines, for example, composition as a discipline has widely documented the benefits of face-to-face instruction and small class sizes for the development of writing skills. In part, this is because effective writing instruction as defined by disciplinary bodies like the Conference on College Composition and Communication (CCCC) relies on active learning and complex feedback mechanisms that historically have taken place in face-to-face settings, including student-teacher conferences, peer feedback, collaborative projects, and a large percentage of instructor-student face time.[1] Think back to your typical first-year composition course that most of us take. Students are assigned readings and a range of different types of writing assignments. Because lecturing on the art of writing, crafting a topic sentence, say, is only of use in its practical application, there is only so much lecturing one can do without devoting a certain amount of class to active learning and practical application. Thus, most composition classrooms are already "flipped" in that content is delivered outside class and students use class time for discussion and practice. Content delivery, however, need not be face to face, and in a sense, traditional composition instruction is one small step away from being blended, as discussed below.

Thus, in many ways, a college composition classroom is not the ideal laboratory for testing the success of blended learning in the same way that other courses described in this book are. Just as technology, however, has redefined the nature of composition, it has redefined the nature of composition instruction. Would a course design centered around the use of a videogame to blend the class solve the problem of low student engagement? Would using a videogame to blend the class increase engagement with writing for students who had no prior interest in either the Italian Renaissance or videogames? I set about designing a course around the use of *Assassin's Creed II* for the spring semester of 2013.

The course was called "The Digital Italian Renaissance" and was a second-semester composition course focused on the Italian Renaissance as a thematic topic and an object of analysis. In lieu of lectures on the period, the students were to play through Ubisoft's videogame, *Assassin's Creed II*. Set in Florence during the second half of the 15th century, the game sends the protagonist Ezio Auditore on a series of missions and interactions, including gameplay with Leonardo da Vinci, diplomatic errands on behalf of the Medici, and interactions with other important political figures, including Caterina Sforza and Cardinal Rodrigo Borgia, later Pope Alexander VI. Developed in consultation with historical experts on the period, the gameplay not only involves interaction with these historical figures but includes participation in historical events, including the infamous Pazzi conspiracy—the attempted assassination of Lorenzo de' Medici on Easter Sunday in 1478. It's one of the bestselling videogames and has now sold copies in the tens of millions. To understand why the game is significant not only for the game industry but also for historians, as a thought exercise, contemplate the tens of millions of players of this game in proportion to the sum total of people alive who have read a scholarly, historical monograph on the Italian Renaissance.

Accordingly, the game has received attention in game studies scholarship (Dow, 2013; Shaw, 2015; Veugen, 2016), and scholars have focused on its storytelling, historical representation, and novel game design. Professional mainstream historians, however, have paid very little attention to the *Assassin's Creed* franchise, despite the fact that it is now in its fifth iteration and the series has made efforts to recreate historically faithful games. Several professional historians have looked at this game and similar games as pointing toward a future when history classrooms and textbooks could become 3D and immersive (Wainwright, 2014). A few scholars have done studies on using the game in the high school classroom (Apperley and Walsh, 2012; Marín et al., 2015). Teaching history with videogames, however, is far from mainstream.

The game is suitable as an interactive lecture for several reasons. First, the developers made an effort to faithfully render in 3D the architecture and landscape of Renaissance Italy, particularly the cities of Florence and Venice, with all possible attentiveness to accuracy. Game players are literally taking a 360-degree virtual tour. Second, gameplay incorporates Renaissance Italian culture without being too anachronistic. For example, as part of the sandbox gameplay (meaning that the player has a lot of choice in how to interact with the environment, rather than a prescribed sequence of events), Ezio gains "notoriety" depending on his actions. If he bumps into too many nuns in the street or starts fights, nonplayer characters react to him in certain ways and he is more likely to be recognized by the police, be pursued, and have the gameplay hindered. This gameplay corresponds with the Renaissance Italian idea of *fama* or reputation in the streets—wherein public actions would hinder or help a person. Finally, the developers also included digital historical placards in the game. When the player encounters a monument, street, or nonplayer character, for example, digital placards will pop up in the game, giving you a historical overview. Because of this design the game is very close to being an interactive historical textbook, and thus lends itself to substituting for lectures.

To put it mildly, however, videogames are more the exception than the rule as assigned texts in writing-intensive introductory courses and undergraduate history courses. While game studies as a discipline has an increasingly prominent seat at the academic table, it is still unusual to find courses that consider these media on an equal footing with Shakespeare's plays or Austen's *Pride and Prejudice*, for example. As other scholars have noted, however, videogames take advantage of research-based pedagogy, including interest-driven learning, active learning theories, and research on student engagement. As Squire notes, "Interest driven learning can be a powerful motivator. When passionate about a topic, students will willingly read and write texts that are far more complicated than texts about topics they are not passionate about" (Squire, 2011, p. 46). Other scholars have noted in quasi-experimental studies that videogames may not increase content knowledge but do promote student engagement (Annetta et al., 2009). A meta-analysis, however, found that games were more effective in certain contexts than traditional instruction, especially at garnering engagement, but did not necessarily increase motivation (Wouters et al., 2013). Other meta-analyses have argued that the effectiveness of videogames for learning is inconclusive (Girard et al., 2013). The research on using games in the classroom is still nascent. As Young et al. point out, "The inconclusive nature of game-based learning research seems to only hint at the value of games as educational tools. ... Many educationally interesting games exist, yet evidence for their impact on student achievement is slim" (Young et al., 2012, pg.80). Indeed, at present most of the studies on game-based learning are more theoretical than practical. What follows is a description of course design and how to incorporate a videogame in the class.

When designing the course, I wanted to be as clear as possible in outlining my course goals, learning outcomes, and expectations so that students would not be too focused on the novelty of having a class designed around a popular videogame—*Assassin's Creed II* was meant to be an immersive textbook, not just a fun alternative to traditional readings. Thus, I scaffolded the game for them with learning goals in the syllabus and introduced up front the idea of reflecting on the learning medium. I wanted students to analyze cultural phenomena, becoming aware of how history becomes incorporated into popular culture and interrogating what it means to use a videogame as a textbook:

Using pop culture adaptations of history and literature as an analytical lens, by the end of this course you will be able to evaluate and construct arguments in a variety of modes. In particular, this course is designed to build upon your critical thinking and evaluative skills, help you develop a research toolbox, aid in honing the principles of effective argumentation and rhetoric, and reinforce best practices for effective writing at the college level. You will demonstrate proficiency in the process of articulating and organizing rhetorical arguments in written, oral, visual, and nonverbal modes, using concrete support and conventional language. (Madden, 2013, p 1)

By explicitly tying the learning goals to the game as an object of inquiry and a medium of delivery, I let the students know that I wanted them to analyze how historical information is delivered and underscored the importance of reflection and metacognition. After setting up these expectations up front in the syllabus, I outlined the course and described the programmatic and other expectations, the required texts, and the assignments, enumerating the goals for each assignment and the overall goals for the course.

Finally, I designed assignments to scaffold the videogame as outlined below. Assignments were also designed to test improvement in rhetorical and analytic skills, reflection, and metacognition as measured by increasingly complex assignments over the course of the semester and as measured by the final portfolio and portfolio reflection. Content-related benchmarks can be hard to assess, as can the development of analytic skills, but I relied on reflective essays to measure student engagement and progress toward outcomes. The assignments were also designed to measure engagement, as students could not complete the assignments while passively reflecting back material.

I also aligned this course design with programmatic guidelines, which provided further structure and scaffolding for the course. Programmatic writing guidelines fostered technology use and multimodal assignments, as discussed below with respect to course design. Students were expected to learn multiple modalities of communication, and irrespective of content, goals for the course were set both by the instructor and programmatically within the Writing and Communication Program (WCP) program to ensure consistency and standardization.

As multimodal communication is defined broadly, programmatic goals are adapted by instructors to their own courses. For example, students in a class studying zombies would watch films and read comics and novels about zombies and might subsequently produce their own artifacts in a variety of media. These artifacts could include everything from analytic essays to a podcast review to a film produced by students that provides their interpretation of the genre. The only programmatic expectation is that students complete artifacts in each one of the Written, Oral, Visual, Electronic, and Nonverbal (WOVEN) genres, instructors plan assignments that incorporate several stages of drafting and feedback, and students create a portfolio at the end of the semester showcasing their best work. Moreover, students in composition classes are required to produce 25 "pages" of polished work to be presented in this final portfolio, whether written or otherwise, which has gone through multiple stages of revision and reflection.

The portfolio is worth, at a minimum, 10% of their grade, as programmatically decided, especially as it gives the Writing and Communication program programmatic assessments as required by the state board of regents and accrediting agencies. The portfolio, however, is not just an assessment tool—it is also a reflection tool for students, giving them a chance to reflect on their development throughout the semester. In the syllabus, students were told:

> Your final project for this class will be a portfolio showcasing the drafts, iterations, revisions, and reflections on the work you have done throughout the semester. As a result, it is important for you to save all the iterations of the drafts that you do. More details forthcoming as the semester progresses.

From the get-go, this set up the expectation that the course would be cumulative and iterative and that students' learning and writing would both be processual. This type of scaffolded assignment can take some of the pressure off students to get it right the first time, so that they can focus on small components of their learning and piece together individual tasks as components of learning how to write.

In addition to these programmatic learning outcomes as outlined in table 10.1, I especially wanted students to improve in the following categories detailed in the table: rhetorical awareness and stance and support.

I felt that focusing on two categories would allow me to better assess my intervention with the videogame. In my experience as a teacher of writing in several disciplines, most students come into introductory-level college writing and composition courses in the developing category. Their rhetorical awareness—understanding of audience, making an original argument—often falls short. Regarding the second category listed in table 10.1, stance and support, students have a difficult time marshaling evidence effectively. My goal is to get them to mature in both instances, so that they are producing original, insightful arguments appropriate for their chosen audience and backed by novel evidence.

Table 10.1

Scale	1: Basic	2: Beginning	3: Developing	4: Competent	5: Mature	6: Exemplary
Rhetorical awareness: Argument considers audience, persona, message, and medium	Ignores two or more aspects of the rhetorical situation and thus does not meet the expectations of the task	Ignores at least one aspect of the rhetorical situation and thus compromises effectiveness	Attempts to be rhetorically aware, but the attempt is inappropriate or insufficient	Addresses the rhetorical situation in a predictable way	Addresses the rhetorical situation with unexpected insight	Addresses the rhetorical situation in a sophisticated, unique manner
Stance and support: Central claim is duly supported by evidence	Involves a confusing or unspecified position that is not effectively supported by evidence	States a trite, overly general position that is supported by weak evidence	Ambiguous claim lacks unity because evidence contradicts or competes	Offers a clear, unified, standard position illustrated by predictable evidence	Offers a clear, unified, distinct position illustrated by compelling evidence	Offers an inventive, well-informed position illustrated by well-chosen evidence
Organization: Clear structure logically moves from introduction to conclusion	Omits a unifying and cohesive claim, exhibits weak paragraph unity, and offers ineffective transitions	Offers ambiguous or unsupportable claims in the thesis and/or topic sentences and uses simple transitions that fail to connect ideas	Uses claims that are sometimes imprecise or poorly matched to content in ways that comprise logical development and transitions	States a unifying claim with clear supporting points, employs a recognizable organizational scheme with mechanical transitions	Asserts and sustains a claim that develops progressively, adapts typical organizational schemes to the context, and achieves substantive coherence	Asserts a sophisticated claim developed with complex, multiple perspectives that are organized to achieve maximum coherence and momentum

Table 10.1 (continued)

Scale	1: Basic	2: Beginning	3: Developing	4: Competent	5: Mature	6: Exemplary
Conventions: Competent adherence to usage standards; skillful integration and citation of sources	Involves excessive grammatical, punctuation, and other mechanical errors that disrupt the message	Involves a major pattern of grammatical and other mechanical errors	Involves some distracting grammatical, punctuation, and other mechanical errors	Adheres to usage standards, with only minor errors	Exhibits mastery of linguistic conventions	Manipulates conventions in ways that advance the argument
Design for medium: Well-chosen design features enhance audience motivation and participation	Lacks the visual features necessary for the document's genre	Involves distracting inconsistencies in features such as headings and type	Uses consistent visual features appropriate for the genre but poorly matched to content	Uses standard, recognizable design features generally suited to genre and content	Creates visual appeal with features that highlight and enhance specific content	Persuades with careful, seamless integration of design and content

Total =

259

I designed my assessments according to these goals. These assessments included a research project and presentation of their research as well as a series of low-stakes digital essays in blog format, in addition to their final portfolio showcasing their best work. I also designed the assignments as temperature tests to be taken throughout the semester so I could intervene and switch things up as needed. The blog in particular was one such assignment. Here is the description of the blog assignment provided to the students, outlining goals and learning outcomes:

Reading Response Group Blog (20% of grade/200 points)
The goal of this assignment is to practice your writing and analytical skills for a wider audience, receive feedback, and create a writing community. Once enrollment has solidified, I will be dividing you into groups of five and you will be creating Word-Press blogs. Throughout the semester you will be using this blog as a sort of collective journal. You will be asked to post reading responses, reviews, and reflections among other short assignments. These posts will be a way for you to work out your ideas as well as a point of departure for deeper reflection. While I will not be correcting these extensively or providing detailed feedback on every blog post (a total of six), I expect you to use these blogs to reflect upon readings, class discussions, and engage with the texts while following the basic rules of composition. Moreover, at the end of the semester I will be assessing your blogs for development and improvement over the course of the semester.

In the blogs, students reflected over the course of the semester on their experience of playing the game. This allowed me to take a temperature test throughout the semester on what students were learning. The answer, it seemed, was a lot. As one student remarked, "One of my favorite parts of the semester was *seeing* Italy." Other students focused on game design, and several students who were as inexperienced gamers as I was reflected not only on their experience playing the game but on becoming self-identified gamers. Several other students remarked on the collaborative nature of learning with the game—one student even mentioned how frustrated they were at not being able to get beyond a certain checkpoint in the game but how relieved they were when their classmates patiently talked them through the checkpoint. Other students noted how their "homework" (i.e., playing the game) became the envy of their friends and that they often played in tandem with their classmates.

Moreover, three-fourths of the way through the semester I asked students to complete a learning reflection essay, reflecting on what they had learned for the course:

Analysis Assignment: For this assignment, you will be asked to analyze and reflect on your experience of learning and writing about the Italian Renaissance in the three modes you have learned about it: reading, playing, and experiencing. To do so, you will take the writings you have done throughout the semester, Blog Post #1 (What I know about the Italian Renaissance), Blog Posts #2 and #3 (Playing *Assassin's Creed II* and Values of the Italian Renaissance), your character creation, the annotated bibliography, and the materials you have used in the feud simulation, to reflect on the following questions: What does it mean to learn by reading? What does it mean to learn by playing? What does it mean to learn by doing? In order to answer these questions, you will take these materials and reflect on them in the following ways in your 5-7 page research and analysis essay. In essence, you will be making an argument, using what you have written and done as evidence for your thesis, and using your experience as evidence to answer the following question: What's the best way to learn? What's the best way to learn how to write?

This reflective essay was the primary way for me to assess the effects of the blended learning intervention on course outcomes and student conceptual gains. A brief aside on research design: quantitative assessment can be inappropriate in humanities courses, particularly writing-intensive courses, as it is hard to administer multiple-choice or other questions with definitively correct answers. Therefore, qualitative data was the primary type of data collected in this class. Qualitative assessment can be more or less subjective depending on what it is measuring. The measures that were used to assess improvement in writing were not subjective because they were examining conventional usage and elements of good writing such as thesis statements, use of evidence, and grammar, for example. The measures that were used to assess deep learning, however, were more subjective because deep learning is not as strictly defined. To measure deep learning and skill transfer, I used the reflective assignments.

With these assignments designed as writing and reflective assessments, and *Assassin's Creed II* serving as the immersive lecture, classroom time would be devoted to discussion and peer review. These assessments also allowed for a more flexible learning environment. Gameplay would drive learning, as would student reflection in regular low-stakes writing assignments and student discussions on the course Piazza discussion board. This flexibility, enabled by this particular blended learning design, allowed me to clarify student questions and direct productive discussion as well as increase student engagement if I felt that students were becoming more interested in certain aspects of the content. For example, when students became especially interested in Dante's *Inferno*, I directed them to several resources including more readings for course discussion. Most importantly, these assessments were designed to assess the effectiveness of the blended learning intervention.

Student response to the course design went better than I could have hoped for or expected. Students responded incredibly favorably to the use of *Assassin's Creed II* as a text. One student succinctly said that "this class is a perfect example of how history/English classes could run in order to get people more inclined to actually learn the material" (3/1/13). Another student cogently remarked in their reflection:

In context, I have just spent twelve years reading textbooks and articles, squeezing the last bit of information therein into a paper or onto a test, and then, more often than not, throwing that knowledge away and moving on.

Over the course of the semester I realized that the class did not need to be this way. I came to enjoy the assigned reading, which was one of the few resemblances this class bore to my previous experiences.

While we did cover some of that information, the material of this class went in depth to a point I would not have thought possible. I firmly believe that this level of immersion could not have been achieved without the combination of learning styles used in the class. I have gained knowledge about the time period while practicing my writing, which, as it turns out, is much better when I have some interest in the subject (3/4/13).

This student's comment is particularly striking in that it neatly hits all of the improved measurements I was hoping to see: reflection, analysis, and cognizance of how using this text shaped their own engagement. The student acknowledged that they came to enjoy reading the "traditional" texts and found themselves more engaged in their writing assignments. Indeed, in an unprompted Piazza forum thread initiated by a student, several other students reflected on how playing the game made them more engaged in the required writing assignments for the class:

Before this class started, I actually didn't know much at all about the Italian Renaissance period. I remember struggling really hard writing the first blog post. I think what helped me the most with understanding the class material was *Assassin's Creed II*. I think the game's accuracy made me get into the game and the class material even more. (4/21/13)

When I was writing the first blog post, I had almost no knowledge of the Italian Renaissance. Though I won't say it helped much information wise, *Assassin's Creed II* did help me write the blog, because it also got me more interested in the topic. I guess being able to visualize the Renaissance era, even graphically, was enough to push me to start learning. (4/21/13)

Not only did students find themselves engaged with their writing assignments, they also found themselves more engaged with the content. As intended, another student noted that the game's historical database drew them even further into the subject matter: "If you encounter something that was placed in the game and was relevant to the history at the time, chances are the database has an entry on it. ACII [*Assassin's Creed II*] taught me a lot about the cultural aspects of the time through these entries and was actually a very informative, fun way to learn about the Italian Renaissance" (4/21/13). Another student remarked: "I found it quite interesting that the developers used real events from the lives of the historical characters to help the plot line develop and seem plausible. I think the Assassin's Creed games are a fun way to learn about historical events, even if you do not realize that you are learning" (3/1/13). Indeed, it is particularly interesting that learning using a videogame prompted reflection on learning.

This type of reflection and self-awareness of learning, called metacognition, is critical to knowledge transfer. It is a habit of mind that is also very hard to teach students. So it was heartening when students reflected on how they learned, as the student did below:

For the same reason, the examples from the assignments I completed during the semester allowed me to directly correlate my personal learning to the different modes. This made it able for me to not only analyze the different modes of learning but also reflect on how each individual assignment affected my learning and which assignment had the largest magnitude. (4/5/13)

The student in question felt that the videogame produced the most personal gains in terms of learning. Several other students shared similarly sophisticated insights into their experience of learning in the class—sophisticated in the sense that most students don't reflect on their own learning habits without scaffolding that teaches them to do so.

In composition courses, assessment is traditionally writing-based and measures improvement in areas such as sophisticated presentation of arguments, effective use of evidence, a firm grasp of conventions like those of grammar, as well as awareness of audience. Students are expected to show improvement over the course of a semester in response to instructor and peer feedback, as well as increased cognizance of process and other expert-level writing behaviors. Instructors diagnose areas for student improvement in beginning writing assignments and provide iterative feedback over the course of a semester.

Student engagement in this process and in higher-level skill transfer of expert-level writing behavior, however, can be harder to measure than things like improved thesis statements and topic sentences. Students may show evidence of increasingly polished argumentation and audience awareness but evince little cognizance of how these skills transfer to a variety of settings, like writing usability reports or user manuals, for example.

In many ways, blending this first-year composition course went far better than I could have hoped. Students responded to the course with increased enthusiasm and engagement, which resulted in better learning outcomes, overall improved writing, and growing metacognition. Interestingly, they appeared to learn more about the Italian Renaissance and to learn more deeply than students in specialized courses on the subject that I had previously taught. Indeed, their learning and engagement were similar to those of upper-level undergraduates majoring in history. They were so eager to learn more about the videogame that they willingly undertook research and analysis and even seemed to look forward to the writing assignments.

My takeaways from this informal experiment were the following. First, course design was key as was scaffolding. From the outset, I designed the course so students could see that this was not just about playing a videogame in lieu of reading a textbook. It was also about increasing their awareness of learning and of learning how to learn. Having students write a blog as a sort of reflection journal on their own learning and on their experience playing the game was key to this. Indeed, having them do this was so successful that I assigned them the reflection assignment so they could tell me more explicitly what they felt they were gaining via this course design. Blending creates metacognition in these contexts, something that deserves further investigation.

Second, humanities courses, especially writing courses, can be blended in interesting ways that increase engagement. As pointed out elsewhere, humanities courses are often flipped by their very nature. With the advent of new technologies, however, more work needs to be done on augmenting and blending these courses in more concerted ways, particularly by exploring more ways to engage students, including engaging them in discussions, working in multiple modalities, and metacognition.

Third, blending this course seemed to engage students with the historical content in ways I had not previously experienced. And it was not just students already predisposed to like the subject. It was all of the students in the class. Blending a course using a videogame or other learning modalities beyond textbooks and academic writing is a very fruitful avenue for exploring how to get students engaged in academic writing. The students enjoyed their research assignments. As Nicolas Trépanier noted in the American Historical Association's publication, *Perspectives*:

It also gave them an alternative way to engage with academic publications. A typical undergraduate history course is defined by a given body of knowledge, typically a chronological narrative that represents a scholarly consensus. Its double objective is to convey this knowledge to students while training them in a number of transferable intellectual skills along the way. When things go well, undergraduates come out of the course knowing more about the War of Spanish succession or the institution of slavery, and with improved thinking and writing abilities. In the end, however, few students truly realize the multitude of debates that have led to the creation of that body of historical knowledge. (Trépanier 2014)

Discipline experts and humanities teachers who want students to engage with history and historical scholarship should take heed.

Note

1. For research and best practices in writing instruction, see the CCCC website, http://cccc.ncte.org/cccc/resources/positions.

References

Anderson, P., Anson, C. M., Gonyea, R. M., & Paine, C. (2015). The contributions of writing to learning and development: Results from a large-scale multi-institutional study. *Research in the Teaching of English, 50*(2), 199.

Annetta, L. A., Minogue, J., Holmes, S. Y., & Cheng, M. T. (2009). Investigating the impact of video games on high school students' engagement and learning about genetics. *Computers & Education, 53*(1), 74–85.

Apperley, T., & Walsh, C. (2012). What digital games and literacy have in common: A heuristic for understanding pupils' gaming literacy. *Literacy, 46*(3), 115–122.

Burnett, R. E., Frazee, A., Hanggi, K., & Madden, A. (2014). A programmatic ecology of assessment: Using a common rubric to evaluate multimodal processes and artifacts. *Computers and Composition, 31*, 53–66.

Casner-Lotto, J., & Barrington, L. (2006). *Are they really ready to work? Employers' perspectives on the basic knowledge and applied skills of new entrants to the 21st century US workforce.* Washington, DC: Partnership for 21st Century Skills.

Chapman, A. (2016). *Digital games as history: How videogames represent the past and offer access to historical practice* (Vol. 7). New York: Routledge.

Cicchino, M. I. (2015). Using game-based learning to foster critical thinking in student discourse. *Interdisciplinary Journal of Problem-Based Learning, 9*(2), 4.

Dow, D. N. (2013). Historical veneers: Anachronism, simulation, and art history in *Assassin's Creed II*. In M. W. Kappell & A. B. Elliott (Eds.), *Playing with the past: Digital games and the simulation of history.* New York: Bloomsbury.

Eichenbaum, A., Bavelier, D., & Green, C. S. (2014). Video games: Play that can do serious good. *American Journal of Play, 7*(1), 50–72.

Gee, J. P. (2005). Learning by design: Good video games as learning machines. *E-Learning and Digital Media, 2*(1), 5–16.

Girard, C., Ecalle, J., & Magnan, A. (2013). Serious games as new educational tools: how effective are they? A meta-analysis of recent studies. *Journal of Computer Assisted Learning, 29*(3), 207–219.

Kirkley, S. E., & Kirkley, J. R. (2005). Creating next generation blended learning environments using mixed reality, video games and simulations. *TechTrends, 49*(3), 42–53.

Liu, X. M., & Murphy, D. (2017). Are they ready? Integrating workforce readiness into a four-year college IT/IS curriculum. In *SAIS 2017 Proceedings*, 8. https://aisel.aisnet.org/cgi/viewcontent.cgi?article=1007&context=sais2017.

Madden, A. (2013). *ENGL1102: The Digital Italian Renaissance.* Course taught at Georgia Institute of Technology, Atlanta, GA.

Marín, V., López, M., & Maldonado, G. (2015). Can gamification be introduced within primary classes? *Digital Education Review, 27*, 55–68.

Meyer, L. (2015). 4 Innovative ways to teach with video games: Educators from around the country share their best practices for using educational and consumer games to improve students' engagement and performance. *THE Journal: Technological Horizons in Education, 42*(5), 20.

Mitchell, A., & Savill-Smith, C. (2004). *The use of computer and video games for learning: A review of the literature.* London: Learning and Skills and Development Agency.

Schiesel, S. (2009, December 9). *Assassin's Creed II*: On the scenic trail of intrigue: Adventures in 15th-century Italy. *New York Times.* https://www.nytimes.com/2009/12/08/arts/television/08assassin.html.

Shaw, A. (2015). The tyranny of realism: Historical accuracy and politics of representation in *Assassin's Creed III. Loading...: The Journal of the Canadian Games Studies Association, 9*(14), 4–24. http://loading.gamestudies.ca.

Squire, K. (2011). *Video games and learning: Teaching and participatory culture in the digital age. Technology, education—connections: the TEC series.* New York: Teachers College Press.

Trépanier, N. (2014). The assassin's perspective: Teaching history with video games. *Perspectives on History, 52*(5).

Veugen, J. I. L. (2016). *Assassin's Creed* and transmedia storytelling. *International Journal of Gaming and Computer-Mediated Simulations (IJGCMS)*, 8(2), 1–19.

Wainwright, A. M. (2014). Teaching historical theory through video games. *History Teacher*, 47(4), 579–612.

Watson, W. R., Mong, C. J., & Harris, C. A. (2011). A case study of the in-class use of a video game for teaching high school history. *Computers & Education*, 56(2), 466–474.

Wouters, P., Van Nimwegen, C., Van Oostendorp, H., & Van Der Spek, E. D. (2013). A meta-analysis of the cognitive and motivational effects of serious games. *Journal of Educational Psychology*, 105(2), 249–265.

Young, M. F., Slota, S., Cutter, A. B., Jalette, G., Mullin, G., Lai, B., et al. (2012). Our princess is in another castle: A review of trends in serious gaming for education. *Review of Educational Research*, 82(1), 61–89.

11

BLENDED LEARNING IN A MIDLEVEL, REQUIRED COURSE WITH STUDENTS FROM TWO MAJORS

Lauren Margulieux

> **MIX taxonomy classification:** This course is blended. Students received content both through technology (an e-textbook) before coming to class and during short in-class lectures. They then spent most of the class time applying content with the instructor providing feedback, moderating discussion, and answering questions. As a result, the instructor received high efficacy ratings at the end of course evaluation.

CHAPTER OVERVIEW

This chapter describes a case study of a blended learning intervention during fall 2015 in a Research Methods course. To situate the key takeaways from this case study, the chapter starts with information about the students, assignments, course design, and physical classroom. With this context in mind, the chapter describes the greatest success and the greatest failure in the course and discusses why these aspects of the course worked or not. The chapter concludes with generalizable lessons learned and ideas for improving similar courses.

COURSE DEVELOPMENT

Research Methods, offered through the psychology department, teaches undergraduate students to conduct human-subjects research with an emphasis on experimental design and methodology. It is a midlevel course with no prerequisites. My course in particular had five main learning objectives:

1. Define research terminology
2. Complete a research project
3. Write reports that apply knowledge of methodology
4. Improve professional skills
5. Be able to identify research questions and conduct research

These learning objectives can be summarized as learn content, apply it inside and outside of the classroom, and develop general professional skills—learning objectives that are common in most courses. I decided to use a blended course design to ensure that the application-focused objectives were thoroughly fulfilled. I wanted to provide plenty of opportunities for students to receive feedback while they were applying content, based on research that suggests that receiving feedback while applying knowledge produces better learning outcomes than applying knowledge without feedback (Freeman et al., 2014; Margulieux, McCracken, and Catrambone, 2016). In Research Methods, as in many courses, if students know the content but cannot apply it, then they might as well not know the content.

The course met on Tuesday and Thursday from 1:35 to 2:55 and was worth four credit hours. The course is typically taught in this time slot with a graduate student as the instructor of record. I was a student in my final year of graduate school when I taught this course. While I taught, I was part of a community of graduate student instructors (four doctoral students and one faculty member) that was organized by the Center for Teaching and Learning, and so I had a lot of support while teaching and a group of people with whom to discuss ideas. The community observed two of my classes to give me feedback (e.g., that I needed to repeat students' questions or answers so that the entire class could hear) and met weekly to discuss our courses. The community helped me work through some in-class activities to make them more effective (or debrief what went wrong), and hearing from other instructors gave me ideas to use in my class. If you want to start blending or improve on your blend and if you have a center for teaching, I highly recommend that you ask them whether they sponsor a group that meets regularly to discuss blended learning. If not, try to find a faculty member who already blends to bounce ideas off of and to observe each other's classes.

Students

The course is required for all psychology majors, who typically take it in their second year, and computer science majors specializing in user design, who typically take it their final or penultimate semester. They can take the course as early as their second year, but some of the computer science majors admitted to me that they put off the course as long as they could and openly questioned its utility. The course is offered through the psychology department, but three-quarters of the students are computer science majors, one-quarter are psychology majors, and a few students are from other majors such as business, taking the course to complete their minor. Initial enrollment was capped at 60 students, but due to high demand from computer science students facing a graduation deadline, overloads pushed enrollment to 75 students. One student dropped the course seven weeks into the semester.

I asked students to complete a short survey during the first week of class to collect information about their major, their year in school, their interest in the course, and their prior experiences with blended learning. All except two students responded. About half the students had prior experiences with blended or flipped courses during college. Students who had prior experiences either had a neutral or slightly negative perception of these types of courses. None of them had strongly negative or strongly positive experiences.

Students' baseline interest in the course depended largely on their major. Nearly all of the students who were psychology majors indicated that they had an interest in the course topic, whereas nearly all of the students who were computer science majors indicated that they needed the course to graduate. These survey results matched my perceptions of the students' engagement.

The psychology students were generally excited and engaged with this course, likely because, as psychology majors, the value of conducting research was evident to them. The course is taught by psychology graduate students (or occasionally psychology faculty), making the instruction and assignments likely to be more relevant to the psychology students than to the computer science students. Because most of the computer science students (i.e., most of the class) indicated that they were only taking the course because it was required, we had a general discussion in class about why they thought it was required and what they wanted to get out of it. I wanted to emphasize the aspects that they would find valuable to increase their motivation (based on the expectancy-value theory; Wigfield, 1994). Many of them said that they did not know why it was required and just wanted to get a good grade with as little work as possible. A few of the students said that they thought it was required so that they could conduct usability testing on the system they developed. For that reason, I included at least one example and activity per class that was related to usability testing. Several of the computer science students, however, seemed generally disengaged with the course throughout the semester.

Class attendance was not required though it was encouraged. For each class period, about 75% of the students were present, except for days on which an assignment was due, then about 95% of the students were present. With a few exceptions, the students who missed class varied from day to day. Based on an end-of-course survey that was distributed by the institution and asked about time spent on the course, attendance, etc., most students attended at least 90% of the classes. Several students attended nearly 100% of the classes, and a few students attended less than 70%. These self-reported numbers matched my perceptions.

Assignments

Because the focus of the course was to apply content knowledge to conducting research, the assignments were mostly project- and paper-based rather than test-based. Students turned in four papers and gave two presentations throughout the course. The first paper was a research report. In this assignment, students were tasked with finding a news or entertainment article discussing a scientific study and asked to describe the methods used and results reported as well as to discuss whether the conclusions of the study were valid. Students completed two of these papers, which were each 5% of their grade and three pages long. The second type of paper was the report on their group projects. In these projects, they completed a research project including all steps from posing a research question, designing methodology, developing a data collection protocol, collecting data, and analyzing data, to writing up and presenting their results. The project included writing an APA-style paper with a literature review, methods section, results section, and discussion section. The first three sections were each turned in as drafts throughout the semester and peer reviewed during class. The group projects also required a 10-minute class presentation and participation in a poster session held in the psychology building. The drafts, peer reviews, final papers, and presentations together were worth 45% of their grades. The last type of paper was a reflection paper completed at the end of the class in lieu of a final exam. Students were asked to reflect on their learning and professional development throughout the course, and this assignment was worth 15% of their grades.

The remaining 30% of their grades was split evenly between two types of low-stakes grades. The first type was called directed paraphrasing. For each reading assignment that students had (18 total throughout the semester), they were given two to four research words to define and provide an example of. The words were typically higher-level concepts, like construct validity, which required a sentence or two to thoroughly define. Asking students to provide an example was intended to make them connect what they were learning with examples from their world. The assignments were due at 8:00 a.m. the day of class, ensuring that the students were not cramming them right before class and giving me flexibility in when to read them. The students turned in the assignments in a Google document that was shared with me. Each student having one document that they added to was considered logistically easier than separate documents on every assignment for both them and me. I decided a few weeks into the semester to ask them to add their newest responses at the top of the document so that I did not have to scroll down to the bottom.

Before each class, I would read about half of the students' responses to gauge their understanding of the concepts. Then I would provide targeted lectures, spending less time on concepts everyone understood and more time on concepts that caused confusion or were misunderstood. Reading assignments before most classes might sound like a lot of extra work for the instructor, but it replaced the time that I would normally have spent preparing lectures. In the end, it did not take me more time to do, and it provided lectures that were much more targeted for the students' knowledge.

The second type of low-stakes grade was a quiz at the end of each of the five content units. These were low-stakes because the quiz asked students to define and provide an example of words from the directed paraphrasing. Therefore, students knew exactly what the content of the quiz could include. I picked five words from the unit, and the quiz was open-ended.

Course Design and Tools

This course was blended. It was similar to a flipped course, but not exactly the same. Students were first introduced to content by reading an e-textbook (http://socialresearchmethods.net/kb/). To ensure that they had read before class, they were asked to complete the directed paraphrasing assignment for each reading. They did not receive direct feedback on these assignments though the predominant right or wrong answers were discussed in class. In class, about a third of the time was devoted to lecture and the other two-thirds was used for group activities. During group activities, the instructor and two teaching assistants were available to answer questions.

In-class activities usually encouraged students to work in groups to apply their knowledge to a research-related scenario or problem that I had created or found on the internet through Google searches or on merlot.org. Many of the activities were practice for the group project. The most common type of activity was think-pair-share in which I would pose a somewhat challenging question (e.g., what would be a suitable and ethical control group for an experiment testing the effect of studying on test performance?) and ask students to think about it by themselves, discuss it with those sitting around them, and then report back to the whole class. To gauge students' base understanding of concepts, I used Socrative, an online quizzing tool, to ask them simple questions (e.g., what type of data is height?).

To facilitate large-group discussions, I also used Google Drive to increase participation from all students. For example, the students collectively created a demographic questionnaire to include in their research projects by using Google Forms in class. By using this tool, I could monitor the activity of a large number of students at once and provide instantaneous feedback to help students apply concepts to authentic problems. Note that no more than 50 people can use the same Google document at the same time.

At least every third week, a class period included time to work on the group projects. On these days, class ended 30 minutes early or more to give students time to work on their project. I remained in the classroom during this time to answer any questions. About half of the students chose to stay in class during this time to work on their project and the other half chose to leave. I was usually constantly answering questions from groups, and most of the questions were specific to the group's project rather than more general questions about the assignment. Mostly, students wanted me to check their work and make sure that they had applied concepts correctly to their project. In addition, a full week of class was devoted to conducting experiments and collecting data. Considerable class time throughout the semester, therefore, was devoted to working on group projects. This use of class time ensured that students were not putting off their projects until the last minute and that they had plenty of opportunities to get my help.

Classroom

The classroom was a large room with theater-style seats. The room did not slope nor was the instructor on an elevated platform. The six rows of seats were placed about three feet (slightly less than a meter) apart; therefore, there was not much room between rows when the seats were folded down—barely enough for a student to squeeze past another student. This limited space also meant that there was little room for storing backpacks in the rows. Each of the 80 chairs had built-in desks that were about half the width of the chairs and about 1.5 feet (0.4 meters) deep.

The room is typically used as a lecture hall. The seating configuration made group work difficult because students could not easily get into groups of more than two or three. Furthermore, I could only easily speak with students at the front or edges of the block of chairs. Because of the room configuration, during the semester I had to change some of the tools and activities that I used for large-group activities to match the room. These changes are discussed further below.

The room had two large whiteboards covering most of two of the walls. One of the other walls had several large windows, and the last wall was immediately behind the last row of seats. The projector screen, when down, covered the middle half of the front whiteboard. The instructor's podium and assorted technology obstructed about a quarter of the front whiteboard on one side. The room had a projector, document camera, sound system, and computer, which I used during lectures or to project instructions for activities.

SURVEY DATA

Four surveys were given throughout the semester. The first, described above in the "Students" section, asked students for information about their major, year in school, interest in the course, and experience with blended learning. The last was the generic Course-Instructor-Opinion-Survey that was administered through the institution. It asks students questions about their participation in the class (how many hours per week they spent, what percentage of classes they attended, what percentage of assignments they completed), the course design (how prepared they were to take the class, how much they learned, how effective the course was), and the instructor (how clear the instructor was, how respectful the instructor was, and how effective the instructor was).

The second and third surveys were both a page long and designed by me to get feedback on how well the class was going. The second survey was given out with the first quiz, four weeks into the semester, so that most students would complete it. It was filled out by 95% of the students. It asked the following questions and, unless otherwise indicated, gave a 7-point scale that ranged from "Not at all the case" to "Completely the case." The mean score for each question is included in parentheses.

1. How long do you spend on each directed paraphrasing activity outside of class (Mode = 31–45 mins.; students selected from 0–15 mins., 16–30 mins., 31–45 mins., and more than 45 mins.)
2. The outside-of-class portion of directed paraphrasing helps me understand course content (M = 5.3)
3. The in-class directed paraphrasing discussion helps me understand course content (M = 5.5)
4. Other in-class activities help me understand course content (M = 5.3)
5. The pace of content in class is (M = 3.5; anchors were too slow and too fast)
6. Activities in class are (M = 3.5; anchors were too easy and too hard)
7. I feel that I understand the course content well (M = 5.2)
8. I like discussing course concepts in small peer groups (M = 4.8)
9. I like discussing course concepts as an entire class (M = 5.2)
10. I feel that the professor cares about my learning (M = 6.4)

I felt generally good about the results of the survey and identified some areas for improvement. I expected that the directed paraphrasing would take 30–45 minutes, so the item 1 response aligned with my expectations. I did not expect students to completely understand content through the directed paraphrasing, so a mean score of 5.3 was good for item 2. I had hoped that the in-class discussion (3) and in-class activities (4) would score higher, but I thought that they were either too slow or not difficult enough in the first several weeks of the course. This guess was backed up by a slightly low score on items 5 and 6. The small-group discussions were particularly shallow or slow-paced during this time as well, explaining the low score on item 8. I aimed to make discussions and activities less shallow to address these issues and also increase the score on item 7. Based on the score on item 9, I resolved to continue large-group discussions despite the difficulties introduced by the classroom. It was after this survey that I started using Google Drive to monitor large-group discussions and activities. I think that the high score on item 10 is a result of the blended course and working on activities during class time. Because I used students' responses from directed paraphrasing in discussions, helped them during activities, and made an effort to learn each of their names, I had more opportunities to individually connect with students and their learning.

The third survey was given out with the third quiz, eight weeks into the semester. It was completed by 97% of the students. It asked the following questions and, unless otherwise indicated, gave a 7-point scale that ranged from "Not at all the case" to "Completely the case." The mean score for each question is included in parentheses.

1. I find the professional development sections beneficial (e.g., for lay writing and group work) ($M = 5.0$)
2. Receiving peer feedback on the project components is helpful ($M = 5.2$)
3. The pace of content in class is ($M = 3.9$; anchors were too slow and too fast)
4. Activities in the class are ($M = 3.7$; anchors were too easy and too hard)
5. What percentage of lectures do you attend (Mode = >90%; students select from < 25%, 26–50%, 51–75%, 76–90%, > 90%)

For some background on item 1, the course included a couple of short (30 minutes or less) discussions or activities to improve general professional skills. For example, to help the students learn how to write for lay audiences, we compared two writings that explained why understanding someone over the telephone can be difficult. Both were written by experts in sound engineering, but one was accessible to a lay audience and the other was not. Students read both of these passages in class and then we discussed and came up with a list of things to do and things to avoid when writing for lay audiences. I wanted to know what each of the students thought about this type of activity, so I included it on the survey. Many of the students rated this item highly, but several gave it the lowest score, which might artificially bring down the average.

The score for item 2 was lower than I expected because the peer feedback that some students received was shallow (e.g., simply said "good job"). For the remaining peer evaluations, I gave at least five questions to answer about the work that they were evaluating in addition to other comments they had. Items 3 and 4 were closer to the midpoint than in the previous survey, so I think the adjustments to the discussions and activities were an improvement. Item 5 affirmed that, even though attendance at each class was only about 75% of the students, most students attended most classes.

GREATEST SUCCESS

The greatest success in this course was the directed paraphrasing assignment (described in the "Assignments" section). First, the assignment moved content delivery outside of class to free up time in class for activities. Based on the surveys, these assignments took only 30–45 minutes for most students. Second, I had a good idea of what students understood coming into class because I had seen their definitions and examples of concepts from the reading assignments. Third, having this information before class allowed me to quickly develop targeted lectures that reviewed well-understood concepts and explained less clear ones. This targeted lecture cut down on lecture time, allowing for more in-class activities. The directed paraphrasing assignment also ensured that students read before coming to class, which reduced lecture time because it was not the students' first exposure to content.

In the end-of-course survey, one student commented that

Before class each student would answer questions about the assigned reading, and then Professor Margulieux would read these answers before getting to class. This ensured that if we had questions about the readings, they would be answered, and we wouldn't even have to stress about asking questions in front of a large class.

Several students made comments like this one. From these comments, I felt like students' questions might have gone unanswered if I had used a different format. Another student described how this helped us to use class time wisely:

Before every lecture, she would read through our homework online to see which parts of the course we understand very well and for which we need assistance or further clarification. Following this, the time in lecture was used wisely. The value of this cannot be understated: no other professor I've had has done this before!

Reading through the direct paraphrasing assignment before each class might seem like it would take a lot of time for the instructor, especially with

75 students, but it was actually quite reasonable. This approach was particularly helpful because this was the first time I taught this course, and so I did not know with which concepts students would struggle. Typically, I would plan in-class activities, which took an hour or less, the day before class and then read the responses and simultaneously develop the lecture the day of class. Reading the responses and developing the lecture together took about an hour, which is about as long as it would have taken me to prepare a full lecture. Part of the reason that this took only an hour was that I sampled half of the responses to read thoroughly. The grades for directed paraphrasing were participation-based, so I only had to check whether the other half of the students completed the assignment. The other reason that this took only an hour was that using the responses as a reference allowed me to know exactly what to include in the lecture.

Using the directed paraphrasing responses to develop lectures made the lectures more like a dialogue between me and the students. I could respond directly to the students and give specific examples of correct or incorrect answers without requiring them to speak in front of a large class. Especially when many students gave similar definitions or examples, I could say something like, "Many of you gave the example [x], and that's right because ..." This dialogue made a class of 75 students much more student-centered than they tend to be. I felt that this method was validated in the feedback survey when many students gave the highest rating on the item that asked about whether I cared about their learning.

Suggestions for Future Implementations

One thing that would have likely streamlined the directed paraphrasing assignment is not requiring definitions of the concepts and requiring only examples of the concepts. The vast majority of students always defined the concepts correctly, but the examples often revealed misconceptions. For example, no students incorrectly defined the concepts "sample" and "population," but many of the examples of samples were populations and many of the examples of populations were samples. Addressing these incorrect examples, and some good or funny correct examples, made up the bulk of the lecture. The definitions did not usually need to be addressed in lecture because they were correct, and so they likely do not need to be included in the directed paraphrasing assignment.

For this assignment, reviewing answers does not have to be completed before class. The idea for this assignment came from a classroom assessment technique that would have students paraphrase concepts in class, and then the instructor would collect the responses and address misconceptions on the spot. When I tested this approach in a workshop with six participants, however, I found that reading responses and aggregating information took too long with a group of students doing nothing but waiting for feedback. If the students had something else to do while I processed the responses, though, the in-class approach could work. In-class directed paraphrasing could also be a good group activity in which the students form groups of four to six, write their responses individually, share with the group, and aggregate their responses into one response to report back to the entire class. This approach would allow for peer teaching within groups and engage all students in the course.

GREATEST FAILURE

The greatest failure in implementing blended learning was not accounting for the physical classroom space in the design of the course. Though I knew which classroom I would use while designing the course, I did not consider how the configuration of seats would affect the implementation of the activities. The course included a lot of group activities during class time, but these activities were impeded by the classroom, which had theater-style, fixed seating with little room between rows. The classroom layout made moving around the classroom difficult for students, and the students could not reasonably work with other students beyond the two students sitting on either side of them. Students could not comfortably turn around to interact with the row behind them because the chairs were placed close together and were immovable. In addition, they could not comfortably sit forward to see around the person sitting next to them because of the built-in desks on the chairs.

I intended to have many more four- to six-person group activities that required longer amounts of time and deep thought to apply concepts, but due to the classroom limitations, there were only a few throughout the semester. These activities were typically discussions that would start in small groups and then combine for a large-group discussion. Because all students were facing toward the front of the class, however, these discussions often felt more like a discussion between me and a group instead of a discussion among groups. Sometimes Google Drive was used to mediate these discussions. Then a representative from a small group could write their group's solution to a problem and get responses directly from other groups. I could monitor these discussions and emphasize important points. For this type of environment, turning people's attention toward their laptop instead of toward the front of the room seemed to facilitate interaction among students much better.

As with most technology-supported activities, though, getting everyone situated and troubleshooting took time, making it impractical to use often. Most of the time, I chose to use shorter and more frequent two- to three-person group activities that required less substantive thought. Most classes had one or two of these activities. On days when students worked in their project groups (of four to six people), many of them would gather in circles on the floor or find other rooms in the building better suited to group work.

Another big problem with the classroom layout was that I could not walk around to talk with students at the center of the classroom. Unless the students were seated in the first couple of rows or at the edges of the rows, I had a difficult time conversing with them. Therefore, if students had questions during one of the activities, they would have to ask the question in front of the entire class instead of having a more personal conversation with me. I also could not walk around to check in with groups while they were working on activities, meaning that groups had to ask for help instead of my dropping by and offering help.

For a course that relies heavily on in-class activities, the right classroom layout is imperative for a highly successful course. One reason for doing many in-class activities is to increase the personal interactions between the instructor and students, and having the wrong classroom layout can hinder interactions.

The wrong layout can also limit the types of activities that can be done in class, further reducing the benefits of a blended course.

If you will not have control over which classroom you use, think about how to support activities in the classroom you have. Online tools like Google Drive and Socrative can give each student a voice, even in a large class. Small group assignments should be achievable in any sort of classroom, but think about how you can use technology to get small groups to talk to each other. Feel free to use space outside of the seats as well. Many classrooms have a lot of space besides just the student seats, and most students are not uncomfortable sitting on the floor.

If you do have control over which classroom you use, finding a classroom that has a good layout for a blended course can be difficult. The classroom might need to be able to support a lecture-type environment with all of the students facing the same direction and having desk space in addition to an activity-based environment. If you do not plan to spend much time on lectures, though, this is not a priority. In addition, the classroom needs to support students grouping in circles to work on activities, preferably with a shared table or at least with each student having a personal desk space. The best layout I have seen is a classroom that had tables that were medium-length (~3–4 feet or 1 meter), narrow-depth (~2 feet or 0.5 meters), and movable with chairs that were not attached to the table, rolling, and had a built-in, retractable desk. The built-in desk on the chair ensured that students had desk space regardless of where in the room they were, and the tables provided shared desk space without taking up too much floor space. Because the tables were small, they were easy to move. In summary, classroom furniture that can easily be reconfigured is the best for a blended classroom.

OTHER LESSONS LEARNED

Perceptions of the Course

I felt that this course went well, despite its challenges and aspects that could have been done better. Based on the student evaluations of the course and instructor (i.e., the final survey that was administered by the institute), the students also thought that the course went well. The overall rating of the course was high, 4.7 out of 5, which is 0.5 points higher than the average rating for courses of this size (50 students or more) in the College of Sciences at Georgia Tech. This rating is particularly noteworthy because, as the coordinator of the courses in the psychology department put it:

As a Methods class, it isn't one that typically leads to high instructor evaluations; it's right down there with statistics in terms of popularity. Please don't tell my colleagues, but I have the distinct feeling it's taught by an advanced, trusted, mature graduate student and not by a faculty member for precisely that reason: Nobody wants to handle that level of disinterest on a regular basis.

In the students' written survey comments, many of them commented that they liked the applied aspects of this course the best. One student wrote:

She spent the first class period setting the students up to work together and stating how important it was that we learn from each other and be respectful of each other. By doing this on the first day of class, she showed that she cared about us as people, and she cared about what we had to say.

Another wrote:

Such a class can easily become a series of lectures and vocabulary and check all of the boxes on the syllabus—however, Prof. Margulieux made our class experience applicable and interesting while making each individual student in a class of over 60 feel valued & respected.

Many students liked that they applied each concept in short activities before integrating and applying the concepts to the long group project. The students appreciated dedicated class time for group projects. One student wrote, "She acknowledged that not all learning must be done in a lecture-hall setting, and would often leave class time open for work days and group collaboration days, allowing us to use the class time as we best saw fit." Many students also commented that they liked replacing tests with individual papers and the group project because those assignments were more similar to how they would apply their knowledge after college and gave them products to put in their portfolios or to discuss at job interviews.

Many of the negative comments about the course were not related to its blended design. For example, the most common negative comment was that students did not understand why they had to take this course and that it was not helpful for them. About 5% of the student comments said that the in-class activities were sometimes too easy or that the pace of the course was too slow. I would concur with these comments, and I also wished that the in-class activities could have been more challenging and more easily accomplished in larger groups.

Perceptions of Assignments

The application-based assignments (i.e., individual papers and group project) were particularly well suited to this course because of the course's learning objectives and in-class activities. The learning objectives focused on what students would be able to do with the knowledge they obtained in this course. For example, one learning objective was "Write reports that apply knowledge of methodology to assess the practical contributions and limitations of scientific research." This learning objective was based on how students might apply their knowledge in their future jobs and could not have been assessed well by anything other than writing a report. Moreover, the in-class activities also focused on applying knowledge. Therefore, a heavy emphasis on testing knowledge would have been incongruent with the goals of the class. Writing reports is not well suited to every course, though. To measure more knowledge-based learning objectives than application-based learning objectives, a test would likely be better than a written report.

It is important for any course to have alignment between learning objectives, daily activities, and assignments. This lesson is an important one that I learned through my instructor community hosted by our Center for Teaching and Learning. If you have a blended course, then it is likely that you are placing an emphasis on application of knowledge instead of or in addition to acquisition of knowledge. Therefore, it is important to align your assignments with the focus on application in the rest of your course.

Communication

I felt that open, two-way communication with students was a big part of what made this course successful. I started the first day by explaining to students how I designed the course and why I believed it was the best option for them (a recommendation that I received from other instructors who had blended their classes). I also explained at the beginning and throughout the semester how to be successful in the course, emphasizing that many of the strategies they use in other courses might not apply. Because students had less experience with this type of class than with more lecture-focused classes, I found that I needed to give them thorough instructions for completing activities. In particular, when students were giving feedback to each other, they needed explicit instructions about aspects of the work to assess and how to give constructive, useful feedback.

Two-way communication includes asking the students for feedback about the course. I found that explicitly asking for anonymous student feedback once or twice in the semester let me know what the students were excited about and what could be improved. After receiving feedback, I shared the results with students and told them how I planned to implement their suggestions or explained why I would not.

Outside of the class, I got a lot of advice and feedback from the instructor group that I had joined as part of the Center for Teaching and Learning. I met with them once or twice a month to share my good experiences, debrief my bad experiences, and run activity ideas past them. Each of the other instructors did the same, giving me ideas for what works well and what does not. I do wish that we had had an instructor in the group who had done several blended courses to be our mentor, but bouncing ideas around was very valuable.

I found my blended course was a great way to make sure that students could apply their knowledge to situations that they might encounter in the future. It was also a great way for students to practice job skills, such as technical writing, that will be highly valued when they enter the workforce. The course offered all of this without greatly increasing the workload of the students or instructor. My best piece of advice if you're thinking about blending your class is to make sure that your course design is aligned across the learning objectives, assignments, activities, and classroom. Write application-focused learning objectives that are assessed by application-focused assignments that are practiced with application-focused activities that are not hindered by the classroom.

References

Freeman, S., Eddy, S. L., McDonough, M., Smith, M. K., Okoroafor, N., Jordt, H., et al. (2014). Active learning increases student performance in science, engineering, and mathematics. *Proceedings of the National Academy of Sciences of the United States of America, 111*(23), 8410–8415.

Margulieux, L. E., McCracken, W. M., & Catrambone, R. (2016). Mixing face-to-face and online learning: Instructional methods that affect learning. *Educational Research Review, 19,* 104–118.

Wigfield, A. (1994). Expectancy-value theory of achievement motivation: A developmental perspective. *Educational Psychology Review, 6*(1), 49–78.

12

THE PROBLEM-SOLVING STUDIO: AN APPROACH FOR STRUCTURING FACE-TO-FACE LEARNING ACTIVITIES IN THE FLIPPED CLASSROOM

Joseph M. Le Doux

This chapter describes a blended course redesign for beginning biomedical engineering students. A midsized course based on the pedagogy of problem-based learning, its purpose is to teach students how to think like an engineer. In a flipped course, according to the MIX taxonomy outlined in the introduction, students receive content before class, then work on group activities in class. The instructor and teaching assistants provide just-in-time information derived from student questions that helps students build nuanced knowledge. All of the just-in-time mini-lectures are driven by students' interests and questions, providing feedback during application of content rather than delivery of content.

INTRODUCTION

Higher education is undergoing substantial changes in how individual instructors and whole institutions structure students' learning experiences, due in part to advances in internet and information communication technologies. Blended learning is one such change. In blended learning, students engage in learning activities both online and in a physical classroom (Horn and Staker,

2015). One approach to blending learning is the flipped classroom. Students rotate between instructor-guided learning activities that take place face to face in a classroom and online delivery of content that students engage with individually at a pace, place, and time they control (Horn and Staker, 2015). The flipped classroom, by delivering basic instruction and content online, frees instructors to create more innovative, cognitively demanding in-class learning experiences for their students. Unfortunately, although there is a growing body of literature that explores the use of the flipped classroom in higher education, most of it focuses on repackaging the content for delivery online and on students' experiences, perspectives, and outcomes (Torrisi-Steele and Drew, 2013). Few publications provide practical guidance for how to create and implement effective in-class learning activities in a flipped classroom (Brown, 2016).

The purpose of this chapter is to help fill this gap by providing a detailed description of three learning activities that introduce students to two important cognitive tools engineers use to solve problems: diagramming and estimation. These learning activities were developed for use in the *Problem-Solving Studio* (PSS). The PSS is an innovative learning environment we initially developed to help entry-level biomedical engineering students develop robust analytic problem-solving skills.

PSS is a powerful learning environment because it is structured to ensure that students are interacting with each other, building on each other's ideas. Learning is maximized when students are interacting in this way (Chi and Wylie, 2014). PSS can be used to teach any subject in which students can benefit from working collaboratively. PSS is particularly effective when it is used in conjunction with digital learning technologies such as online instructional videos that students watch prior to, or after, class.

PSS is an example of the *cognitive apprenticeship model* of teaching and learning that is well suited for use in active learning (Brown, Collins, and Newman, 1989; Le Doux and Waller, 2016). The cognitive apprenticeship model recognizes that learning is situated—that is, knowledge production is inextricably linked to the activities and situations that produce it, and knowing and doing cannot be separated (Brown et al., 1989). According to Brown et al., "Cognitive apprenticeship methods try to enculturate students into authentic practices through activity and social interaction in a way similar to that evident in craft apprenticeship," except that the emphasis is on the development of cognitive, rather than physical, skills (Brown et al., 1989, p. 37). PSS provides concrete guidance for instructors who wish to use a cognitive apprenticeship model, or who want to flip a single lesson, a module, or an entire course.

In PSS, students engage in the authentic problem-solving practices used by professional engineers (Le Doux and Waller, 2016). First and foremost, PSS activities are *process-focused*, not product-focused. Students receive feedback and are primarily assessed on the soundness of their problem-solving approaches, with little emphasis placed on evaluating their final solution. Critically, the problems students work on are sufficiently complex and ill-structured that a team of two can typically solve only one or two problems in a two-hour class period (Jonassen and Hung, 2008). Second, the PSS learning environment is highly collaborative and public. Students work in teams of two (usually on the other side of a table from another team) on a shared large pad of paper, which makes their work visible to their peers and instructors. Externalizing their thinking processes in this way reveals their otherwise tacit cognitive and metacognitive thinking processes and promotes critical dialogue among the students and between the students and instructor. In short, PSS makes students' thinking visible. The fact that students' thinking is visible makes it possible for instructors to evaluate their students' learning and to make adjustments, as needed, to ensure each student is meaningfully engaged in the problem-solving process. One approach instructors can use to make adjustments during class is called *just-in-time teaching*. In just-in-time teaching instructors give minilectures or lead whole-class discussions that are tailored to meet the students' current needs, rather than giving scheduled long-form lectures on predetermined topics. In a flipped classroom, instructors may also choose to post short minilectures online before class for students to review at their own pace. Another approach instructors can use to make adjustments during class is called *dynamic scaffolding*. In dynamic scaffolding, instructors modify in real time the support they provide, as well as the difficulty level of the problems, to help ensure each student is challenged at a level that is beyond what they could accomplish on their own, but at the upper end of what they can accomplish in the PSS setting. These modifications can be made for a single team, for multiple teams, or for the entire class.

The PSS learning environment was originally developed in a course titled Conservation Principles of Biomedical Engineering. It is one of the first required engineering courses biomedical engineering students take at Georgia Tech. The class meets two times a week for two hours each, in the PSS learning environment. It is a four-credit-hour course. The primary objective of the course is to introduce students to one of the most powerful approaches engineers use to help them deal with complex real-world systems: model-based reasoning. We have found that students struggle with two key steps of the modeling process: generating diagrams and making estimates. We therefore introduce and emphasize the importance of these two skills right away, in the first two PSS sessions of the course. The first day we meet with the students, we employ the "Rotten Tomatoes for Diagrams" learning activity, which introduces them to the idea that diagrams are used by engineers as tools for thinking and solving problems. During the next PSS session, we carry out the "Destination Estimation" learning activity, which introduces students to the importance of estimation and the idea that estimation is a skill that can be learned. Later in the semester we use the "Diagram Swap" learning activity to provide students with powerful feedback on the current state of their diagramming skills.

Below, I describe in detail these three learning activities. These descriptions are intended to serve as detailed examples of the kinds of exercises that work well in the PSS learning environment, so that they can serve as useful templates to help instructors create new activities that target their course's most challenging learning outcomes. Each exercise leverages the features of the PSS learning environment by requiring students to work interactively to diagram, estimate, problem-solve, and reflect while being apprenticed by their instructor.

Each learning activity is described in significant detail so that even teachers who are new to using the PSS or flipped-classroom approach can follow the step-by-step procedures with confidence. These step-by-step instructions are intended to serve as helpful guides and are not intended to be used as rigid procedures that must be precisely followed at all times. We fully expect and hope that instructors will experiment with them and fine-tune them to suit their learning objectives, teaching style, and classroom's culture. The reader is encouraged to focus his or her attention on any one of these; they are independent and need not be read in any particular order. Learning activity 1 teaches students the usefulness of diagrams and sketches for solving problems. Learning activity 2 introduces students to techniques for making good estimates. Learning activity 3 teaches students how difficult it can be to work collaboratively with others while at the same time increasing their awareness, in a memorable way, of what the critical features of diagrams are.

LEARNING ACTIVITY 1: ROTTEN TOMATOES FOR DIAGRAMS

Overview

The instructor provides students with several diagrams of a complex process (examples in the sections that follow), as well as a verbal description of that process. The description should provide some context for the purpose of the diagrams, such as the problem they will help solve. Even though the diagrams describe the same process and share the same purpose, they should all differ. To what extent they differ from each other, and how they differ, depend on the instructor's goals. Students analyze the diagrams to identify characteristics they have in common and how they differ. Next, they rank the diagrams from best to worst, after which they make a case for why they ranked them the way they did. The instructor facilitates a whole-class discussion to help the class understand how similar diagrams can differ in meaningful ways and to help them determine how to assess the quality of an engineering diagram as a tool for thinking.

Purpose

This exercise encourages students to think deeply about what constitutes an effective diagram, helps then identify which aspects of diagrams make them powerful thinking and problem-solving tools, and alerts them to the fact that diagrams of the same process can differ significantly from each other, either because they were constructed for different purposes or because some were constructed more skillfully than others.

Step-by-Step Directions

1. Consider your learning objectives for the course. Identify which aspects of the generation or use of diagrams are important for your students to learn, are particularly difficult to master, or tend to be underappreciated by students.

2. Create (or acquire) several diagrams that depict the same object, system, or process but vary in the aspects that you want to call your students' attention to. Ideally, there will be no clearcut best or worst diagram. This will promote controversy and a vibrant discussion in which students share differing opinions about which diagrams are better or worse than others and why. You can create the diagrams yourself, or you may be able to locate examples created by others (prior students, professionals, colleagues, etc.).

3. Create a packet, one for each student, that includes the backstory of the diagrams, the diagrams themselves, and directions for what to do with them. Print each diagram on its own sheet of paper. Give each diagram a name or label. Consider labeling each diagram with the name of a color, since it is best to avoid numbering or lettering them (to avoid confusion between the diagrams' identification and its quality ranking). Consider asking two students to share one set of diagrams to save paper (since they will be working in teams of two for most of the exercise).

4. Instruct the students to silently read the backstory. The story should describe a realistic scenario for why the diagrams were created. The students must know the purpose of the diagrams in order to have a basis for ranking them.

5. The case write-up should instruct the students to work alone, initially, to examine the diagrams and rank them from best to worst according to their effectiveness in achieving their stated purpose. The packet should include a table for the students to record their rankings.

6. After a few minutes, ask students to pair up with another student. Students should compare their rankings. If there are differences, they should explain to each other the basis for their rankings and negotiate a team ranking that they

both agree with. Encourage them to take notes on their discussion, especially noting points of contention and how (or if) they were resolved. The handout should include a table for the students to record their team rankings, as well as a place to record their discussion notes.

7. Finally, ask the student teams to concisely summarize the criteria by which they ranked the diagrams. Ideally, their criteria would be sufficiently clear that another person or team could apply them to the diagrams and end up with the same rankings as the authors of the criteria.

8. After student teams have established mutually agreed-on rankings and ranking criteria, lead a whole-class discussion. Start by listing the names of the diagrams on the classroom's whiteboard. Go through each diagram one by one, asking students to raise their hands if they ranked that diagram as the best or the worst diagram of the lot. Record the results of the voting on the whiteboard. Often, the best discussions happen when one or more of the diagrams are ranked as the best by some students and as the worst by others.

9. Use the results of the voting to focus a classwide discussion whose goal is to develop a rubric to evaluate diagram quality. For example, suppose four students ranked a diagram (let's call it "diagram blue") as the best, and six students ranked diagram blue as the worst. Ask two or more of the students who ranked the diagram as the best to provide one reason, one criterion, for why they ranked it that way. Record their answers on the whiteboard. Next, ask two or more of the students who ranked diagram blue as the worst to provide one reason, one criterion, for why they ranked it that way. Repeat with other controversial diagrams. Lump similar criteria together as you proceed. Continue until several independent criteria have been identified.

10. Next, ask the students to return to their teams of two to work together to organize the criteria into a smaller number of "metacategories." Try to limit the number of metacategories to a very small number, say three or four. Challenge them to establish metacategories that are orthogonal or independent of each other.

11. After a few minutes, ask some of the groups to share their metacategories and work as an entire class to establish a small set of metacategories by which the quality of diagrams can be assessed.

12. Conclude the discussion by sharing with the students what your metacategories are for evaluating and grading diagrams. Compare and contrast your categories with those developed by the class. Often, students miss one or more features of diagrams that the instructor considers critically important.

EXAMPLE LEARNING ACTIVITY 1

The Backstory

You've come up with a brilliant idea for a start-up business that you call the "Wash and Walk Company." Similar to car wash companies such as the Cactus Car Wash, which offer customers full-service car washing, your idea is to provide customers with a full-service, real-time clothes washing service. Unlike how you wash clothes at home, your company must develop an industrial clothes washing process that is operated continuously (at steady state) by moving clothes through multiple machines, each of which performs one specific function. To keep the price you charge for this amazing service low, you need to determine how to run the process in a way that washes and dries clothes in the most economical manner possible.

Your initial design of the process works as follows: dirty clothes are introduced to the first unit of the system, where they are washed with water and soap to remove all the dirt from the clothes. Next, the clean clothes are rinsed with water to remove all the excess soap, after which they are spun (centrifuged) to remove most of the water from the clothes. The wet but clean clothes are then transferred to a dryer, which exposes the clothes to hot air. (Note: The hot air is generated by a preheater, which takes air from outside the building and heats it up.) Two streams exit the dryer—dry clothes and hot humid air.

The enigmatic multibillionaire Sir Yugo Next has decided to invest in your company. Using the funds he has provided, you hire an engineer, Ms. Sparkle, to begin evaluating the process. Sparkle focuses her initial analysis on the dryer and preheater units. Sparkle's initial design produces 100 pounds per hour of clean dry clothes. Twenty percent of the weight of the wet clothes that enter the dryer is water. The air that enters the preheater is at 70°F and has a dewpoint of 50°F. The preheater uses 2 kW of power to operate and the dryer has a volume of 400 ft³. Air exits the preheater (and enters the dryer) at 200°F, and exits the dryer at 180°F. The entire process operates at 1 atmosphere of pressure (i.e., 14.7 psia).

Sparkle is a newbie engineer and isn't quite sure how to begin, so she produces several diagrams of this part of the process and asks your advice on which diagram she should use to continue her analysis.

THE RANKING INSTRUCTIONS AND TABLE

Team Ranking Sheet

Working with the person next to you, discuss your individual rankings and create a team ranking, from best to worst, according to their effectiveness in continuing your analysis. Feel free to make notes to help you. Aim for being able to say, "Although I might have ranked them differently working alone, I can support this team ranking."

Also, answer the following questions:

1. Consider the diagram you ranked as #1 (the best). Why did you rank it #1?
2. Consider the diagram you ranked as #6 (the worst). Why did you rank it #6?
3. Please describe your ranking criteria as well as you can.

An Example of the Criteria That Might Be Developed or Discussed

For this example, the diagrams are similar to process flowsheets that chemical engineers use. Chemical engineering process flowsheets track the flow of

Table 12.1

Rank	Diagram(s) names	Notes
1 (best)		
Above average		
Below average		
6 (worst)		

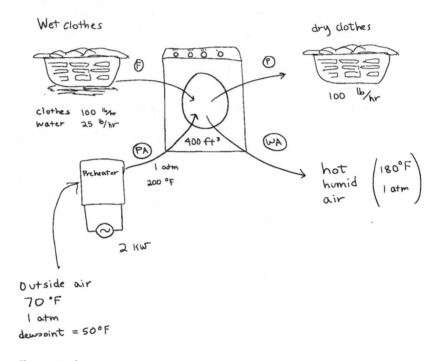

Figure 12.1a, b

This figure shows two of the seven diagrams we use to run this exercise. The diagrams contain the same information, but they differ in two ways in how that information is displayed: (1) in the diagram on the left (L), objects are sketched; in the diagram on the right (R), objects are depicted as icons, and (2) in L, quantitative information appears next to the relevant area of the process; in R, quantitative information is separated from the process, in a table.

material and energy into and out of systems. By the culmination of this exercise, we introduce our students to the idea that there are three major characteristics that good diagrams have whose importance is related in a hierarchical manner. Most important is that the diagram does not violate the conservation principles of mass and energy. Next most important is that the diagram correctly reflects the structure or topology of the real system it is describing. Least important, but still desirable, is that the diagram is computationally efficient—

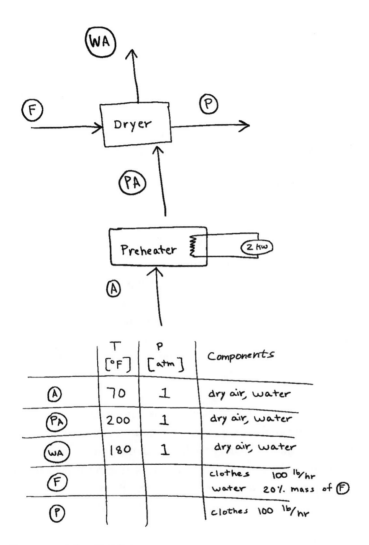

Figure 12.1a, b (continued).

that is, that all relevant data, and no irrelevant data, are included and located on the diagram near the part of the system it describes.

Alternative Approaches

1. Instead of giving examples of diagrams that vary in quality (i.e., in their usefulness as thinking tools), give students examples of outstanding diagrams that differ because they were made for different purposes (e.g., consider comparing a circuit diagram, a free-body diagram, and a process flowsheet of the same system or process). This emphasizes to the students that what a diagram looks like is strongly connected to its purpose. This is similar to the age-old credo that one must "use the right tool for the job."

2. Consider extending the transition from teams of two to the whole-class discussion that occurs between steps 7 and 8. To do this, after step 7 is completed, have student teams split up and walk around the room to talk to others about their rankings. When they find a team with rankings similar to theirs, they can form a four-member team to work together to refine their ranking criteria. Alternatively, ask students to join with a team who ranked their diagrams differently. In this case, each two-member team should present their approach to the other team. Each team can comment on or question the other about their approach, which may lead the teams to refine or revise their ranking criteria.

3. Instead of giving students examples of engineering diagrams, give them exemplars of a different kind of assignment or product that it is important for your students to learn how to produce by the end of the course. For example, you might ask them to compare experimental designs, research papers, project reports, physical prototypes, or videos of oral presentations, just to name a few.

SUGGESTIONS FOR BLENDING AND OTHER INFORMATION

For students to master the ability to generate high-quality diagrams that are useful as thinking tools, it is important that they clearly understand the criteria by which their diagrams are being assessed and graded. Therefore, by the end of this exercise it is a good idea to establish a final assessment rubric that everyone in the class agrees to use for the remainder of the course. Then, as an after-class assignment, ask your students to rerank the diagrams based on the finalized set of grading criteria just developed.

Alternatively, or in addition, ask them to find one or more real-world diagrams online. Ask them to post an image of the diagram to the course website, along with their critique of it using the rubric developed in class. In addition, ask them to critique the rubric itself—did it work well for this real-world diagram? If not, make recommendations for how to modify the rubric. What aspects of the real-world diagram did they notice that were similar to, or different from, the diagrams they worked with in class? What symbols or icons did they see in the real-world diagram that they were curious about? Ask them to search the web or other sources to identify what they mean or what the origin and purpose of the symbols are. Do they relate to the subject matter of the course, or to the diagrams that we will be creating?

Additional resources: For additional information, see Ferguson (1992), Larkin and Simon (1987), and Schwartz and Bransford (1998).

EXAMPLE LEARNING ACTIVITY 2: DESTINATION ESTIMATION

Overview

This activity teaches the students about estimation. The instructor provides students with an artifact whose properties are to be estimated. The artifact can be a physical object, picture, or diagram. Students carefully observe the artifact and identify its characteristics or physical properties that can be estimated. Alternatively, they are told what physical properties to estimate. Next, they make their estimates and then rank them in order of their level of confidence in them. Students then partner with another student, share the processes they used to make their estimates and their level of confidence in them, and then negotiate with each other to create a new estimate they both agree on. The instructor then facilitates a whole-class discussion to help students see the extent to which their estimates differ, to realize that some quantities are much harder to estimate than others, to share the different approaches they used, and to develop a set of best practices for making good estimates.

Purpose

The purpose of this exercise is to introduce students to the idea that estimation is a legitimate professional practice of working engineers, that estimates are not guesses, and that estimation is a skill that can be practiced and learned. Estimation is part of a broader skill set that supports an individual's engineering judgment. Engineers that have good judgment are esteemed by their colleagues. Many authors have noted the importance of engineering judgment, but perhaps none as eloquently as Henry Petroski, who said:

The first and most indispensable design tool is judgment. It is engineering and design judgment that not only gets projects started in the right direction but also keeps a critical eye on their progress and execution. Engineering judgment, by whatever name it may be called, is what from the very beginning of a conceptual design identifies the key elements that go to make up an analytical or experimental model for exploration and development. It is judgment that separates the significant from the insignificant details, and it is judgment that catches analysis from going astray. (Petroski, 1985, p. 189)

Engineering judgment is required to engage in model-based reasoning, since to create a diagrammatic representation of a complex process, the engineer must identify which aspects of the real-world process are significant and which are not. This requires judgment and strong estimation skills. Because of this, we frequently precede this learning activity with the "Rotten Tomatoes of Diagrams" exercise.

Step-by-Step Directions

1. Consider the learning objectives for the course and identify the properties or quantities that are important for your students to be able to estimate.

2. Create or find a picture or diagram that represents a process or object that has one or more of these properties. It is a good strategy, when students are new to making estimates, to depict an object or process they are somewhat

familiar with. This enables students to anchor their initial estimates in their own personal experiences.

3. Create a problem statement that includes a backstory explaining why the estimates are needed as well as the picture or diagram itself.

4. Form small groups of students. Groups of two are ideal, with students seated at tables of four students each. Students on the same team should sit side by side.

5. Give each student the problem statement. Instruct them to silently read the problem statement and to make the requested estimates on their own.

6. After a few minutes, ask the students to share their estimates with their partner. Ask them to come up with a new estimate that they are both comfortable with.

7. Hold a whole-class discussion. First, call on a few random groups to write down their estimates—what they were when they did it alone and then as a team. Write these on the whiteboard. Ask students what they observe about these estimates. This should elicit some discussion about the variability (or similarity) of the answers. Often, students will give estimated values without units and with more than one significant figure. This is a good time to discuss best practices such as *Never give a number without its units* and *When making an estimate, report your estimate with just one significant figure*. Also, if more than one quantity was estimated, ask students to share the relative level of difficulty they had in making these estimates. Students' estimates will generally vary more (have a higher standard deviation) for quantities that are perceived as being harder to estimate.

8. End the whole-class discussion by asking students to discuss with their partner how they arrived at their estimates. Encourage them to keep pushing each other until they can explain what they did to the best of their ability. Challenge them not to simply say that they pulled a number out of thin air.

9. After a few minutes, hold another whole-class discussion. Ask several groups to share at least one strategy they used to make their estimates. If more than one quantity was estimated, ask them to also think about why some quantities were so much harder to estimate than others. Write the students' observations on the whiteboard. Group the observations into categories.

10. Use the discussion to identify some of the key features, best practices, and lessons learned with respect to the art of making estimates. Key points to make include that there are well-established heuristics that experienced people use to make estimates. These include (a) anchoring their initial estimate to a quantity they have high confidence in or that they can relate, through one or more steps, to the quantity they are trying to estimate; (b) breaking something that is hard to estimate off the top of their head into a set of subquantities for which they can give a reasonable estimate based on their prior experience or knowledge; (c) estimating a quantity by taking the geometric mean of its upper and lower bounds; (d) using scaling to move from a quantity they are confident in to a quantity they are less confident in; and (e) working in the unit system they are most comfortable with. These and other techniques are discussed in various papers and books, some of which are cited in the "Additional Resources" section below.

11. In addition to discussing estimation techniques, it is also valuable to discuss why estimation is important and its role in the engineering problem-solving process, or other related concepts such as what the difference is between an assumption and an estimate, what the term *order of magnitude* means, how to calculate a geometric mean, the meaning of *significant figures*, the meanings of precision, accuracy, and trueness, and how to determine if a solution is "reasonable" or not.

Example Handout for This Exercise

Please take 20 minutes to complete the following problem on your own:

Consider an industrial process for washing and drying clothes. Unlike how you wash clothes at home, the industrial process is operated continuously (at steady state) by moving clothes through multiple machines, each of which performs one specific function. You wish to determine how to run the process in a way that washes and dries clothes in the most economical manner possible. Your goal is to produce 100 lb/hour of dry, clean clothes.

The process works as follows: dirty clothes are introduced to the first unit of the system, where they are washed with water and soap to remove all the dirt from the clothes. Next, the clean clothes are rinsed with water to remove all the excess soap, after which they are spun (centrifuged) to remove most of the water from the

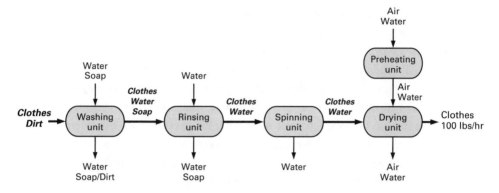

Figure 12.2

A diagram to be included with the handout

clothes. The wet but clean clothes are then transferred to a dryer, which exposes the clothes to hot air. (Note: The hot air is generated by a preheater, which takes air from outside the building and heats it up.) Two streams exit the dryer—dry clothes and hot humid air.

Briefly, roughly estimate the mass of each component (i.e., mass of clothes, dirt, soap, water, air) in (1) the two streams entering the washing unit and in (2) the two streams entering the drying unit."

Alternative Approaches

1. Ask students to help determine the scenario or backstory. This can be done as part of the first class on estimation, or as an extension to this activity. In the latter case, challenge students, before the next class, to notice systems and processes in the real world. Ask them to sketch them out and estimate one or more quantities associated with or passing through the system.

2. Practice short estimation problems, emphasizing the specific heuristics that can be used to make an estimate. Excellent resources for example estimation problems and/or heuristics for carrying out estimates are listed below in the "Additional Resources" section.

Suggestions for Blending and Other Information

Give the students a follow-up assignment to complete after class that builds on what they learned, or that connects what they learned with other aspects of the course. To build on what they learn, ask them to read a paper or book chapter on estimation or watch a video in which you model for them the estimation process. You might assign a video for them to watch of an object or process you want them to make estimates of or ask them to create such a problem for themselves or their peers. For example, I once showed a clip from *Spiderman 2* (2004) of Spiderman stopping a train (https://youtu.be/GYOYewO_Veg). I asked the students to estimate the power required, and the work done by Spiderman, to stop the train. To connect what they learned to other aspects of the course, ask them to create a diagram of a process without giving them a lot of quantitative information about the process. This will require them to make estimates as they generate the diagram, further solidifying their understanding of the connection between estimation and engineering model–based reasoning and problem solving.

Additional resources: For additional information, see Mahajan (2014), Petroski (1985), Weinstein and Adam (2008), and Weinstein (2012).

EXAMPLE LEARNING ACTIVITY 3: DIAGRAM SWAP

Overview

In diagram swap, a group of students receives a problem statement that includes a verbal description of a system. The group creates a diagrammatic representation of the system that is described in their problem statement. In parallel, other groups of students are doing the same thing, but with different problem statements. Next, the student groups swap diagrams and then attempt to solve the problem statement using only the diagrammatic representation provided to them. This brings into sharp relief the diagrams' weaknesses and deficiencies. In addition to trying to solve the problem, each group analyzes and evaluates the quality of the diagram they were given and provides feedback to its creators.

Purpose

The primary purpose of this exercise is to alert students to the most critical features of useful diagrams. This is accomplished by engaging students in three activities: diagram generation, problem solving, and diagram evaluation. The purpose of the first activity is to provide students with an opportunity to practice and learn together how to create a diagrammatic representation of a system. Often, students think they understand how to do this well and do not attend to critical features of diagrams that help make them powerful problem-solving tools. The purpose of the second activity is to provide students with the opportunity to practice solving problems using only a diagrammatic representation of the system of interest. The purpose of the third activity is to help students discern which features of diagrams are most important for helping them serve as useful tools for problem solving, and to provide them with practice in articulating these to another person or team.

Step-by-Step Directions

1. Create two (or more) unique problems that are similar in terms of their complexity and the topics and skills they require. Give a unique name to each problem that the students will easily remember and enjoy (e.g., Problem Voldemort and Problem Harry Potter, terms that will be used in the example that follows). The problems should describe a system or process that is too complex to comprehend without the aid of a diagram. At the end of the problem statement, ask the students to create a diagram that faithfully represents the system or process. Do not ask them to solve anything about the system. Do not include any other instructions on the written problem statement.

2. Form small groups of students. Groups of two are ideal. Having groups with more than two students raises the likelihood that some students will not fully engage with the exercise. Ideally, student groups should sit at separate tables. For example, a class of 48 students might have twelve tables of four students (i.e., each table has two teams of two students).

3. Distribute the problem statements to each group. Each team at a table should get the same problem statement. Do not let students know that some groups are solving a different problem.

4. Instruct the teams to read and complete the problem statement, which includes generating a diagrammatic representation of the system described. Give them a challenging time limit for completing the diagram to keep them focused. Monitor their progress and allow them extra time if needed. Make sure they are satisfied with their diagram before proceeding to the next step. Ideally, the students have large sheets of paper to work on so that they feel free to create a large, easy-to-read diagram.

5. Once the teams are satisfied with their diagram, call "time." Have the students write their names on their diagram.

6. Reveal to the class that they were working on two (or more) different problems. Ask the students to swap their diagram with another team that was working on a different problem. This can be done relatively easily by first having students working on Problem Voldemort raise their hands, followed by students working on Problem Harry Potter, and then having them swap their diagrams with each other.

7. Explain to the students that they now are going to be asked to solve one or more problems associated with the system diagram they just received. Explain that they will not receive the verbal description of the system that the diagram is based on.

8. Distribute to each table the question that they are tasked with answering about their system. The question should say something like, "Use the diagram of the process Harry Potter, drawn by another student team, to answer the following question ..." The question should be challenging to answer even if the diagram they are working with is an excellent representation of the system.

9. Give the students time to fully engage with the task of trying to answer the question they have been asked using the diagram they have been given. They may realize, in just a few minutes, that they cannot answer the question due to deficiencies in the diagram.

10. Carry out a brief, whole-class discussion about what is going on—that many of the diagrams are not of high enough quality to enable them to answer the question. Instruct the students to write a note of feedback to the authors of the diagram. This note should include both positive and negative construc-

tive feedback about the diagram. What about the diagram did they appreciate? What about the diagram needed improvement in order for them to be able to solve the problem they were asked to solve? What information was missing that they needed?

11. Carry out a whole-class discussion about what was learned. Ask groups to summarize what they found was missing or inadequate about the diagrams they were provided with. List and categorize the responses on the whiteboard. Solicit recommendations from the students about how they could improve their diagrams in the future.

12. Conclude the day by having the teams return the diagrams to their owners, along with their feedback and the question that they were supposed to answer. Ask the students to revise their diagrams based on their peers' feedback, and to answer the question that was asked about their system.

Example Problems

Problem #1: Process Harry Potter

Description of the Harry Potter Process

Oilseed is a crop grown mainly to produce vegetable oil and protein. Examples include soybean, cottonseed, and flax. Solvent extraction is used to isolate the oil from the seed proteins. Consider a process that obtains oil and protein from flax. Raw flax is composed of 39% oil, 22% protein, 32% fiber, and 7% hull. First, the raw seeds are processed to remove the hulls and fiber from the rest of the seed components, yielding clean seeds that are composed of only oil and protein. The clean seeds are sent to an extractor where they are incubated with solvent. Two flow streams provide solvent to the extractor: a "solvent makeup" stream and a stream of pure solvent that exits a separator (described below). About 1.8 pounds of solvent must be used per pound of clean seeds processed. Two streams exit the extractor: an oil-rich solvent stream and an oil-free protein stream that is 0.6% solvent. The oil-rich solvent stream is sent to a separator that generates a stream of pure oil and a stream of pure solvent. The pure solvent stream exiting the separator is fed back to the extractor.

Work with your teammate to draw a community-sanctioned diagram of the Harry Potter process described above.

DO NOT SOLVE for anything—simply work to create a diagram that faithfully represents the process.

Harry Potter problem statement (give to a team that drew the Voldemort process)

Use the diagram of the Harry Potter Process, drawn by another team, to answer the following question:

If 100 pounds of raw seeds are processed per hour, what are the flow rates of (1) the pure oil stream, (2) the oil-free protein stream produced, and (3) the pure solvent stream that is fed back to the extractor?

Problem #2: Process Voldemort

Description of the Voldemort Process

Instant coffee is made as follows: 11 lb/hr of roasted ground coffee (modeled as being composed of "solubles" and "insolubles") and 14 lb/hr of water are fed to a percolator. Two streams exit the percolator: coffee extract, which is 30.0% solubles and water, and a waste stream composed of water, solubles, and insolubles. The ratio of solubles to water in each of these streams is the same. The extract is sent to a dryer to remove almost all of the water from the solubles. The dried solubles are the desired product, instant coffee. The waste stream is partially dewatered prior to sending it to a landfill. A press and a dryer are used, in series, to remove water from the waste stream. The waste stream, which is 24% insolubles, enters a press, which "squeezes" out a lot of the water. The waste that exits the press contains 55% insolubles. It is sent to a dryer, which removes even more water. The waste that exits the dryer, which contains 72% insolubles, is sent to the landfill.

Work with your teammate to draw a community-sanctioned diagram of the Voldemort process describe above.

DO NOT SOLVE for anything—simply work to create a diagram that faithfully represents the process.

Voldemort problem statement (give to a team that drew the Harry Potter process)

Use the diagram of the Voldemort Process, drawn by another team, to answer the following question:

Calculate the fraction of solubles lost in the waste stream.

Alternative Approaches

A variation of this exercise is to give student teams a chance to revise and improve their diagrams in class, based on their peers' feedback, after step 10. Once they believe they have a good diagram, they can return it to the team that was trying to use it to answer a question. The team can now attempt once again to answer the question using the revised diagram. If they are still unable to do so, provide the team with the original verbal description of the system and ask them to prepare a second feedback report for the team that generated the diagram.

Suggestions for Blending and Other Information

It is a good idea to ask students to reflect on this activity and post it online, on a classroom blog or in a discussion forum, for example. Student reflections can help solidify the learning experience in their minds; it can also give the instructor insights into the impact of the exercise and may stimulate ideas for improvement. As an example, ask students to answer the following questions on their course blog: What did you learn? How do you know you learned it? What got in the way of your learning? What helped your learning? and How did you feel? In addition, ask them to post a comment on at least two of their peers' posts. Set a deadline for these activities to take place, such as before the next time the class meets face to face.

Additional resources: For additional information, see Boyd and Fales (1983), Davis (2008), Dunning (2011), and Palincsar (1998).

References

Boyd, E. M., & Fales, A. W. (1983). Reflective learning: Key to learning from experience. *Journal of Humanistic Psychology, 23*(2), 99–117.

Brown, J. S., Collins, A., & Duguid, P. (1989). Situated cognition and the culture of learning. *Educational Researcher, 18*(1), 32–42.

Brown, M. G. (2016). Blended instructional practice: A review of the empirical literature on instructors' adoption and use of online tools in face-to-face teaching. *Internet and Higher Education, 31,* 1–10.

Chi, M. T. H., & Wylie, R. (2014). The ICAP Framework: Linking cognitive engagement to active learning outcomes. *Educational Psychologist, 49*(4), 219–243.

Collins, A., Brown, J. S., & Newman, S. E. (1989). Cognitive apprenticeship teaching and the crafts of reading, writing, and mathematics. In L. B. Resnick (Ed.), *Knowing, learning, and instruction.* Hillsdale, NJ: Lawrence Erlbaum Associates.

Davis, A. (2008). "Reflecting on their learning." Edublog Insights. http://anne.teachesme.com/2008/10/16/reflecting-on-their-learning/.

Dunning, D. (2011). The Dunning-Kruger effect: On being ignorant of one's own ignorance. *Advances in Experimental Social Psychology, 44,* 247–296.

Ferguson, E. S. (1992). *Engineering and the mind's eye.* Cambridge, MA: MIT Press.

Horn, M. B., & Staker, H. (2015). *Blended: Using disruptive innovation to improve schools.* Hoboken, NJ: Wiley.

Jonassen, D. H., & Hung, W. (2008). All problems are not equal. *Interdisciplinary Journal of Problem-Based Learning, 2*(2), 6–28.

Larkin, J. H., & Simon, A. H. (1987). Why a diagram is (sometimes) worth ten thousand words. *Cognitive Science, 11,* 65–99.

Lazebnik, Y. (2002). Can a biologist fix a radio?—Or, what I learned while studying apoptosis. *Cancer Cell, 2*(3), 179–182.

Le Doux, J. M., & Waller, A. (2016). The problem solving studio: An apprenticeship environment for aspiring engineers. *Advances in Engineering Education, 6*(2), 1–27.

Mahajan, S. (2014). *The art of insight in science and engineering: Mastering complexity.* Cambridge, MA: MIT Press.

Palincsar, A. S. (1998). Social constructivist perspectives on teaching and learning. *Annual Review of Psychology, 49*(1), 345–375.

Petroski, H. (1985). *To engineer is human: The role of failure in successful design.* New York: St. Martin's Press.

Schwartz, D. L., & Bransford, J. D. (1998). A time for telling. *Cognition and Instruction,* 16(4), 475–522.

Torrisi-Steele, G., & Drew, S. (2013). The literature landscape of blended learning in higher education: The need for better understanding of academic blended practice. *International Journal for Academic Development,* 18(4), 371–383.

Weinstein, L. (2012). *Guesstimation 2.0: Solving today's problems on the back of a napkin.* Princeton, NJ: Princeton University Press.

Weinstein, L., & Adam, J. A. (2008). *Guesstimation: Solving the world's problems on the back of a cocktail napkin.* Princeton, NJ: Princeton University Press.

13

GLOBAL ISSUES AND LEADERSHIP: GEORGIA TECH AS A LABORATORY FOR THE FUTURE OF EDUCATION

Joe Bankoff and Kenneth Knoespel

This chapter describes the course design of a seminar called Global Issues and Leadership. The blended design of a midsized course for advanced students from multiple disciplines at Georgia Tech and master's students from Sciences Po in Paris asks students to work in groups of four to five on current global issues. Each team presents their work to local, and sometimes national, leaders in the community. This design helps manage the difficulties associated with multidisciplinary teams, especially those with members on two continents. While according to the MIX taxonomy, mixing two groups of students who have different instructional experiences does not constitute a blended or hybrid course, we have defined this course as blended as it challenges us to reconceptualize mixing face-to-face and online learning.

OVERVIEW OF COURSE

The course titled Global Issues and Leadership has been taught in a blended format to undergraduate and graduate students since spring 2013. As an interdisciplinary course, it has attracted students from multiple disciplines—including the sciences, engineering, the humanities, and the social sciences—who have worked together to address global issues such as energy policy and cybersecurity. In the version offered in fall 2016, the seminar included Georgia Tech students from multiple disciplines and MS students in international affairs and public policy at Sciences Po, Paris. In fall 2017, the seminar included the participation of faculty from Moscow State University. The seminar has become a setting for exploring the practices of blended learning as a valuable pedagogy for engaging interdisciplinary education. As a result, digital technology has become a central participant and agent in the development of the seminar.

The seminar alerts us to ways the integration of new learning technologies requires us not only to become absorbed in the analysis of technology but also to become alert to the challenges posed to ingrained and often unquestioned structures of the university—including disciplinary boundaries. Above all we have learned that technology does not simply blend classrooms, it blends disciplines. While the disciplinary knowledge associated with a major is clearly important, a single discipline by itself will hardly solve the big problems we are challenged to confront. Educational environments that bring together students from multiple disciplines to address common global problems both affirm disciplinary integrity and anticipate the broad, mixed disciplinary settings and diverse participants that students will meet after graduation.

Our course also demonstrates how blended learning enables and realizes the active integration of analytic and human-centered disciplines envisioned in a required core but less frequently practiced in upper-level courses in a major. Learning how to work with others who think differently is not just an academic exercise, but a skill that only comes from confronting real issues and expending real effort. The integration of international affairs, science and technology competencies, as well as leadership, also demonstrates the ways blended learning can build on the momentum of a core curriculum at Georgia Tech—a curriculum that requires work in multiple areas such as calculus, writing and communication, lab sciences, and computer programming for all students regardless of majors. The core focus of the course is challenging students to combine their life experiences and perspectives as well as their areas of study to explain global issues in a cogent fashion to a policymaker.

Since its inception, the seminar has brought together from 18 to 30 students each semester from disciplines across Georgia Tech to present prepared briefings to experts. Participating students are selected by application and faculty recommendations. The selection process is designed to achieve a cross-section in terms of age, academic field, and career plans as well as to represent gender, racial, and ethnic diversity. In particular, ethnic diversity is emphasized to draw on the broad range of international students at Georgia Tech and call attention to the multiple ways that background shapes problem-solving strategies.

To provide context for the students' backgrounds: significant international student enrollment (countries represented to date include China, France, India, Jordan, South Korea, Lebanon, Nigeria, and Pakistan) contributed in substantial ways to the global objectives of the seminar. Well beyond the diversity of experience represented, the international breadth of the course underscored the crucial importance of working in languages other than English. The seminar repeatedly offered native English speakers the opportunity to use the other languages they were learning. Arabic, Chinese, Farsi, French, German, Korean, and Spanish were among the languages being studied by the US-born students. Repeated reference to online news sources other than English language sources underscored the reality that we were working in settings that were hardly monolingual. When students were asked to introduce themselves to each other in their favorite language other than English, 12 languages were represented in the seminar. Students from Sciences Po also represented a range of nationalities and language backgrounds that contributed significantly to the seminar's multilingual setting. The digital setting of course inherently reinforced building educational environments that reflect the critical importance of moving beyond a monolingual framework.

While it is true that the majority of the students participating in the first three sessions came from the humanities, the last session included a number of graduate student engineers. For a breakdown, see table 13.1.

The class demonstrates ways the disciplinary boundaries are changing. In addition, other global institutions have now expressed interest in such "virtual classrooms." The success of the seminar comes with the challenge to

Table 13.1

Enrollment figures including Sciences Po for 2013–2017

GT majors	Spring 2013	Fall 2013	Fall 2014	Fall 2015	Fall 2016	Fall 2017
Engineering	2	9	6	5	5	4
Humanities	1	1	1	2	0	2
Social sciences	12	7	6	5	8	7
Sciences/bio	1	1	3	0	2	1
Computing	1	0	0	0	0	2
Business	0	0	3	2	1	0
Independent	0	1	3	0	0	0
Totals	17	19	22	14/28	16/31	16/31

consider the ways that it serves as a model for the robust integration of multiple disciplines in settings for problem-based learning. The seminar has already served to reinforce the development of broadly integrated courses within the engineering curriculum. The most significant challenge faced by the seminar is institutional interest in having successful courses scaled up to meet the interests of a larger number of students.

The learning outcomes shared at the beginning of the seminar (see figure 13.1) emphasize that it is not intended to satisfy degree requirements alone but also to create meaningful opportunities to work in diverse teams to explore complex global issues through a blended convergence of disciplinary experience. The integration of disciplinary competency, international perspective, and leadership (indicated by the sides of the triangle) depends on developing the students' skills identified within the triangle through repeated practice. While the learning objectives identified by the triangle are utilized in all facets of the course, they also provide a reminder that so-called core skills continue to develop at all levels.

The briefings, which constitute the major assignment for the course, are substantially different from any other course assignment due to their formal nature. Modeled on briefings given in multiple government or corporate organizations, the briefings are not more than 12 to 14 minutes in length and are reinforced by weeks of research. Their formal nature is further reinforced by the national and international leaders that respond to them.

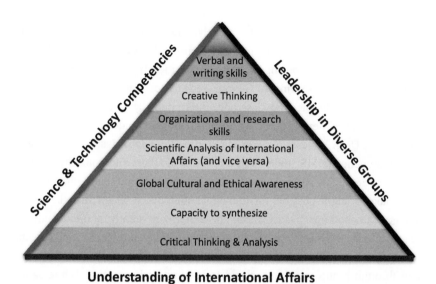

Understanding of International Affairs

Figure 13.1
Learning objectives for Global Issues

In the spring 2013 semester, briefings were devoted to the topics of "Russia and Nuclear Arms Control," "Urban Planning," "Global Health/Urban Health," and "The Challenge Charter Schools Pose for Public Education." In fall 2013, topics included "Atoms and Adoption," "Sustainable Development in Africa," "Choices in Education: A Debate," and "Privacy in the Age of Snowden." In fall 2014, briefings were presented on "Pirates and Privacy: Global Commerce," "The Politics of Energy: Gas and Guns," "Rising Expectations and Failing States," and "Education and the Role of Women."

All the chosen topics represent complex issues that require more than a single disciplinary persuasion. Work on the topics chosen for briefings underscored the ways that blended learning cannot be restricted to a discussion of the efficacy of electronic platforms. By engaging students from disciplines across the university to work together, these topics demonstrate the multiple ways that the impact of blended learning extends beyond university curricula. Students live in educational settings where their experience of seeking information or resources on the internet is blended already. The seminar draws on these available resources and makes students more aware of the ways education within a university setting is becoming fused with education from the internet.

The success of the seminar at Georgia Tech in 2013 and 2014 led to an interest in extending the blended classroom internationally, and the seminar has become an experiment in building an international blended classroom. With the help of Dean Vanessa Scherer at Sciences Po, Global Issues and Leadership was opened to MS students in international affairs and policy in Paris in the fall of 2015.[1] The ability to record each seminar session using BlueJeans™ technology made it possible for individual students to review their briefings and evaluate their own participation. The course consistently required students to attend to the ways integrating disciplines and indigenous experience inflects the approach to problem solving via interaction during the seminar meetings and through group meetings related to briefing assignments.[2] At the same time that technology enables international links, it also reinforces collaborative thinking among an ever-expanding community.

Well beyond digital links in the US and Europe, students themselves enable and explore the ways that digital technology makes possible their work with each other, whether in Atlanta or in Paris. But while technology enables the virtual classroom, it is above all the productive multidisciplinary interaction made possible by the technology that generates blended learning and substantial educational outcomes. The inclusion of remote participants such as a Georgia Tech PhD student at Oak Ridge National Laboratory or Georgia Tech colleagues teaching at our campus in Metz, France, demonstrated the usefulness of extending both outreach and response with blended learning. Some of our prior participants included Lisa O. Monaco, then assistant to President Obama for Homeland Security and Counterterrorism, who gave a live presentation to the seminar from the Briefing Room of the White House. During the fall term of 2017, Mikhail Troitskiy from Moscow State Institute of International Relations (MGIMO), Petr Topychkanov from the Carnegie Endowment for International Peace, and Elena Chernenko of *Kommersant* gave invaluable presentations on cybersecurity from Moscow.

During the last few iterations of the course, prior students' positive responses to the blended seminar resulted in ongoing engagement with former students. A former undergraduate member of the seminar returned to participate in meetings after he joined CXS Railroad as a designer. A graduate student who was completing a PhD in international affairs facilitated briefings related to her work in Geneva on a UN Committee on the Non-Proliferation of Nuclear Weapons. A former student, who graduated with a degree in aeronautical engineering, has worked to extend the model of the blended seminar in the College of Engineering.

Student engagement in the seminar was remarkable in terms of time invested, and students motivated each other. Through briefings, blogs, papers, and personal interaction, they began to recognize that they were not only learning together but were teaching one another. By broadening the idea of teaching, the blended seminar challenged deeply ingrained stereotypes of the classroom as a place where the professor dispenses information to be absorbed by students. The mutual learning environment that has evolved in the course of the seminar was clearly reinforced by the blended classroom.

Student interaction and engagement can clearly be seen in the briefing assignment. Returning to the details of that assignment, after the formation of research groups of four to five persons for each briefing, groups were given a scenario that formulated the problem to be addressed. Membership of the groups would rotate for each briefing so that the students were put in a different cohort for each assignment. Students got together regularly outside of seminar meetings to divide research assignments and draw on the particular expertise of the group. Rotation required students to work with colleagues from different disciplines. Each group would have three weeks to prepare their 12- to 14-minute policy briefing. While the briefing assignment required students to give polished presentations to professionals chosen for their expertise, it did not require them to demonstrate exhaustive mastery of the topic in only three weeks. It challenged them to identify and explain the core problem(s) to a policy maker.

Preparation for the briefings was complemented by having each student contribute a weekly blog post or comment that emphasized the importance of regular discussion and debate among students about current issues.[3] The students were also challenged to regularly write in their own voice from their own perspective. As the seminar developed, written interaction among students reinforced their interaction both within the assigned briefing groups and in seminar discussions. This evolving interaction became another benefit of the blended seminar. The blended learning environment made it possible for individuals to understand how the integration of material from multiple disciplines does not equate with "general speak" but enables a perspective unique to their personal identity and experience.

Evaluation of the briefings came from the written response of the expert visitors as well as from the evaluation of students that were not part of the briefing. Students also did self-evaluations after examining digital video recordings that were made of each briefing. The remainder of the evaluations in the course included a midterm or paper as well as a final paper devoted to the analysis of a recommended strategy for dealing with an identified issue. Overall, students in the seminar submitted approximately 25–30 pages of written work.

Discussions outside the seminar were devoted to analysis of presentation style (voice, stance, projection) as well as the substance of the arguments presented. An important feature of the seminar became the opportunity it gave students to practice formal presentations and become comfortable with public speaking. The blended classroom and its diversity in terms of disciplines, experience, language, and cultural background made students more self-aware of how their perspectives had been shaped by their individual experience and encouraged them to develop their unique voice in making public presentations.

Regular meetings between faculty and individual students enabled by the blended format also promoted the success of the seminar. At Georgia Tech, meetings took place outside of classroom time and in person. At Sciences Po, meetings took place via Skype. As soon as the students understood that they were being trusted to shape the discussion, their engagement and responsibility for the seminar developed substantially. For example, each student was required to spend considerable time outside the seminar doing research and meeting with other members of the briefing group. As they came to know each other, they became increasingly frank in their assessment of their mutual work. Strong briefings from one group prompted the development of ever-stronger briefings from other groups as the semester progressed.

To provide an example, at a briefing on chemical weapons in Syria given to Senator Sam Nunn during the first semester the course was taught, the presentation showed recent satellite reconnaissance photos of the Russian naval base in Syria. Senator Nunn was astonished by the images and learned that the woman making the initial comments was an aeronautical engineering graduate student who had acquired the images through her own work on aerial reconnaissance. In his subsequent comments on the presentation, Senator Nunn asked if he might use the slides in a presentation he was giving in Europe during the coming week! The exchange between the student and Senator Nunn demonstrated the high level of student research being done. It also showed how the seminar fostered a beneficial learning setting for both students and experts. In addition, the exchange emphasized the multiple ways that the blended seminar could draw on and expand the expertise of a wide range of individuals and organizations through a practiced use of technology.

As the course developed, the briefings grew in sophistication. In one notable presentation, a biology student analyzed the environmental implications of bilgewater from the China Sea being pumped into the Atlantic Ocean off the coast of Savannah, Georgia. Other presentations included an urban planning analysis of Atlanta's beltline and a survey of grid maps that identified food deserts in Atlanta. Still other presentations highlighted the ongoing work of nongovernmental organizations (NGOs) in Uganda on water purification issues. The seminar also served as an incubator for research that extended into subsequent semesters. A civil engineering student working with Engineers Across Borders applied her seminar research to her work on water purification for an African village. In tandem with a Brazilian graduate student in economics who was also in the seminar, she created the project "Application of Ceramic Filters in Northern Uganda: A Feasibility Study." The work they did in the seminar led to significant roles for both after graduation.

While the faculty and outside experts that participated in the briefings created a framework for the seminar, the students themselves created the learning environment. Once more we would emphasize how the seminar gave students the ability to "learn how to learn." Where one student was prepared to do a detailed urban planning analysis of Census Bureau data, another was ready to provide an analysis of oil reserves in Russia, another a commentary on religious minorities in Lebanon, and another on NGOs in Nigeria. Well beyond the range of topics addressed by the student briefings, the seminar recognized the close relation between the blended classroom and pragmatic problem-based learning. A common response to the seminar has been student pride and even astonishment that they were able to teach each other to work together. The human connections that arose from the virtual were real and very meaningful. While data is preliminary, the results appear encouraging. Engaging students at Sciences Po in Paris has given real texture to the process and perception of diversity.[4]

COMMENTARY

The success of the seminar may also be seen in the superior Georgia Tech student evaluations (4.9–5.0 on a scale of 5) and through the written comments of participants who evaluated the briefings. The seminar that included Sciences Po also received strong support, with an overall evaluation of 92% in other blended settings. This commentary from Sciences Po was positive. As one student commented:

This class was a great surprise! The interaction and communication with American students was not always easy but really enriching—and I think that both elements were the whole point of the class. We learned as much from team work as we did during the lectures and in the realization of the policy briefs, an exercise most of us had never done before. All scenarios were tackling current affairs, and this is also a great strength of the class, since it puts us into real situations where we have to find solutions to issues of *real politik*. The aim of the class—learning about leadership in its different forms—was fully reached.

These positive evaluations should be recognized as a consequence of the multiple ways the students taught each other.

As another measure of success, the course has become a blueprint for similar courses at Georgia Tech. For example, two former students have decided to use the Global Issues and Leadership seminar as a model for a capstone course for all majors within the Ivan Allen College of Liberal Arts at Georgia Tech.

A further indication of success comes from the number of requests for follow-up research projects pursued in subsequent semesters. In the spring term of 2017, a student with a detailed focus on Latin America and who worked as an intern at the Carter Center requested an independent study course to work on an analysis of the art market for indigenous Native American material objects. Her analysis led to an evaluation of pre-Columbian art collections in Europe and the United States. A number of graduating seniors who took the class were also accepted into premier graduate programs. The woman student active in Engineers Without Borders, referred to earlier, was accepted into the PhD program in Science Policy at UC-Berkeley. Another student who had also worked as an intern in the Georgia state legislature during the time she was in the seminar was accepted into Duke's PhD program in public policy. These examples show the ways the blended seminar provided a setting reinforcing student accomplishment. Even more, the examples suggest how the focus on problem solving in the seminar contributed to students' decisions to work in areas where they could continue to engage with complex social issues.

The success of the seminar depended on its digital infrastructure. While the technology at times could seem an assumed presence, the seminar would have been impossible without the technological structure that enabled our blended work. The students' ability to teach others was a consequence of the virtual classroom, as was the student need to use technology to prepare and coordinate their efforts over six time zones and 4,300 miles. The ways the students taught each other also certainly depended on the structure and trust provided by participating faculty. The definition of briefing topics, the preparation of problem scenarios, and the task of inviting visiting experts involved continuous faculty engagement and monitoring. This shared commitment to use technology to foster such student development reinforced the vital relation between blended and problem-based learning.

This mutual commitment was based on the disciplinary blending that students experienced in the seminar. Individual students majoring in international affairs frequently called attention to what they learned from their fellow students in engineering. Undergraduate students who worked in briefing groups with graduate students quickly learned to use databases or formulate issues in ways that extended well beyond their undergraduate experience.

In one instance in 2015, a graduate student from Sciences Po who had completed an internship in the Bulgarian Foreign Ministry engaged General Philip Breedlove, who was then Supreme Allied Commander in Europe, in an extended video-linked conversation about Eastern Europe and NATO. In another briefing, a five-minute film with a soundtrack made by an undergraduate on food deserts in Atlanta elicited admiration and surprise that something so professional could be prepared in three weeks.

The seminar Global Issues and Leadership serves as an enhanced example of blended learning through its integration of diverse disciplines and problem-based learning. While blended learning has become associated with educational settings that integrate traditional classroom experiences (whether lectures or discussions) and classroom experiences that are virtual, Global Issues offers another dimension to the model of blended learning. Rather than being a lecture course offered to a large number of students potentially in many locations, the Global Issues model provides blended learning by also blending disciplines. As with other examples of blended learning, its success has been fostered by digital technologies. The effectiveness of the course can be measured by the ways that it has blended technology with an emphasis on creating settings where diverse students may learn and work together.

The learning outcomes in this effort inevitably extend beyond the predefined objectives often expected within university systems. The goals for the seminar are different from the goals defined for a calculus class or course in computer programing. In contrast to courses developed to teach particular analytic skills, the skills developed in Global Issues are above all synthetic because they require the simultaneous engagement of multiple skills. Given its synthetic character, the seminar most importantly provides a learning laboratory for the imaginative engagement of technology and a range of analytic skills. Synthesis is required under time pressure through the integration of disciplines and personalities. Research universities such as Georgia Tech and Sciences Po that produce students with accomplished discipline skills are uniquely situated to give strong students the experience of integrating learning on all levels.

The seminar has demonstrated that digital technology cannot be viewed as a simple add-on but should be regarded as an integral participant in education. It is not a matter of simple connectivity but of the expectation that students continuously coordinate their work both within the realm of their own networks and within the networks developed through the work in the seminar. But while digital technology has become like a mathematical function that appears to permeate all aspects of education, it places in strong relief the ways that educational communities reinforce interaction between the spectrum of participants. While digital technology within educational settings may appear top-down if not totalizing, such technology enhances multiple levels of learning. In effect, our experience shows how we are learning to learn within a digitally linked society.

The seminar has also stressed the challenges of leadership in a global environment where there are diverse participants and frequently sharp differences in perspective. Reference to leadership, however, has also served as a means to challenge the popular—dare one say faddish—emphasis on leadership. Rather than viewing leadership as a term that too often moves in the direction of making business decisions ahead of one's colleagues, we have stressed the ways leadership involves the capacity to work with colleagues from multiple backgrounds. The seminar has emphasized that the capacity to be effective in diverse groups and cultures requires more than a winning personality, brains, and technical competence. It requires an understanding of how differently the same issues are seen based on differences in culture, history, language, gender, generation, technology, and political structures. The capacity to lead in a global or multicultural environment is about more than just asserting a compelling solution; it is about listening and understanding the strengths and fears of others. Through the detailed group discussions required by the briefings, the blended seminar has provided rich and numerous settings for the practice of cooperative leadership.

Finally, the seminar shows that leadership must also be linked to the digital environments. The work groups established for each briefing required students to assign each other roles for the briefing. Such assignments were not a matter of a decision by a single leader but emerged as a consequence of the growing recognition of particular strengths in the group. Leadership involved shared orchestration of the project and the learned responsibility to work within limited time frames.

The success of the seminar brings with it the challenge to consider the ways it serves as a model for the robust integration of multiple disciplines in settings for problem-based learning. The seminar has already reinforced the development of broadly integrated courses within the engineering curriculum. The most significant challenge faced by the seminar is institutional interest in having successful courses scaled up to meet the demands of a larger number of students. Given our experience in building the blended Global Issues and Leadership seminar, we are optimistic that evolving institutional strategies will give ongoing support to a range of courses that complement evolving institutional commitment to blended learning. While it would not be possible to offer Global Issues and Leadership as a MOOC, multiple opportunities exist for integrating upper-level seminars using Global Issues as a model.

Besides shaping a multidisciplinary setting for problem solving, the course has demonstrated the viability of building courses that can be shared between international institutions. It is even more important to recognize how the combined classroom experience with Sciences Po anticipates major opportunities for university education and the ways it forecasts educational development. Multiple challenges face such collaboration as well. Beyond the immediate importance of course development and coordination, there are issues involving (1) business models that would sustain participating institutions, and (2) the legal implications of institutional restriction of property rights particularly involving R&D for science and technology.

While impediments clearly exist, what appear to be impediments may well be addressed by further experimentation. Existing models of shared research, particularly in the social sciences and humanities, already anticipate shared courses and the eventual development of combined curricula.

BLENDED LEARNING AND THE FUTURE OF UNIVERSITY EDUCATION

The Global Issues and Leadership seminar will continue to provide a setting in which to approach the role of blended learning for the future of education. The current scrutiny of American university education reminds us that we are in the midst of a societal transformation affecting both the structure and purpose of education. While the problem-oriented emphasis of the seminar resonates with the ideals of American education espoused by John Dewey and other pioneering educators, it expands the scope and impact of a blended pragmatic approach. Above all, the seminar has shown us the importance of asking how an *"intentional" learning environment* within a blended setting can be created using a three-dimensional matrix of opportunity of (1) engaged diversity among participants, (2) rich interaction with multiple foreign news and information sources, and (3) an objective focused more on defining root problems than on finding solutions. The three components are premised on the notion that the situation is not static and that both the "problems" and the "solutions"— from various perspectives—are evolving. The three components, illustrated in figure 13.2, are premised on the notion that the situation is not static and that both the "problems" and the "solutions"—from various perspectives—are evolving.

While we have embraced the use of a range of digital technologies in the seminar, the most influential technology has been the internet itself. Access to instantaneous information and shared video has transformed the challenges of learning from obtaining access to information to knowing how to evaluate it and what to do with it. While there remains unchallenged value in the face-to-face interaction between faculty and students on a campus, we suspect that

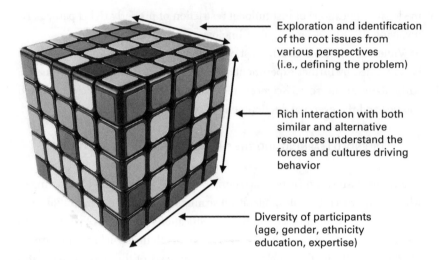

Exploration and identification of the root issues from various perspectives (i.e., defining the problem)

Rich interaction with both similar and alternative resources understand the forces and cultures driving behavior

Diversity of participants (age, gender, ethnicity education, expertise)

Figure 13.2
Rubik's Cube of intentional learning

the percentage of learning (and attention) enjoyed by the traditional approaches to learning has greatly diminished.

The seminar has become a powerful example of the ways blended learning enables "real-world" learning experiences with real-time access to both global issues and a global diversity of views and will yet require continuing experimentation. Because learning styles and expectations differ among cultures and not just languages, careful attention must be given to the ways the global community may be usefully included in the virtual classroom experience.

In conclusion, we would share three observational questions that arise from the blended seminar. First, what does the blended seminar on Global Issues and Leadership indicate about the ways we build new course clusters or modules that allow students to work with each other? The seminar invites the development of courses that carry the spirit of integrated learning through their very conception. Such courses would emphasize the expertise and experience in separate disciplines but would provide settings for the necessary skills to build bridges to evolving careers and professional identity. The growing disparities in global societies require the institutions responsible for educating future leadership to find new ways in which the collective understanding is greater than the sum of the mastery of the parts. The relevance of the university of the future will rest not only on excellence in its disciplines, but on creating leaders with the capacity to engage that expertise usefully across diverse disciplines and cultures. Certainly, blended-classroom approaches can be important in creating both the skills and knowledge to do so.

The seminar offers a strong argument for the ways blended learning impacts new institutional configurations. Collaboration between Georgia Tech and Sciences Po is not anomalous or eccentric but demonstrates how the electronic infrastructures are enabling new modes of international education. They urge us to envision new institutional formations, which will require us to rethink faculty and student affiliation, particularly from the vantage point of contract, copyright, and patent law. There is absolutely no reason that a student from one institution couldn't participate in coursework or research projects at another institution. For example, conversations with colleagues at Sciences Po have underscored the resonance between Global Issues at Georgia Tech and a course offered by Vincent-Antonin Lépinay and Thomas Tari that examined multidisciplinary vantage points on "grand" global problems.

Second, how are we to understand the relation between the technological platforms crucial for blended learning and the individual experience of learning? At the same time the blended seminar underscores the fundamental importance of technology for education, it reminds us that the technology is hardly impassive or self-executing. Whatever the strength of the digital infrastructure, multiple levels of administrative coordination fused with pragmatic experimentation are essential for shaping future blended courses. Such coordination and experimentation include students as well as instructors. The creative engagement of students, faculty, and staff is essential. Such multifaceted engagement shows how the blended classroom provides new modes of educational experience that students may carry into their professional work.

Third, how does the blended seminar contribute to fostering a continuous learning ecosystem for the university? Beyond what we have learned about the use of robust technological platforms for international education, we have more fully understood the role of the university in fostering a continuous learning ecosystem. Further education no longer means only graduate school but education throughout the lifespan. The extensive learning community that has surrounded Global Issues and Leadership has expanded perspectives and connections for the significance of blended learning beyond a single course or the configuration of disciplinary degrees. In the broadest sense, we must build university curricula that expect and encourage extended learning experiences. At a time when broad analysis draws attention to the very future of university education, it is essential to gather examples of promising situated work that may provide insight into these broader issues. The seminar Global Issues and Leadership provides an evolving experiment that participates in the complex process of changing the university curricula while simultaneously inviting us to understand the ways we are participating in the ongoing transformation of university structure. Given our experience in building the blended seminar Global Issues and Leadership, we are optimistic that evolving institutional strategies will give ongoing support to a range of courses that reflect evolving institutional commitment to blended learning. Multiple opportunities exist for integrating upper-level seminars using Global Issues as a model.

Notes

1. With the support of colleagues in Paris and Atlanta, the international format has now been offered three times—in 2015, 2016, and 2017—and it is offered in real the time (Atlanta EST 12:00–15:00; Paris 18:00–21:00; Moscow 20:00–23:00). In addition to Dean Scherer, Peter Herrly, Ronald Hatto, and Henri Landes have reinforced our work in innumerable ways.

2. Although courses are conducted in English, the seminar repeatedly emphasizes multilingual backgrounds of students both at Georgia Tech and Sciences Po. On an occasion when students were asked to introduce themselves in a language other than English, 12 languages were represented.

3. To provide an example of a briefing, in a briefing on the international control of chemical weapons presented to Senator Sam Nunn, a student in aerospace engineering

who was experienced in digital reconnaissance provided visual examples of chemical weapons depots in Syria. Her work complemented that of others in the group, who drew on their language training in Arabic and Farsi.

4. Wholly apart from the drama of the November attacks in Paris (as we prepared students to brief on "Responding to Terror"), the sense of connection has proved greater than the sense of distance. When the terrorist bombings in Paris happened in November 2015 close to where our Sciences Po students lived, the Atlanta students were frankly frightened, immediately checked on their friends, and shared similar signs of post-traumatic stress.

14

CONCLUSION

Amanda G. Madden, Lauren Margulieux, Robert S. Kadel, and Ashok Goel

This volume was designed with a single, broad purpose: to provide novel perspectives on and evidence-based assessments of blended learning, adhering to a central understanding of the blended learning pedagogy. It highlights the extensive benefits of blended learning, illustrates some of its instantiations, describes strategies to implement the pedagogy, and provides pointers for effective research. It uses the MIX taxonomy for classifying the blended learning strategies along two axes: delivery via instructor to delivery via technology; and receiving content to applying content.

There is a continuum in the literature on blended learning. At one end, much of the existing literature on blended learning is written for researchers and includes evaluations that can be difficult to follow for the nonspecialist. At the other end of the continuum, there are informal guides written for practitioners lacking strategies for formal evaluation of effectiveness. This volume fills the gap somewhere in the middle as a guidebook for those interested in blended learning and research. The goal of this book is to empower deliberative educators—teachers, instructional designers, and administrators—to develop curricula, courses, and tools for blending learning while also encouraging data-driven evaluation and research.

This book also provides perspective on the ongoing debates about the nature of higher education and its future directions. Blended learning provides insight on one of the foci of the debate—the nature of pedagogy. The conversation over the benefits and risks of technology-enabled learning is ongoing and likely to be so for some time. On one side are educators committed to on-campus education and skeptical of the quality of online learning, and on the other are educators who see online courses as critical to the future, in part for economic and demographic reasons. While a majority of educators likely are somewhere between these two extremes, advocates for either side often tend to be the most vocal. This book bridges the two as it is directed toward both advocates and detractors of online education, as well as toward those in between. Blended learning provides a more balanced and nuanced perspective on these debates.

The reader will no doubt have noticed that certain themes prevail across multiple chapters, and they all center on how blending can open new horizons for the classroom. Blended learning can positively impact consistency and quality as well as enabling the process of scaling up learning. Blended learning can also impart a greater degree of flexibility for both student and instructor. The contributions to this book have also explored how blended learning can overcome or confront common obstacles, including spatial constraints and low student engagement. Finally, several contributions break down how blended learning can further other successful pedagogical strategies like project-based learning and peer learning. We expand on these points in the following pages.

KEY TAKEAWAYS

There are important lessons from each chapter that can be used to weigh the costs and benefits of implementing a blended course:

• In chapter 2, Ferri, Harris, and Ferri have demonstrated that providing common resources for multiple sections of the same course creates consistency and quality, but it can also constrain autonomy. They offer three models on a spectrum from less freedom and more consistency to more freedom and less consistency. The benefit is that practitioners choosing to experiment with blended learning in a large, multisection course will find a variety of options to explore.

• Goel has pointed out in chapter 3 that online education and blended learning are ripe with opportunities for developing new technologies. There is at present no specific prescriptive or analytic model for designing a blended learning course. Educators considering blended learning will often make use of extant technologies such as videos, online discussion forums, and learning management systems to support learning; however, this perspective limits the degree to which instructors can try new technologies. Goel's advice is that instructors design their blended learning for the course and students they have, incorporating new technologies such as cognitive tutors. They should not become constrained by the tools currently at their disposal. And they should keep the problem they are trying to solve first and foremost in mind and exploit opportunities to experiment.

• In chapter 4, Joyner has shown that there is no specific required ratio of online and face-to-face work in a blended course. In his Introduction to Computing course, he shared resources such as the help desk and tutoring support between a section conducted primarily online and a section conducted largely face to face. Further, the Smartbook described in chapter 4 is a competency-based tool for learning mastery, which was applicable across both the online and face-to-face sections. To what degree can other instructors combine competency-based learning with adaptive learning? By blending his course, Joyner demonstrated that there are opportunities for adaptive learning across different types of courses when capitalizing on the use of technology to deliver instruction.

• The contribution by Braunstein et al. (chapter 5) features an example of problem-based learning in a scaled environment enabled by blended learning. In this environment, it was possible to involve medical professionals in the process of designing applications to fit their needs. These types of opportunities provide greater intensity of learning—when some of the content delivery is offloaded to technology, project time can be filled with greater interaction with practitioners. This flexibility is a key advantage of the blended environment.

- Kadel and Margulieux (chapter 6) and Margulieux and Kadel (chapter 8) have provided valuable guidance for conducting research in blended classrooms. The data collection and analysis strategies they describe can be applied across a range of different types of blended courses. To demonstrate this point, chapters 7 and 9 serve both as examples of quality research and as evidence of the effectiveness of blending in their own right.
- In chapter 7, Burnett, Menagarishvili, and Frazee showed that blended learning can include authentic projects and can be a valuable strategy for teaching technical communication to students in STEM majors. Further, in comparing a face-to-face section of a course with one that is blended, Burnett et al. found that there were no greater or fewer challenges in the blended section than in the face-to-face section, indicating that the modality did not have a notable effect on the quality of teamwork.
- In chapter 9, Webster, Kadel, and Madden have demonstrated that flipping a course can work at scale to improve performance as well as student satisfaction with the course. In typical large-format courses, the larger they become, the more anonymous they become. Students are less likely to raise their hands, ask questions, and seek guidance. But when flipped, opportunities arise for students to interact regularly with the professor and teaching assistants.
- Madden showed in chapter 10 that blending does not need to rely on typical technological platforms or even on strictly educational technology at all. Her incorporation of the *Assassin's Creed II* videogame is a prime demonstration of Goel's earlier point about experimenting with different technologies. Combined with Piazza discussion forums, the result was greater student engagement and even excitement to learn the content.
- In chapter 11, Margulieux's demonstration of flipping a social research method course showed the importance of providing students with preclass work that the instructor could review before coming to class. The blended format allowed students to work on activities that were interesting to them, and Margulieux could be more focused in her lecturing by incorporating student work and comments on an ongoing basis.
- Le Doux demonstrated the value of a blended-format class in modeling expert behavior (chapter 12). By being encouraged to think like engineers, students

learned design-based thinking and the value of diagramming problems toward a solution. The blended format provided valuable face-to-face time during class, where students could work through a problem together with guidance from the instructor.

• Finally, in chapter 13 Bankoff and Knoespel have shown the value of inter-disciplinary team learning and the opportunities that come from engaging students from multiple policy perspectives. Further, the authentic learning experiences provided by interacting with students from Sciences Po in Paris helped students to think like global citizens, again modeling the behavior and mindset of experts in the field.

What all the above chapters have in common is that they demonstrate the importance of using the blended classroom to teach students how to com-municate in different ways, how to better invest their out-of-class time, and how to enhance peer-to-peer interaction—either with technology, in the phys-ical space, or both. The next section provides more detail on these common themes.

COMMON THEMES

One of these themes is that blended learning can provide *consistency and quality of learning* for students. In chapter 2, Ferri, Harris, and Ferri demonstrated that the use of an electrical engineering MOOC across a large, multisection course provided consistency across a course with multiple instructors teach-ing different sections. In a similar experiment with multiple sections, Goel showed that residential and online students performed almost equally well on skill assessments and content-based tests after online lecture videos were incorporated into the on-campus course (see chapter 3). The contribution by Braunstein et al. (chapter 5) underscored that blended learning can promote consistency as well as innovation in both online and on-campus MS degree programs. These instructors found that using MOOCs in this way removed a barrier to blended learning at scale, namely inconsistency across multiple sections or in large courses.

Closely related to our discussion of consistency, another theme of this book has been *scale of learning*. As several chapters have demonstrated effectively, class size may be less of a challenge for adopting blended learning than previously thought. Joyner's chapter (chapter 4) examined the outcomes of an Introduction to Computing course that used a MOOC and an adaptive ebook to teach a high-demand topic. Chapters 9 and 11—by Webster, Kadel, and Madden and by Margulieux, respectively—demonstrated that even with required courses with enrollments approaching 90 students, student performance and the perception of the benefits of the blended environment were on par with smaller sections. Moreover, blended learning can introduce scale in ways that are productive for community formation, cross-cultural interaction, and learning from multiple professionals. In chapter 7, Burnett, Menagarishvili, and Frazee explored how blended learning can scale up a traditionally small-enrollment communication class. In chapter 13, Bankoff and Knoespel described how blending made it possible to include students from France in their course. Finally, Goel, Joyner, and Braunstein et al.'s contributions (in chapters 3, 4, and 5, respectively) exemplify how blending can involve a successful application of online lecture videos that scales learning in ways not previously possible. As these contributions show, blending a course can work at scale without sacrificing student performance or satisfaction with the course.

In part, scaling up blended learning has traditionally been constrained by traditional on-campus spaces. One challenge that many instructors faced was teaching in a physical space that did not provide enough flexibility for students to work in groups or for the teacher to move among the students. While many classrooms are being renovated or built to encourage and facilitate student interaction and working in groups, many instructors still teach in spaces that make interaction more challenging. With a little creativity, several instructors made blended learning work for them despite space limitations. Margulieux addressed this issue explicitly in chapter 11 and gave some pointers on how to overcome spatial constraints—including using technology to create groups and letting students find spaces that work for them in large lecture halls. Following this and other examples, we encourage our readers not to let space become a barrier to implementation and hope our contributors have provided some inspiration and ideas in this regard.

Flexibility and *adaptivity* are two common themes. Blended learning allows instructors the flexibility to incorporate diverse student populations and to use pedagogical strategies that are not as feasible in a traditionally formatted classroom. Indeed, such flexibility is particularly beneficial when one class serves the needs of multiple populations of students. Braunstein et al. and Margulieux worked with multiple student populations in the same course, the former mixing residential and remote learners, and the latter seeking to integrate populations from both psychology and computer science. In chapter 13, Bankoff and Knoespel described how they blended their class, not only to enable project-based learning but to combine geographically distant graduate and undergraduate students from Georgia Tech and Sciences Po, Paris, in the projects. In all cases, this mixing of student populations as enabled by blended learning proved extremely beneficial for both students and instructors.

Student engagement has been another focus of this book. Blended learning fosters the ability to use pedagogical strategies that are more appealing to students than traditional strategies often are. In chapter 10, Madden showed this in describing her creative use of *Assassin's Creed II* to teach students about writing and the Italian Renaissance—the use of this videogame kept students highly engaged with the course material. In chapter 9, Webster, Kadel, and Madden demonstrated the engagement value in allowing students in a Dynamics course to work in pairs in class to solve complex engineering problems. Problem solving of this type was shown to be more interesting than usual to students, resulting in better outcomes. At least half of the instructors represented in this volume took advantage of blended strategies to incorporate project-based learning and based the projects on authentic practices in the real world. Blended learning offers opportunities to model expert behavior with students. Braunstein et al., Le Doux, and Bankoff and Knoespel all provided students with assignments that required them to work in interdisciplinary, collaborative teams similar to what they will find in the workplace. Students invariably found this real-world model of assignments highly engaging.

There are key takeaways that can be used specifically for the task of weighing the costs and benefits of implementing a blended course. As discussed above, readers are encouraged to design blended learning for the courses and students they have, including incorporating new technologies such as cognitive tutors, adaptive ebooks, and games. Teachers should keep the problem they are trying to solve first and foremost in mind and maximize their opportunities to experiment. Instructors should not become constrained by the tools currently at their disposal. To provide some guidelines for overcoming commonly encountered challenges and issues, the next section presents some of the lessons learned by the editors and authors of this book.

LESSONS LEARNED

While blended learning brings the potential of collaboration, engagement, and flexibility, the chapters included in this volume also demonstrate many of the common challenges. While every instructor should try blended learning, those considering blending a course might find it useful to seek guidance and assistance from others, including and especially those who have blended their own courses previously. Blended learning necessarily involves exploration and experimentation, failure and iteration. As in every experiment, it's also important to embrace failures, reflect on them, seek guidance from others, make small adjustments, and try again.

Readers may expect the first time they blend a class to be like any other first offering of a course. Unexpected issues will come up and some level of confusion will emerge for both instructors and students. Teachers should try to anticipate issues beforehand but should not get discouraged when they arise. The course will be much better the second time it is offered, and readers can make consistent, minor improvements every offering afterward until the course runs smoothly. Even then, they should expect to make changes as the demographics and dynamics of the student groups change from term to term.

Institutions can support their instructors in this process in the following ways: encourage experimentation, reward innovation, invest in technology, and where possible, provide financial support for redesign. Most large institutions have a center for teaching and learning that can provide consultation and support, helping instructors design the classroom, construct a syllabus, and evaluate effectiveness. Even at schools without such a resource, creating a working group of instructors who seek to blend their courses can be enormously beneficial. The process of experimenting, failing, seeking support, and making small changes over time requires a change in mindset, which a faculty support group can also foster. Collaborate as much as feasible, whether with such a faculty group, an instructional designer, or a researcher, to restructure a course, gather feedback, and make additional changes. Instructors will find it helpful to consult with their students and seek their feedback.

Students sometimes resist blended learning, and a change is required in their mindset as well. To a certain extent, this is already happening in K–12 environments, where more teachers are blending their classes, engaging students with the material and with each other, and encouraging teamwork. However, while a trend toward blended K–12 classrooms appears to be growing (though reliable statistics are scarce), it has not yet reached a critical mass to the point that all undergraduates would be expecting such a model in college. One avenue for understanding how students are responding to a shift toward blended classes is to collect data on the process. Referring back to the chapters on research design, using short surveys to gather information and to gauge students' opinions at the beginning, middle, and end of the first few times an instructor blends a course can be helpful. This data is valuable for reflection and for making adjustments.

Instructors seeking to blend their courses might find it helpful to be up front and open with their students about it. They should explain the costs and benefits, share research with them (the research in this book will help), and give them opportunities to provide feedback. Like an ethnographer, teachers need to be willing to observe. When students are working in peer-to-peer situations, collaborating on projects or problems, or creating work products as a team, the instructor should take time to watch and listen to them. This is valuable as a research tool and also encourages on-the-spot refinements to the lessons as students demonstrate what they're learning and where they're struggling. As has been discussed throughout the book, one of the bigger advantages to blended learning is its flexibility and adaptivity.

LOOKING INTO THE FUTURE

This volume has focused almost exclusively on blended learning in college education, especially at Georgia Tech. However, blended learning is now being explored in a variety of educational contexts around the world from STEM education to education in the arts and literature, from K–12 to college to post-graduate education, and from formal to informal education. The scope and variety of blended learning will continue to increase because of its power and impact.

As the scope and variety of blended learning applications increase, it will be useful to study their relationship to various demographic groups. As at many US universities, the demographics of the Georgia Tech student body are becoming more diverse. Thus, the students come from more varied back-grounds and have a wider range of goals and objectives. However, it is not yet clear whether different varieties of blended learning, such as those described in this book, are more or less suited to different student demographics. It seems possible, perhaps likely, that blended learning can be better tuned to various prior experiences, and even more, to individual students, than the traditional lecture hall with its one-size-fits-all view of classroom education. Exploring and adapting blended learning to the educational backgrounds and learning needs of future students is an important topic.

Given that blended learning is based in part on technologies developed for online education, what new technologies currently under development may further promote this approach to learning and how? Parallel advances in educational technologies—especially in computing, networking, media, virtual reality, artificial intelligence, machine learning, and data analytics—are making many familiar models of learning scalable and also introducing new models of learning. It is not easy to fully fathom the impact of these new technologies on the classrooms of tomorrow. Nevertheless, it seems fair to say that due to ongoing advances in the cognitive, social, and learning sciences on the one hand, and progress in the technologies of artificial intelligence, machine learning, data analytics, virtual reality, and social media on the other, the future of blended learning looks very bright and promising.

CONTRIBUTORS

EDITORS

Ashok Goel is a Professor of Computer Science and the Director of the PhD Program in Human-Centered Computing in the School of Interactive Computing at Georgia Institute of Technology. Goel conducts research into artificial intelligence, cognitive science, and human-centered computing, with a focus on computational design, modeling, and creativity. He is the editor in chief of AAAI's *AI Magazine*. Goel serves on Georgia Tech's Commission on Next in Education and co-leads its task forces on the Future of Pedagogy and Future Learning Systems. As part of Georgia Tech's Online Master of Science in Computer Science program, he developed a graduate-level course on AI, and as part of this class, he developed Jill Watson, an AI teaching assistant for answering questions in the online class discussion forum. The *Chronicle of Higher Education* has included virtual assistants exemplified by Jill Watson in its list of transformative educational technologies over the last fifty years.

Robert S. Kadel is Assistant Director for Research in Education Innovation with Georgia Tech's Center for 21st Century Universities. His research emphases include measuring the effectiveness of online and blended learning strategies, building communities of inquiry in MOOCs, leveraging learning analytics for student success, and implementing tools/strategies to help close the digital divide for economically disadvantaged students. He spent seven years as an independent educational technology research consultant, with clients across the US, and six years with Pearson Education, where he regularly extolled the virtues of quality research design with clients worldwide. Kadel continues to teach online courses in the sociology of education, criminology, and juvenile delinquency for the University of Colorado, Denver.

Amanda G. Madden is a Research Scientist at the Center for 21st Century Universities at Georgia Tech. A former Marion L. Brittain postdoctoral fellow in digital pedagogy with the Writing and Communication Program at Georgia Tech, she has published on writing assessment and blended learning. In 2012–2013, she provided instructional design for one of the first composition MOOCs, First-Year Composition 2.0 (Coursera, 2013; funded by the Gates Foundation and Georgia Tech's Office of the Provost). Her research interests include digital pedagogy, student engagement, and improving diversity in higher education. She continues to maintain an active research agenda on the history of women and gender in early modern Europe and history pedagogy.

Lauren Margulieux is an Assistant Professor in the Learning Sciences Department at Georgia State University. While pursuing her doctorate at Georgia Tech, she worked in the Center for 21st Century Universities. Her research interests are in educational technology and online learning, particularly for science, technology, engineering, and mathematics (STEM) education. She focuses on designing instructions to support online students who do not necessarily have immediate access to an instructor or professor to ask questions or overcome problem-solving impasses. Margulieux explores factors that affect the success of hybrid, blended, flipped, and inverted courses.

AUTHORS

Joe Bankoff is the Chair of the Sam Nunn School of International Affairs at Georgia Tech. He was appointed to his position in spring 2012 following six years as president and CEO of the Woodruff Arts Center and 32 years as a senior partner at the Atlanta-based law firm of King & Spalding. Bankoff's expertise ranges across law and policy, economic development, government legislation, fiscal planning, and global issues. In 1992, he took a sabbatical from his law firm to accept an appointment as a visiting scholar at the Max Planck Institute for Intellectual Property & Competition Law, Munich, Germany. He also served as counsel to Atlanta's Olympic Organizing Committee, negotiating the television rights agreements for Europe (EBU), Canada, Australia, Latin America, and the United States. For an exploration of international property law see Joe Bankoff, "Building an Internationalized City," Shenzhen Symposium, Shenzhen, China, September 17, 2014.

Paula Braun is an Instructor at the Rollins School of Public Health at Emory University and an Entrepreneur in Residence in the division of Vital Statistics at the National Center for Health Statistics. Before coming to Emory, Braun worked at Elder Research, Inc., and was an Analyst in Charge for the Special Inspector General for Afghanistan Reconstruction in Kabul, where she received the Sentner Award for Dedication and Courage. She holds an MS in Analytics from the Institute for Advanced Analytics at North Carolina State University, as well as an MS in Mathematics from the University of Toledo.

Mark L. Braunstein is a Professor of the Practice in the School of Interactive Computing at Georgia Tech. He was a pioneer in the field of clinical health informatics, and for the past decade he has been teaching Georgia Tech's introductory graduate seminar in the field. Over time, the course evolved using blended learning technologies into what is widely regarded as a model for project-based learning in the field, and he will be replicating the course at the University of Queensland in Australia in the second half of 2018 using many of the same blended learning technologies described in his chapter. He is interested in teaching more nontechnical learners and offers them a public MOOC and a series of books. He is engaged in a number of research projects in collaboration with several faculty at Georgia Tech and elsewhere.

Timothy G. Buchman is a Professor of Surgery, of Anesthesiology, and of Biomedical Informatics at the Emory University School of Medicine. He is also the founding director of the Emory Critical Care Center, which integrated ICUs throughout the Emory Healthcare System by bringing together clinicians and investigators from diverse disciplines to conduct research to define best clinical practices and inform public health policy. Buchman's research has encompassed physiological dynamics, predictive biology, patient monitoring, the genetics of sepsis, and ICU end-of-life care. Before joining Emory, he was an Edison Professor of Surgery, Anesthesiology, and Medicine at Washington University in Saint Louis.

Rebecca E. Burnett is Director of Writing and Communication at Georgia Tech and holds the Class of '58 Endowed Professorship in Georgia Tech's School of Literature, Media, and Communication. Her research includes risk communication, collaboration, technical communication, assessment, multi-modality, digital pedagogies, large-scale pedagogies, and visual literacies, supporting both her interest in innovative pedagogies and her work as an expert witness in litigation. She sees blended learning as a way to enhance existing face-to-face classes, to appeal to nontraditional students, to engage students with limited access, and to attract international students (including those in countries where she's worked, including Canada, Japan, Mexico, Saudi Arabia, and South Africa).

Aldo Ferri is Professor and Associate Chair for Undergraduate Studies in the George W. Woodruff School of Mechanical Engineering at Georgia Tech. As Associate Chair, he has worked extensively on mechanical engineering curriculum development. He has also been active in educational research pertaining to laboratory courses, hands-on learning, and blended teaching methods. He is the recipient of the Class of 1940 W. Howard Ector Outstanding Teacher

Award from Georgia Tech and is a fellow of the American Society of Mechanical Engineering (ASME). He received his BS from Lehigh University in 1981 and his PhD from Princeton University in 1985.

Bonnie Ferri is the Vice Provost for Graduate Education and Faculty Development as well as a Professor in Electrical and Computer Engineering at Georgia Institute of Technology. She has won several awards for her work in blended and hands-on learning, including the IEEE Undergraduate Teaching Award and the Regents Award for the Scholarship of Teaching and Learning. She has been very active in promoting hands-on learning in traditional and flipped courses to other faculty through workshops and training videos.

Andy Frazee is the Associate Director of the Writing and Communication Program at Georgia Tech, managing courses in first-year composition, technical communication, and research writing as well as the day-to-day processes of the Marion L. Brittain Postdoctoral Fellowship. Holding a PhD in English and Creative Writing (University of Georgia, 2010), his research interests include postmodern and contemporary poetry, higher education administration, pedagogy and pedagogical innovation, and faculty development. In 2012–2013, he served as co-PI and project manager of one of the first composition MOOCs, First-Year Composition 2.0 (Coursera, 2013; funded by the Gates Foundation and Georgia Tech's Office of the Provost). In collaboration with Writing and Communication Program colleagues, Frazee investigates how digital technologies reshape the teaching of writing and communication, particularly in relation to active learning, experiential learning, and student engagement.

Mohammad Ghassemi will be joining the faculty of Computer Science and Engineering as an Assistant Professor at Michigan State University in the fall of 2019. He received his PhD from the Massachusetts Institute of Technology's department of Electrical Engineering and Computer Science. His projects include a large open-access intensive care database, an algorithm for real-time social analysis using wearable data, and a tool for the automated transcription of paper spreadsheets that combines machine learning and crowd-sourcing.

Alyson B. Goodman is a medical epidemiologist and pediatrician at the US Centers for Disease Control in Decatur, Georgia, and an Adjunct Professor in the Emory University School of Medicine.

Joyelle Harris is an academic faculty member and Director of the Engineering for Social Innovation Center at the Georgia Institute of Technology. She has ten years of combined experience in industry and academia, and she incorporates her industry experience when teaching her engineering students. Harris focuses on engineering education, design for usability, and problem-based learning. She aims to create consistent, quality content and structure for large, multisection courses.

Cheryl Hiddleson is a master's-prepared registered nurse and the Director of the Emory eICU Center. She practiced at the bedside in critical care for twenty years before appointment to her current position. She had oversight of the development and implementation of the Emory eICU program in 2013. Over the last five years, she has become involved in research and development of various remote monitoring and analytic predictive applications focused on reducing serious complications for critical care patients. She has also developed a first of its kind remote satellite location for the Emory eICU Center in Perth Australia. Emory intensivists and nurses are relocated there to allow them to provide care to cover Emory patients in Georgia at night during the daytime hours in Australia.

David Joyner is a Senior Research Associate and Associate Director of Student Experience in Georgia Tech's College of Computing. His research interests focus on online education and learning at scale, especially as they intersect with for-credit offerings at the graduate and undergraduate levels. Toward this end, his focus is on designing learning experiences that leverage the opportunities of online learning to compensate for the loss of synchronous collocated class time. This includes leveraging artificial intelligence for student support and assignment evaluation, facilitating student communities in large online classes, and investigating strategies for maintainable and interactive presentation of online instructional material. As part of his work, Joyner teaches online versions of CS6460: Educational Technology, CS6750: Human-Computer Interaction, and CS1301: Introduction to Computing.

Kenneth J. Knoespel is McEver Professor of Engineering and the Liberal Arts at Georgia Tech. He has participated in building undergraduate and graduate programs at Georgia Tech as a faculty member, school chair, associate dean, and interim dean. He has contributed to program development at universities in France, Russia, and Sweden. At Georgia Tech he has worked to establish several degree programs, including the undergraduate BS in Science, Technology, and Culture (STAC), the BS in Computational Media (CM), and the PhD and MS in Digital Media. He has held research appointments at the University of Uppsala, the University of Paris 8, Cornell University, the Hebrew University of Jerusalem, and the Russian Academy of Science.

Joseph M. Le Doux is an Associate Professor and the Associate Chair for Undergraduate Learning and Experience in the Wallace H. Coulter Department of Biomedical Engineering at Georgia Tech and Emory University. Early in his career, Le Doux engineered viruses to improve their ability to transfer genes to cells for the purpose of human gene therapy. He has since shifted his research focus to the learning sciences and engineering education. Le Doux's current projects are focused on creating interactive learning environments, fostering an entrepreneurial mindset through reflection and personal narrative, and promoting inclusion in engineering education.

Olga Menagarishvili is an Assistant Professor in the Department of English at Appalachian State University. She was a Marion L. Brittain Postdoctoral Fellow in the School of Literature, Media, and Communication at Georgia Institute of Technology (2012–2016). She currently teaches Technical Writing, Technical Writing for Computer Science, Business Writing, and Introduction to Professional Writing at Appalachian State University. Menagarishvili has also taught technical, scientific, and professional communication at the University of Minnesota, the Royal Institute of Technology in Stockholm, Sweden, and Ivanovo State University in Ivanovo, Russia. She has been teaching blended courses since 2008. Her research interests include scientific and technical communication, technical communication pedagogy, online and blended learning pedagogy, multimodality, rhetoric, and lexicography.

Shamim Nemati is an Assistant Professor in the Department of Biomedical Informatics at the Emory University School of Medicine. He received his PhD in Electrical Engineering and Computer Science from MIT in 2013. He was the James S. McDonnell Foundation postdoctoral fellow in complex systems at the Harvard Intelligent Probabilistic Systems group. His research focuses on physiological signal processing, modeling, and control for real-time clinical decision support; deep learning and reinforcement learning for optimizing sequential decision making in medicine; and computational neuroscience and deep brain stimulation.

Donald R. Webster is the Karen & John Huff School Chair and Professor in the School of Civil and Environmental Engineering at the Georgia Institute of Technology. His research expertise lies in environmental fluid mechanics, focusing on the influence of fluid motion and turbulence on biological systems. Webster's educational activities include serving as the co-PI on an NSF-supported Integrative Graduate Education and Research Training (IGERT) program that trains graduate students in the physics, chemistry, and ecology of chemical and hydrodynamic signaling in aquatic communities. He also has been a faculty mentor for an NSF-supported Research Experience for Undergraduates (REU) program addressing the interdisciplinary area of Aquatic Chemical Ecology. Starting in 2013, Webster implemented a blended classroom pedagogy in his junior-level Fluid Mechanics and sophomore-level Dynamics courses.

BIBLIOGRAPHY

Accreditation Board for Engineering and Technology (ABET). (n.d.). About ABET. http://www.abet.org/about-abet.

Albers, L., & Bottomley, L. (2011). *The impact of activity based learning, a new instructional method, in an existing mechanical engineering curriculum for fluid mechanics.* Paper presented at the 118th ASEE Annual Conference & Exposition, Vancouver, BC.

Allen, I. E., & Seaman, J. (2017). *Digital learning compass: Distance education enrollment report 2017.* Oakland, CA: Babson Survey Research Group.

Ammerman, N. T. (1992). *Bible believers: Fundamentalists in the modern world.* New Brunswick, NJ: Rutgers University Press.

Anderson, J., Corbett, A., Koedinger, K., & Pelletier, R. (1995). Cognitive tutors: Lessons learned. *Journal of the Learning Sciences, 4,* 167–207.

Anderson, P., Anson, C. M., Gonyea, R. M., & Paine, C. (2015). The contributions of writing to learning and development: Results from a large-scale multi-institutional study. *Research in the Teaching of English, 50*(2), 199.

Apperley, T., & Walsh, C. (2012). What digital games and literacy have in common: A heuristic for understanding pupils' gaming literacy. *Literacy, 46*(3), 115–122.

Argote, L., & Ingram, P. (2000). Knowledge transfer: A basis for competitive advantage in firms. *Organizational Behavior and Human Decision Processes, 82*(1), 150–169.

Aristotle. n.d. *Rhetoric*, book 1, chap. 2. https://rhetoric.eserver.org/aristotle/rhet1-2 .html.

Azevedo, R., & Aleven, V. (Eds.). (2013). *International handbook of metacognition and learning technologies (Vol. 26)*. New York: Springer.

Babbie, E. (2012). *The practice of social research* (13th ed.). Belmont, CA: Wadsworth.

Baker, R., & Inventado, P. (2014). Educational data mining and learning analytics. In J. Larusson & B. White (Eds.), *Learning analytics* (pp. 61–75). New York: Springer.

Bartsch, R. A., & Murphy, W. (2011). Examining the effects of an electronic classroom response system on student engagement and performance. *Journal of Educational Computing Research, 44*, 25–33.

Beatty, B. (2014). Hybrid courses with flexible participation: The HyFlex course design. In L. Kyei-Blankson & E. Ntuli (Eds.), *Practical applications and experiences in K-20 blended learning environments* Hershey, PA: Information Science Reference.

Beckem, J., & Watkins, M. (2012). Bringing life to learning: Immersive experiential learning simulations for online and blended courses. *Journal of Asynchronous Learning Networks, 16*(5), 61–70.

Beichner, R. J., Saul, J. M., Allain, R. J., Deardorff, D. L., & Abbott, D. S. (2000). *Introduction to SCALE-UP: Student-centered activities for large enrollment university physics*. ASEE Annual Conference & Exposition, Washington, DC.

Bender, D., & Sartipi, K. (2013). HL7 FHIR: An agile and RESTful approach to healthcare information exchange. In *Proceedings of the 26th IEEE International Symposium on Computer-Based Medical Systems*.

Bergmann, J., & Sams, A. (2012). *Flip your classroom: Reach every student in every class every day*. Eugene, OR: International Society for Technology in Education.

Bergmann, J., & Sams, A. (2014). *Flipped learning: Gateway to student engagement*. Eugene, OR: International Society for Technology in Education.

Biddix, J. P., Chung, C. J., & Park, H. W. (2015). The hybrid shift: Evidencing a student-driven restructuring of the college classroom. *Computers & Education, 80*, 162–175.

Bishop, J. L., & Verleger, M. A. (2013, June). *The flipped classroom: A survey of the research*. Paper presented at the 120th ASEE Annual Conference & Exposition, Atlanta.

Bloom, B. S. (1984a). The search for methods of group instruction as effective as one-to-one tutoring. *Educational Leadership, 41*(8), 4–17.

Bloom, B. S. (1984b). The 2 sigma problem: The search for methods of group instruction as effective as one-to-one tutoring. *Educational Researcher, 13*(6), 4–16.

Bloom, B. S., & Krathwohl, D. R. (1956). *Taxonomy of educational objectives: The classification of educational goals, by a committee of college and university examiners. Handbook I: Cognitive domain.* New York: Longmans, Green.

Bonk, C. J., & Graham, C. R. (2012). *The handbook of blended learning: Global perspectives, local designs.* Hoboken, NJ: Wiley.

Bonk, C. J., Wisher, R. A., & Nigrelli, M. L. (2004). Learning communities, communities of practice: Principles, technologies, and examples. In K. Littleton, D. Miell, & D. Faulkner (Eds.), *Learning to collaborate, collaborate to learn.* Hauppauge, NY: NOVA Science.

Bonwell, C. C. (1991). *Active learning: Creating excitement in the classroom* (ASHE-ERIC Higher Education Report, *Vol. 1*). Washington, DC: School of Education and Human Development, George Washington University.

Boyd, E. M., & Fales, A. W. (1983). Reflective learning: Key to learning from experience. *Journal of Humanistic Psychology, 23*(2), 99–117.

Boyer, E. L. (1990). *Scholarship reconsidered: Priorities of the professoriate.* New York: Carnegie Foundation for the Advancement of Teaching.

Brame, C. (2013). *Flipping the classroom.* Vanderbilt University Center for Teaching. https://cft.vanderbilt.edu/guides-sub-pages/flipping-the-classroom.

Bransford, J., Brown, A., & Cocking, R. (2000). *How people learn: Mind, brain, experience, and school.* Washington, DC: National Research Council.

Bransford, J., Sherwood, R., Vye, N., & Rieser, J. (1986). Teaching thinking and problem solving. *American Psychologist, 41*(10), 1078–1089.

Brooks, D. C., & Sandfort, J. R. (2014). Trial and error: Iteratively improving research on blended learning. In A. G. Picciano, C. D. Dziuban, & C. R. Graham (Eds.), *Blended learning: Research perspectives* (Vol. 2, pp. 141–149). New York: Routledge.

Brown, A. (1992). Design experiments: Theoretical and methodological challenges in creating complex interventions in classroom settings. *Journal of the Learning Sciences, 2*(2), 141–178.

Brown, J. S., Collins, A., & Duguid, P. (1989). Situated cognition and the culture of learning. *Educational Researcher, 18*(1), 32–42.

Brown, M. G. (2016). Blended instructional practice: A review of the empirical literature on instructors' adoption and use of online tools in face-to-face teaching. *Internet and Higher Education, 31,* 1–10.

Bruffee, K. (1995). Sharing our toys: Cooperative learning versus collaborative learning. *Change: The Magazine of Higher Learning, 27*(1), 12–18.

Burnett, R. E. (1991). Cooperative, substantive conflict in collaboration: A way to improve the planning of workplace documents. *Technical Communication (Washington, DC), 38*(2), 532–539.

Burnett, R. E. (1996). Some people weren't able to contribute anything but their technical knowledge: The anatomy of a dysfunctional team. In A. H. Duin & C. Hansen (Eds.), *Nonacademic writing: Social theory and technology* (pp. 123–156). Hillsdale, NJ: Erlbaum.

Burnett, R. E., Cooper, L. A., & Welhausen, C. A. (2013). How can technical communicators develop strategies for effective collaboration? In J. Johnson-Eilola & S. A. Selber (Eds.), *Solving problems in technical communication* (pp. 454–478). Chicago: University of Chicago Press.

Burnett, R. E., Frazee, A., Hanggi, K., & Madden, A. (2014). A programmatic ecology of assessment: Using a common rubric to evaluate multimodal processes and artifacts. *Computers and Composition, 31,* 53–66.

Carbonaro, M., Montgomery, A., Mousavi, A., Dunn, B., & Hayward, D. (2017, June). Learning analytics in a blended learning context. In J. Johnston (Ed.), *Proceedings of EdMedia 2017* (pp. 62–66). Washington, DC: Association for the Advancement of Computing in Education (AACE).

Carey, K. (2016, September 29). An online education breakthrough? A master's degree for a mere $7,000. *New York Times.* https://www.nytimes.com/2016/09/29/upshot/an-online-education-breakthrough-a-masters-degree-for-a-mere-7000.html.

Cash, R. M. (2017). *Advancing differentiation: Thinking and learning for the 21st century.* Minneapolis: Free Spirit.

Casner-Lotto, J., & Barrington, L. (2006). *Are they really ready to work? Employers' perspectives on the basic knowledge and applied skills of new entrants to the 21st century US workforce.* Washington, DC: Partnership for 21st-Century Skills.

Catalano, G. D., & Catalano, K. (1999). Transformation: From teacher-centered to student-centered engineering education. *Journal of Engineering Education, 88*(1), 59–64.

Center for Postsecondary Research. (2012). *National Survey of Student Engagement.* Bloomington: Indiana University School of Education.

Chadwick, S. (1999). Teaching virtually via the web: Comparing student performance and attitudes about communication in lecture, virtual web-based, and web-supplemented courses. *Electronic Journal of Communication, 9.* http://www.cios.org/EJCPUBLIC/009/1/00915.HTML.

Chapman, A. (2016). *Digital games as history: How videogames represent the past and offer access to historical practice (Vol. 7).* New York: Routledge.

Chen, J. C., Whittinghill, D. C., & Kadlowec, J. A. (2010). Classes that click: Fast, rich feedback to enhance students' learning and satisfaction. *Journal of Engineering Education, 99*(2), 158–169.

Chi, M. T. H., Glaser, R., & Farr, M. J. (1988). *The nature of expertise.* Hillsdale, NJ: Erlbaum.

Chi, M. T. H., & Wylie, R. (2014). The ICAP Framework: Linking cognitive engagement to active learning outcomes. *Educational Psychologist, 49*(4), 219–243.

Christensen, G., Steinmetz, A., Alcorn, B., Bennett, A., Woods, D., & Emanuel, E. (2013). The MOOC phenomenon: Who takes massive open online courses and why? https://doi.org/10.2139/ssrn.2350964.

Cicchino, M. I. (2015). Using game-based learning to foster critical thinking in student discourse. *Interdisciplinary Journal of Problem-Based Learning, 9*(2), 4. https://docs.lib.purdue.hedu/cgi/viewcontent.cgi?referer=https://scholar.google.com/&httpsredir=1&article=1481&context=ijpbl.

Clark, R., & Mayer, R. (2016). *E-learning and the science of instruction: Proven guidelines for consumers and designers of multimedia learning* (4th ed.). Hoboken, NJ: Wiley.

Coe, R. (2002). *It's the effect size, stupid: What effect size is and why it is important.* Paper presented at the British Educational Research Association Annual Conference, Exeter, UK.

Cohen, J. (1988). *Statistical power analysis for the behavioral sciences* (2nd ed.). Hillsdale, NJ: Erlbaum.s

Collins, A. (1989). *Cognitive apprenticeship and instructional technology* (Technical Report No. 474). Urbana-Champaign: Center for the Study of Reading, University of Illinois.

Collins, A. (1992). Toward a design science of education. In E. Scanlon & T. O'Shea (Eds.), *New Directions in Educational Technology* (pp. 15–22). New York: Springer-Verlag.

Connelly, D., & Goel, A. (2013). *Paradigms of AI programming in Python*. Paper presented at the Fourth Symposium on Educational Advances in AI (EAAI-2013), Bellevue, WA.

Cook, D. A. (2007). Web-based learning: Pros, cons and controversies. *Clinical Medicine*, 7(1), 37–42.

Cooper, I. M., Williams, C. G., Ivins, W. K., Jones, C. M., & Turner, M. S. (2016). Developing work-ready software engineers using real-world team-based projects as a catalyst for learning. *Journal of Computing*, 5(2), 24–33.

Cox, J. C., Sadiraj, V., Schnier, K., & Sweeney, J. F. (2016). Higher quality and lower cost from improving hospital discharge decision-making. *Journal of Economic Behavior & Organization*, 131, 1–16.

Creswell, J. W. (2013). *Research design: Quantitative, qualitative, and mixed methods approaches* (4th ed.). Thousand Oaks, CA: Sage.

Creswell, J. W., & Plano Clark, V. L. (2011). *Designing and conducting mixed methods research*. Thousand Oaks, CA: Sage.

Daniel, J. (2012). Making sense of MOOCs: Musings in a maze of myth, paradox and possibility. *Journal of Interactive Media in Education*, 2012(3). https://doi.org/10.5334/2012-18.

Davis, A. (2008). "Reflecting on their learning." Edublog Insights. http://anne.teachesme.com/2008/10/16/reflecting-on-their-learning/2016.

Day, J., & Foley, J. (2006). Evaluating a web lecture intervention in a human-computer interaction course. *IEEE Transactions on Education*, 49(3), 420–431.

DeCarrio Voegele, J. (2016). Student perspectives on blended learning through the lens of social, teaching, and cognitive presence. In A. G. Picciano, C. D. Dziuban, & C. R. Graham (Eds.), *Blended learning: Research perspectives* (Vol. 2, pp. 93–103). New York: Routledge.

DeMillo, R. A. (2011). *Abelard to Apple: The fate of American colleges and universities*. Cambridge, MA: MIT Press.

Dias, S. B., Hadjileontiadou, S. J., Hadjileontiadis, L. J., & Diniz, J. A. (2015). Fuzzy cognitive mapping of LMS users' quality of interaction within higher education blended-learning environment. *Expert Systems with Applications, 42*(21), 7399–7423.

Dochy, F., Segers, M., Van den Bossche, P., & Gijbels, D. (2003). Effects of problem-based learning: A meta-analysis. *Learning and Instruction, 13,* 533–568.

Dow, D. N. (2013). Historical veneers: Anachronism, simulation, and art history in *Assassin's Creed II.* In M. W. Kappell & A. B. Elliott (Eds.), *Playing with the past: Digital games and the simulation of history.* New York: Bloomsbury.

Dringus, L. P., & Seagull, A. B. (2016). A five-year study of sustaining blended learning initiatives to enhance academic engagement in computer and information sciences campus courses. In A. G. Picciano, C. D. Dziuban, & C. R. Graham (Eds.), *Blended learning: Research perspectives* (Vol. 2, pp. 122–140). New York: Routledge.

Duderstadt, J. J. (2000). *A university for the 21st century.* Ann Arbor: University of Michigan Press.

Duderstadt, J. J., & Womack, F. W. (2003). *The future of the public university in America: Beyond the crossroads.* Baltimore: Johns Hopkins University Press.

Dunleavy, M., & Dede, C. (2014). Augmented reality teaching and learning. In *Handbook of research on educational communications and technology.* New York: Springer.

Dunning, D. (2011). The Dunning-Kruger effect: On being ignorant of one's own ignorance. *Advances in Experimental Social Psychology, 44,* 247–296.

Dziuban, C. D., Picciano, A. G., Graham, C. R., & Moskal, P. D. (2016). *Conducting research in online and blended learning environments: New pedagogical frontiers.* New York: Routledge/Taylor & Francis.

Eichenbaum, A., Bavelier, D., & Green, C. S. (2014). Video games: Play that can do serious good. *American Journal of Play, 7*(1), 50–72.

Eichler, J. F., & Peeples, J. (2016). Flipped classroom modules for large enrollment general chemistry courses: A low barrier approach to increase active learning and improve student grades. *Chemistry Education Research and Practice, 17,* 197–208.

Ensign, P. C. (2008). *Knowledge sharing among scientists: Why reputation matters for R&D in multinational firms.* London: Palgrave Macmillan.

Felder, R. M., & Brent, R. (2004). The intellectual development of science and engineering students. Part 2: Teaching to promote growth. *Journal of Engineering Education, 93,* 279–291.

Ferguson, E. S. (1992). *Engineering and the mind's eye.* Cambridge, MA: MIT Press.

Ferri, A. A., & Ferri, B. H. (2016a). *Blended learning in a rigid-body dynamics course using on-line lectures and hands-on experiments.* Paper presented at the 123rd ASEE Annual Conference & Exposition, New Orleans.

Ferri, B. H., & Ferri, A. A. (2016b). A controls approach to improve classroom learning using cognitive learning theory and course analytics. In *Proceedings of the American Control Conference.* https://doi.org/10.1109/ACC.2016.7526828.

Ferri, B. H., Ferri, A. A., Majerich, D. M., & Madden, A. G. (2016). Effects of in-class hands-on laboratories in a large enrollment, multiple section blended linear circuits course. *Advances in Engineering Education, 5*(3), 1–27.

Ferri, B. H., Majerich, D. M., Parrish, N. V., & Ferri, A. A. (2014, June). *Use of a MOOC platform to blend a linear circuits course for non-majors.* Paper presented at the 121st ASEE Annual Conference & Exposition, Indianapolis.

Fisher, D. H., Burge, J., Maher, M. L., & Roth, J. (2015). Blended CS courses using massive, open, online courses (and other online resources). In *Proceedings of the 46th ACM Technical Symposium on Computer Science Education.* New York: ACM. https://doi.org/10.1145/2676723.2691864.

Flaherty, C. (2013, November 8). AAUP asserts that instructors should control classroom curricular decisions. *Inside Higher Ed.* https://www.insidehighered.com.

Forrester, J. (1968). *Principles of systems* (2nd ed.). Arcadia, CA: Pegasus Communications.

Fowler, F. J. (2013). *Survey research methods* (5th ed.). Thousand Oaks, CA: Sage.

Freeman, S., Eddy, S. L., McDonough, M., Smith, M. K., Okoroafor, N., Jordt, H., et al. (2014). Active learning increases student performance in science, engineering, and mathematics. *Proceedings of the National Academy of Sciences of the United States of America, 111*(23), 8410–8415.

Friedman, T. (2005). *The world is not flat: A brief history of the 21st century.* New York: Farrar, Straus and Giroux.

Friese, S. (2014). *Qualitative data analysis with ATLAS.ti.* Thousand Oaks, CA: Sage.

Garrison, D. R., & Kanuka, H. (2004). Blended learning: Uncovering its transformative potential in higher education. *Internet and Higher Education, 7*(2), 95–105.

Garrison, D. R., & Vaughan, N. D. (2008). *Blended learning in higher education: Framework, principles, and guidelines.* Hoboken, NJ: Wiley.

Gee, J. P. (2005). Learning by design: Good video games as learning machines. *E-Learning and Digital Media*, 2(1), 5–16.

Ghassemi, M. M., Richter, S. E., Eche, I. M., Chen, T. W., Danziger, J., & Celi, L. A. (2014). A data-driven approach to optimized medication dosing: A focus on heparin. *Intensive Care Medicine*, 40(9), 1332–1339.

Gibson, W., & Brown, A. (2009). *Working with qualitative data*. Thousand Oaks, CA: Sage.

Glass, G., McGaw, B., & Smith, M. L. (1981). *Meta-analysis in social research*. London: Sage.

Goel, A. (1994). *Teaching introductory artificial intelligence: A design stance*. Paper presented at the AAAI Fall Symposium on Improving Introductory Instruction of Artificial Intelligence, New Orleans, LA.

Goel, A., & Davies, J. (2011). Artificial intelligence. In R. Sternberg & S. Kauffman (Eds.), *Handbook of intelligence* (pp. 468–484). Cambridge: Cambridge University Press.

Goel, A., & Joyner, D. (2016). An experiment in teaching cognitive systems online. *International Journal for the Scholarship of Technology Enhanced Learning*, 1(1), 3–23.

Goel, A., & Joyner, D. (2017). Using AI to teach AI. *AI Magazine*, 38(2), 48–59. https://doi.org/10.1609/aimag.v38i2.2732.

Goel, A., Kunda, M., Joyner, D., & Vattam, S. (2013). *Learning about representational modality: Design and programming projects for knowledge-based AI*. Paper presented at the Fourth AAAI Symposium on Educational Advances in Artificial Intelligence, Bellevue, WA, July 15–16.

Goel, A., Newstetter, W., Jacobs, L., Blum, T., Kim, J., Ludovice, P., et al. (2016). Future of pedagogy: Main findings from the discovery phase. Georgia Tech Commission on Next in Education. http://www.provost.gatech.edu/education-commission/discovery-reports/future-pedagogy.

Gray, G. L., Costanzo, F., Evans, D., Cornwell, P., Self, B., & Lane, J. L. (2005). *The Dynamics Concept Inventory Assessment Test: A progress report and some results*. ASEE Annual Conference & Exposition, Portland, OR.

Guo, P. J., Kim, J., & Rubin, R. (2014). How video production affects student engagement: An empirical study of MOOC videos. In *Proceedings of the First (2014) ACM Conference on Learning @ Scale* (pp. 41–50). New York: ACM.

Gwet, K. L. (2012). *Handbook of inter-rater reliability: The definitive guide to measuring the extent of agreement among multiple raters (3rd ed.)*. Gaithersburg, MD: Advanced Analytics.

Hallgren, K. A. (2012). Computing inter-rater reliability for observational data: An overview and tutorial. *Tutorials in Quantitative Methods for Psychology, 8*(1), 23.

Halverson, L. R., Graham, C. R., Spring, K. J., Drysdale, J. S., & Henrie, C. R. (2014). A thematic analysis of the most highly cited scholarship in the first decade of blended learning research. *Internet and Higher Education, 20,* 20–34.

Hanushek, E. A., & Jackson, J. E. (1977). *Statistical methods for social scientists.* New York: Academic Press.

Harris, K. M., Phelan, L., McBain, B., Archer, J., Drew, A. J., & James, C. (2016). Attitudes toward learning oral communication skills online: The importance of intrinsic interest and student-instructor differences. *Educational Technology Research and Development, 64*(4), 591–609.

Henrie, C. R., Bodily, R., Manwaring, K. C., & Graham, C. R. (2015). Exploring intensive longitudinal measures of student engagement in blended learning. *International Review of Research in Open and Distributed Learning, 16*(3), 131–155.

Hollands, F., & Tirthali, D. (2014). *MOOCs: Expectations and reality.* New York: Center for Benefit-Cost Studies of Education, Teachers College, Columbia University.

Holmes, W. M. (2014). *Using propensity scores in quasi-experimental designs.* Thousand Oaks, CA: Sage.

Holton, J. A. (2007). The coding process and its challenges. In A. Bryant & K. Charmaz (Ed.), *The Sage handbook of grounded theory* (Part *III*, pp. 265–289). Thousand Oaks, CA: Sage.

Horn, M. B., & Staker, H. (2015). *Blended: Using disruptive innovation to improve schools.* Hoboken, NJ: Wiley.

Hotle, S. L., & Garrow, L. A. (2016). Effects of the traditional and flipped classrooms on undergraduate student opinions and success. *Journal of Professional Issues in Engineering Education and Practice, 142.* https://doi.org/10.1061/%28ASCE%29EI.1943-5541 .0000259.

Howell, J. T. (1972). *Hard living on Clay Street: Portraits of blue-collar families.* Prospect Heights, IL: Waveland Press.

Hübler, M. J., & Buchman, T. G. (2007). Mathematical estimation of recovery after loss of activity: I. Renal failure. *Journal of Trauma and Acute Care Surgery, 63*(1), 232–238.

Johnson, D., Johnson, R., & Smith, K. (1998). *Active learning: Cooperation in the college classroom.* Edina, MN: Interaction Book Co.

Johnson, S. D. (1988). Cognitive analysis of expert and novice troubleshooting performance. *Performance Improvement Quarterly, 1*(3), 38–54.

Johnson, S. D., & Chung, S. P. (1999). The effect of thinking aloud pair problem solving (TAPPS) on the troubleshooting ability of aviation technician students. *Journal of Industrial Teacher Education, 37*(1), 7–25.

Jonassen, D. H. (1999). Designing constructivist learning environments. In C. M. Reigeluth (Ed.), *Instructional design theories and models: A new paradigm of instructional theory* (Vol. 2, pp. 215–239). New York: Routledge.

Jonassen, D. H., & Hung, W. (2008). All problems are not equal. *Interdisciplinary Journal of Problem-Based Learning, 2*(2), 6–28.

Jovanović, J., Gašević, D., Dawson, S., Pardo, A., & Mirriahi, N. (2017). Learning analytics to unveil learning strategies in a flipped classroom. *Internet and Higher Education, 33,* 74–85.

Joyner, D. (2017). Scaling expert feedback: Two case studies. In *Proceedings of the Fourth (2017) ACM Conference on Learning @ Scale* (pp. 71–80). New York: ACM.

Joyner, D., Ashby, W., Irish, L., Lam, Y., Langston, J., Lupiani, I., et al. (2016). Graders as meta-reviewers: Simultaneously scaling and improving expert evaluation for large online classrooms. In *Proceedings of the Third (2016) ACM Conference on Learning @ Scale* (pp. 399–408). New York: ACM.

Joyner, D., Bedwell, D., Graham, C., Lemmon, W., Martinez, O., & Goel, A. (2015). Using human computation to acquire novel methods for addressing visual analogy problems on intelligence tests. In *Proceedings of the Sixth International Conference on Computational Creativity.*

Joyner, D., Goel, A., & Isbell, C. (2016). The unexpected pedagogical benefits of making higher education accessible. In *Proceedings of the Third (2016) ACM Conference on Learning @ Scale* (pp. 117–120). New York: ACM.

Kahneman, D. (2011). *Thinking fast and slow.* New York: Farrar, Straus and Giroux.

Kassin, M. A., Owen, R. M., Perez, S. D., Leeds, I., Cox, J. C., Schnier, K., et al. (2012). Risk factors for 30-day hospital readmission among general surgery patients. *Journal of the American College of Surgeons, 215*, 322–330.

Kegan, R., Lahey, L., Miller, M., Fleming, A., & Helsing, D. (2016). *An everyone culture: Becoming a deliberately developmental organization.* Boston: Harvard Business Review.

Kemp, N., & Grieve, R. (2014). Face-to-face or face-to-screen? Undergraduates' opinions and test performance in classroom vs. online learning. *Frontiers in Psychology, 5*, 1–11.

Kenney, J., & Newcombe, E. (2011). Adopting a blended learning approach: Challenges encountered and lessons learned in an action research study. *Journal of Asynchronous Learning Networks, 15*(1), 45–57.

Keppel, G., & Wickens, T. D. (2004). *Design and analysis: A researcher's handbook* (4th ed.). Upper Saddle River, NJ: Pearson Prentice Hall.

Kirkley, S. E., & Kirkley, J. R. (2005). Creating next generation blended learning environments using mixed reality, video games and simulations. *TechTrends, 49*(3), 42–53.

Krathwohl, D. R. (2002). A revision of Bloom's taxonomy: An overview. *Theory into Practice, 41*(4), 212–218.

Krueger, R., & Casey, M. A. (2008). *Focus groups: A practical guide for applied research* (4th ed.). Thousand Oaks, CA: Sage.

Ku, H.-Y., Tseng, H. W., & Akarasriworn, C. (2013). Collaboration factors, teamwork satisfaction, and student attitudes toward online collaborative learning. *Computers in Human Behavior, 29*, 922–929.

Langley, P. (2011). Artificial intelligence and cognitive systems. *AISB Quarterly, 133*, 1–4.

Langley, P. (2012). The cognitive systems paradigm. *Advances in Cognitive Systems, 1*, 3–13.

Larkin, J. H., & Simon, A. H. (1987). Why a diagram is (sometimes) worth ten thousand words. *Cognitive Science, 11*, 65–99.

Lazebnik, Y. (2002). Can a biologist fix a radio?—Or, what I learned while studying apoptosis. *Cancer Cell, 2*(3), 179–182.

Le Doux, J. M., & Waller, A. (2016). The problem solving studio: An apprenticeship environment for aspiring engineers. *Advances in Engineering Education, 6*(2), 1–27.

Leeds, I. L., Sadiraj, V., Cox, J. C., Gao, S. X., Pawlik, T. M., Schnier, K. E., & Sweeney, J. F. (2017). Discharge decision-making after complex surgery: Surgeon behaviors compared to predictive modeling to reduce surgical readmissions. *American Journal of Surgery, 213*(1), 112–119.

Leeds, I. L., Sadiraj, V., Cox, J. C., Schnier, K. E., & Sweeney, J. F. (2013). Assessing clinical discharge data preferences among practicing surgeons. *Journal of Surgical Research, 184*, 42–48.

Likert, R. (1932). A technique for the measurement of attitudes. *Archives de Psychologie, 140*, 1–55.

Lim, D. H., Morris, M. L., & Kupritz, V. W. (2007). Online vs. blended learning: Differences in instructional outcomes and learner satisfaction. *Journal of Asynchronous Learning Networks, 11*(2), 27–42.

Linton, D. L., Pangle, W. M., Wyatt, K. H., Powell, K. N., & Sherwood, R. E. (2014). Identifying key features of effective active learning: The effects of writing and peer discussion. *Life Sciences Education, 13*(3), 469–477.

Liu, Q., Peng, W., Zhang, F., Hu, R., Li, Y., & Yan, W. (2016). The effectiveness of blended learning in health professions: Systematic review and meta-analysis. *Journal of Medical Internet Research, 18*(1). http://doi.org/10.2196/jmir.4807.

Liu, X. M., & Murphy, D. (2017). Are they ready? Integrating workforce readiness into a four-year college IT/IS curriculum. *SAIS 2017 Proceedings, 8*. https://aisel.aisnet.org/cgi/viewcontent.cgi?article=1007&context=sais2017.

López-Pérez, M. V., Pérez-López, M. C., & Rodríguez-Ariza, L. (2011). Blended learning in higher education: Students' perceptions and their relation to outcomes. *Computers & Education, 56*(3), 818–826.

Lovelace, M., & Brickman, P. (2013). Best practices for measuring students' attitudes toward learning science. *CBE Life Sciences Education, 12*(4), 606–617.

Lunsford, A., & Ede, L. (1990). *Singular texts/plural authors: Perspectives on collaborative writing*. Carbondale, IL: SIUP.

Lyman, F. (1992). Think-pair-share, thinktrix, thinklinks, and weird facts: An interactive system for cooperative thinking. In N. Davidson & T. Worsham (Eds.),

Enhancing thinking through cooperative learning (pp. 169–181). New York: Teachers College Press.

Mahajan, S. (2014). *The art of insight in science and engineering: Mastering complexity.* Cambridge, MA: MIT Press.

Mandel, J. C., Kreda, D. A., Mandl, K. D., Kohane, I. S., & Ramoni, R. B. (2016). SMART on FHIR: A standards-based, interoperable apps platform for electronic health records. *Journal of the American Medical Informatics Association, 23*(5), 899–908.

Margulieux, L. E., Bujak, K. R., McCracken, W. M., & Majerich, D. (2014). *Hybrid, blended, flipped, and inverted: Defining terms in a two-dimensional taxonomy.* Paper presented at the 12th Annual Hawaii International Conference on Education, Honolulu.

Margulieux, L. E., McCracken, W. M., & Catrambone, R. (2016). A taxonomy to define courses that mix face-to-face and online learning. *Educational Research Review, 19,* 104–118.

Marín, V., López, M., & Maldonado, G. (2015). Can gamification be introduced within primary classes? *Digital Education Review, 27,* 55–68.

Marino, M. P. (2011). High school world history textbooks: An analysis of content focus and chronological approaches. *History Teacher, 44*(3), 421–446.

Marra, R., Jonassen, D. H., Palmer, B., & Luft, S. (2014). Why problem-based learning works: Theoretical foundations. *Journal on Excellence in College Teaching, 25*(3–4), 221–238.

McGinnis, J. M., Stuckhardt, L., Saunders, R., & Smith, M. (Eds.). (2013). *Best care at lower cost: The path to continuously learning health care in America.* Washington, DC: National Academies Press.

Meadows, D. (2008). *Thinking in systems: A primer.* White River Junction, VT: Chelsea Green.

Means, B., Toyama, Y., Murphy, R., & Baki, M. (2013). The effectiveness of online and blended learning: A meta-analysis of the empirical literature. *Teachers College Record, 115*(3), 1–47.

Menand, L. (2010). *The marketplace of ideas: Reform and resistance in the American university.* New York: Norton.

Merchant, Z., Goetz, T., Cifuentes, L., & Davis, T. (2014). Effectiveness of virtual reality–based instruction on students' learning outcomes in K-12 and higher education: A meta-analysis. *Computers & Education, 70,* 29–40.

Mergendoller, J. R., Bellisimo, Y., & Maxwell, N. L. (2000). Comparing problem-based learning and traditional instruction in high school economics. *Journal of Educational Research, 93*(6), 374–383.

Meriam, J. L., & Kraige, L. G. (2012). *Engineering mechanics: Dynamics* (7th ed.). Hoboken, NJ: Wiley.

Meyer, L. (2015). 4 Innovative ways to teach with video games: Educators from around the country share their best practices for using educational and consumer games to improve students' engagement and performance. *THE Journal: Technological Horizons in Education, 42*(5), 20.

Miles, M. B., Huberman, A. M., & Saldana, J. (2014). *Qualitative data analysis: A methods sourcebook.* Thousand Oaks, CA: Sage.

Mills, J., Bonner, A., & Francis, K. (2006). The development of constructivist grounded theory. *International Journal of Qualitative Methods, 5*(1), 1–10.

Mitchell, A., & Savill-Smith, C. (2004). *The use of computer and video games for learning: A review of the literature.* London: Learning and Skills Development Agency.

Moreland, R. L., & Myaskosky, L. (2000). Exploring the performance benefits of group training: Transactive memory or improved communication? *Organizational Behavior and Human Decision Processes, 82*(1), 117–133.

Mulryan-Kyne, C. (2010). Teaching large classes at college and university level: Challenges and opportunities. *Teaching in Higher Education, 15*(2), 175–185.

Nat, M. (2015). A Flipped classroom model for universities in developing countries. *Global Learn, 1,* 597–604.

National Academy of Sciences. (2010). *Exploring the intersection of science education and 21st century skills: A workshop summary.* Washington, DC: National Academies Press.

National Research Council. (2003). *Beyond productivity: Information, technology, innovation, and creativity.* Washington, DC: National Academies Press.

Nielsen, M. A. (2015). *Neural networks and deep learning.* Determination Press. http://neuralnetworksanddeeplearning.com.

Osguthorpe, R. T., & Graham, C. R. (2003). Blended learning environments: Definitions and directions. *Quarterly Review of Distance Education, 4*(3), 227–233.

Ou, C., Goel, A., Joyner, D., & Haynes, D. (2016). Designing videos with pedagogical strategies: Online students' perceptions of their effectiveness. *Proceedings of the Third (2016) ACM Conference on Learning @ Scale* (pp. 141–144). New York: ACM.

Owston, R., York, D., & Murtha, S. (2013). Student perceptions and achievement in a university blended learning strategic initiative. *Internet and Higher Education, 18,* 38–46.

Palincsar, A. S. (1998). Social constructivist perspectives on teaching and learning. *Annual Review of Psychology, 49*(1), 345–375.

Papert, S., & Harel, I. (1991). *Constructionism*. New York: Ablex.

Parker, M. C., Guzdial, M., & Engleman, S. (2016). Replication, validation, and use of a language independent CS1 knowledge assessment. *Proceedings of the 2016 ACM Conference on International Computing Education Research* (pp. 93–101). New York: ACM.

Parraguez, P., Eppinger, S. D., & Maier, A. M. (2015). Information flow through stages of complex engineering design projects: A dynamic network analysis approach. *IEEE Transactions on Engineering Management, 62*(4), 604–617.

Passow, H. J. (2012). Which ABET competencies do engineering graduates find most important in their work? *Journal of Engineering Education, 101*(1), 95–118.

Pellegrino, J., & Hilton, M. (2013). *Education for life and work: Developing transferable knowledge and skills in the 21st century*. Washington, DC: National Academies Press.

Perrin, K., Rusnak, L., Zha, S., Lewis, D., & Srinivasan, S. (2009). Using blended learning to ensure consistency and quality in multiple course sections. *Journal of the Research Center for Educational Technology, 5*(1), 42–48.

Petroski, H. (1985). *To engineer is human: The role of failure in successful design*. New York: St. Martin's Press.

Picciano, A. G. (2014). Big data and learning analytics in blended learning environments: Benefits and concerns. *Interactive Journal of Artificial Intelligence and Interactive Multimedia, 2*(7), 35–43.

Picciano, A. G. (2016). Qualitative research in online and blended learning. In C. D. Dziuban, A. G. Picciano, C. R. Graham, & P. D. Moskal (Eds.), *Conducting research in online and blended environments: New pedagogical frontiers* (pp. 106–118). New York: Routledge.

Porter, W. W., Graham, C. R., Bodily, R. G., & Sandberg, D. S. (2016). A qualitative analysis of institutional drivers and barriers to blended learning adoption in higher education. *Internet and Higher Education, 28*, 17–27.

Prince, M. (2004). Does active learning work? A review of the research. *Journal of Engineering Education, 93*, 223–231.

Rayyan, S. (2015). Upper level physics MOOCs for online and blended learning. *Bulletin of the American Physical Society, 60*(5). http://meetings.aps.org/Meeting/NES15/Event/24945.

Roach, T. (2014). Student perceptions toward flipped learning: New methods to increase interaction and active learning in economics. *International Review of Economics Education, 17*, 74–84.

Ruiz-Primo, M. A., Briggs, D., Iverson, H., Talbot, R., & Shepard, L. A. (2011). Impact of undergraduate science course innovations on learning. *Science, 331*(6022), 1269–1270.

Sapsford, R. (2006). *Survey research* (2nd ed.). Thousand Oaks, CA: Sage.

Saqr, M., Fors, U., & Tedre, M. (2017). How learning analytics can early predict underachieving students in a blended medical education course. *Medical Teacher, 39*(7), 1–11.

Sauret, E., & Hargreaves, D. (2015). *Collaborative learning approach to introduce computational fluid dynamics. Paper presented at the 2015 Australasian Association for Engineering Education (AAEE) Conference*, Geelong, Victoria, Australia.

Schank, R. (2011). *Teaching minds: How cognitive science can save our schools.* New York: Teachers College Press.

Schaubroeck, J. M., & Yu, A. (2017). When does virtuality help or hinder teams? Core team characteristics as contingency factors. *Human Resource Management Review, 27*(4), 635–647.

Schiesel, S. (2009, December 9). *Assassin's Creed II*: On the scenic trail of intrigue: Adventures in 15th-century Italy. *New York Times.* https://www.nytimes.com/2009/12/08/arts/television/08assassin.html.

Schwartz, D. L., & Bransford, J. D. (1998). A time for telling. *Cognition and Instruction, 16*(4), 475–523.

Scott, C. E., Green, L. E., & Etheridge, D. L. (2016). A comparison between flipped and lecture-based instruction in the calculus classroom. *Journal of Applied Research in Higher Education, 8*, 252–264.

Shadish, W. R., Cook, T. D., & Campbell, D. T. (2001). *Experimental and quasi-experimental designs for generalized causal inference* (2nd ed.). Independence, KY: Cengage.

Shavelson, R. J., Ruiz-Primo, M. A., & Wiley, E. W. (2005). Windows into the mind. *Higher Education, 49*(4), 413–430.

Shaw, A. (2015). The tyranny of realism: Historical accuracy and politics of representation in *Assassin's Creed III. Loading...: The Journal of the Canadian Games Studies Association, 9*(14), 4–24.

Skibba, K. (2016). Choice does matter: Faculty lessons learned teaching adults in a blended program. In A. G. Picciano, C. D. Dziuban, & C. R. Graham (Eds.), *Blended learning: Research perspectives* (Vol. 2, pp. 203–211). New York: Routledge.

Smith, K. A., Sheppard, S. D., Johnson, D. W., & Johnson, R. T. (2005). Pedagogies of engagement: Classroom-based practices. *Journal of Engineering Education, 94*, 87–101.

Spinuzzi, C. (2007). Technical communication in the age of distributed work. *Technical Communication Quarterly, 16*(3), 265–277.

Spinuzzi, C. (2012). Working alone, together: Co-working as emergent collaborative activity. *Journal of Business and Technical Communication, 26*(4), 399–441.

Squire, K. (2011). *Video games and learning: Teaching and participatory culture in the digital age. Technology, education—connections: the TEC series.* New York: Teachers College Press.

St. Amant, K. (2015). Culture and the context of communication design. *Communication Design Quarterly Review, 4*(1), 6–22.

Stephens, P. R., McGowan, M. K., & Pape, V. (2015). Blended learning in the introductory computer skills course. *Issues in Information Systems, 16*(3), 43–53.

Stickel, M., & Liu, Q. (2015). *Engagement with the inverted classroom approach: Student characteristics and impact on learning outcomes.* Paper presented at the 2015 Canadian Engineering Education Association Conference, Hamilton, Ontario.

Strayer, J. F. (2012). How learning in an inverted classroom influences cooperation, innovation and task orientation. *Learning Environments Research, 15*(2), 171–193.

Swithenbank, S. B., & DeNucci, T. W. (2014). *Using a "flipped classroom" model in undergraduate Newtonian dynamics.* Paper presented at the 121st ASEE Annual Conference & Exposition, Indianapolis.

Taplin, R. H., Kerr, R., & Brown, A. M. (2013). Who pays for blended learning? A cost-benefit analysis. *Internet and Higher Education, 18*, 61–68.

Tew, A. E., & Guzdial, M. (2010). Developing a validated assessment of fundamental CS1 concepts. In *Proceedings of the 41st ACM Technical Symposium on Computer Science Education* (pp. 97–101). New York: ACM.

Tokunaga, H. T. (2016). *Fundamental statistics for the social and behavioral sciences.* Thousand Oaks, CA: Sage.

Torrisi-Steele, G., & Drew, S. (2013). The literature landscape of blended learning in higher education: The need for better understanding of academic blended practice. *International Journal for Academic Development, 18*(4), 371–383.

Trépanier, N. (2014). The assassin's perspective: Teaching history with video games. *Perspectives on History, 52*(5).

Tyler, K. M., & Dolasky, K. C. (2016). Educating warrior diplomats: Blended and unconventional learning for special operations forces. In A. G. Picciano, C. D. Dziuban, & C. R. Graham (Eds.), *Blended learning: Research perspectives* (Vol. 2). New York: Routledge.

US Centers for Disease Control and Prevention (CDC). (2016, February 23). *Chronic disease overview.* http://www.cdc.gov/chronicdisease/overview.

Valiathan, P. (2002). Blended learning models. *Learning Circuits, 3*(8), 50–59.

Vattam, S., Goel, A. K., Rugaber, S., Hmelo-Silver, C. E., Jordan, R., Gray, S., et al. (2011). Understanding complex natural systems by Articulating Structure-Behavior-Function Models. *Journal of Educational Technology & Society, 14*(1), 66–81.

Velegol, S. B., Zappe, S. E., & Mahoney, E. (2015). The evolution of a flipped classroom: Evidence-based recommendations. *Advances in Engineering Education, 4*(3), 1–37.

Veugen, C. (2016). *Assassin's Creed* and transmedia storytelling. *International Journal of Gaming and Computer-Mediated Simulations (IJGCMS), 8*(2), 1–19.

Vroom, V. H. (1964). *Work and motivation.* New York: Wiley.

Vygotsky, L. (1978). *Mind in society: The development of higher psychological process.* Cambridge, MA: Harvard University Press.

Wainwright, A. M. (2014). Teaching historical theory through video games. *History Teacher, 47*(4), 579–612.

Wang, Y., Xibin, H., & Yang, J. (2015). Revisiting the blended learning literature: Using a complex adaptive systems framework. *Journal of Educational Technology & Society, 18*(2), 380–393.

Watson, W. R., Mong, C. J., & Harris, C. A. (2011). A case study of the in-class use of a video game for teaching high school history. *Computers & Education, 56*(2), 466–474.

Webster, D. R., Majerich, D. M., & Madden, A. G. (2016). Flippin' fluid mechanics—Comparison using two groups. *Advances in Engineering Education, 5*(3), 1–20.

Weinstein, L. (2012). *Guesstimation 2.0: Solving today's problems on the back of a napkin.* Princeton, NJ: Princeton University Press.

Weinstein, L., & Adam, J. A. (2008). *Guesstimation: Solving the world's problems on the back of a cocktail napkin.* Princeton, NJ: Princeton University Press.

Wenger, E. (1998). *Communities of practice: Learning as a social system.* Cambridge: Cambridge University Press.

Whorley, W. L., & Tesdell, L. S. (2009). Instructor time and effort in online and face-to-face teaching: Lessons learned. *IEEE Transactions on Professional Communication, 52*(2), 138–151.

Wigfield, A. (1994). Expectancy-value theory of achievement motivation: A developmental perspective. *Educational Psychology Review, 6*(1), 49–78.

Wouters, P., Van Nimwegen, C., Van Oostendorp, H., & Van Der Spek, E. D. (2013). A meta-analysis of the cognitive and motivational effects of serious games. *Journal of Educational Psychology, 105*(2), 249–265.

Yalcin, M. A., Gardner, E., Anderson, L. B., Kirby-Straker, R., Wolvin, A. D., & Bederson, B. B. (2015). *Analysis of consistency in large multi-section courses using exploration of linked visual data summaries.* PeerJ PrePrints.

Yildiz, M. N., Petela, A., & Mahoney, B. (2014). Global kitchen project: Promoting healthy eating habits and developing 21st century skills among children through a flipped classroom model. In J. Keengwe, G. Onchwari, & J. N. Oigara (Eds.), *Promoting active learning through the flipped classroom model*. Hershey, PA: IGI Global.

Zacharis, N. Z. (2015, October). A multivariate approach to predicting student outcomes in web-enabled blended learning courses. *Internet and Higher Education, 27,* 44–53.

Zhang, P., Ding, L., & Mazur, E. (2017). Peer instruction in introductory physics: A method to bring about positive changes in students' attitudes and belief. *Physical Review Physics Education Research, 13.* https://doi.org/10.1103/PhysRevPhysEducRes.13 .010104.

INDEX

Abbott, D. S., 216

A/B testing, 62

Academic freedom, 20, 33, 40

Academy of Medicine, 98

Accreditation, 21

Accreditation Board for Engineering and Technology (ABET), 164, 166, 183

Active learning, 2, 9, 40, 60–61, 156, 161–162, 163, 167, 174, 179, 181–183, 184, 214, 216, 252

Adam, J., 306

Adaptive learning, 1, 2, 82

Administrators, xvii, xix

Admission, 70, 96, 186n6

Aerospace engineering, 23, 332n3

AI teaching assistant, 49

Akarasriworn, C., 162

Albers, L, 215

Alcorn, B., 54

Allain, D. L, 216

American Cancer Society, 103

Anderson, L. B., 18

Annetta, L. A., 255

APIs, 118, 122

Apperley, T., 254

Apps, 7, 99, 101, 122

Archer, J., 181

Argote, L., 166

Aristotle, 163

Artifacts, 151, 155, 161, 167, 171, 182, 186n4, 256

Artificial intelligence, xii, 6, 48, 64, 344, 345

Assessments, 3, 4, 6, 7, 11, 18–20, 23, 47, 49, 51, 54, 57, 59, 61–63, 72, 81–83 99, 224, 254, 260–262, 335, 339. *See also* Concept Inventories; Exams

automated, 3, 64, 72, 81

formative, 18, 51, 81, 231

rubric, 172, 227, 295, 301, 322

summative, 6, 18, 19, 21, 23, 172, 213

written, 47, 52, 60, 62, 157